The Sex Life of

FOOD

Other Books by Bunny Crumpacker

FOR CHILDREN

Alexander's Pretending Day

NONFICTION

The Old-Time Brand-Name Cookbook
Old-Time Brand-Name Desserts

COWRITTEN WITH CHICK CRUMPACKER

Jazz Legends

The Sex Life of

FOOD

BUNNY CRUMPACKER

THOMAS DUNNE BOOKS
St. Martin's Griffin
New York

THOMAS DUNNE BOOKS.
An imprint of St. Martin's Press.

www.thomasdunnebooks.com
www.stmartins.com

Design by Kathryn Parise

LIBRARY OF CONGRESS CATALOGING-IN-PUBLICATION DATA

Crumpacker, Bunny.
    The sex life of food / Bunny Crumpacker.
        p.   cm.
    Includes index.
    ISBN-13: 978-0-312-36376-5
    EAN-10: 0-312-36376-1
        1. Food habits—Psychological aspects. 2. Food preferences—Psychological aspects. 3. Sex (Psychology) I. Title.

GT2850.C77 2006
394.1'2—dc22   2005048493

D   10   9   8   7   6   5   4

Contents

Contents

To my parents

They dined on mince, and slices of quince
Which they ate with a runcible spoon;
And hand in hand, on the edge of the sand,
They danced by the light of the moon.

—*The Owl and the Pussycat,*
by Edward Lear

My thanks to Susan Clement Cohen,
Ruth Cavin, Toni Plummer, and Chick.

Introduction

It started with a bacon, lettuce, and tomato sandwich. (On white, please, lightly toasted, with mayo.) I was unhappy—I don't remember why—and it was lunchtime, and I was eating out and that's what I ordered. And it was perfect. It was perfectly made. The bacon was sweet and savory, the mayonnaise was creamy and tangy, the bread ... no, no more: It was just perfect. And I felt better while I was eating it, and still better after I had finished it. But nothing else had changed. The only thing that had happened was that I had ordered a sandwich, and I had eaten it, and I felt better.

There *is* magic in a good sandwich, the most potent magic: the magic of food. Simple, basic food. Our first encounter with the world—well, after our tiny bottoms have been slapped and our footprints taken and a blanket wrapped around us—is with food, though we begin to suck our thumbs well before we're born. Once here, we suck again; our stomachs fill; we fall in love. We sleep, and then we wait, hungry, angry, and alone, until someone comes back, and—magic!—there is food again. And we love again. And so it goes, forever.

All cooking is Mother's. (Or, now, parental. But mothers still get blamed for it.) Good, bad, as we imagined it to be, as we would have liked it to have been ... it's Mother's. It's home. Food is love. Or its absence. Food is also anger, sustenance, deprivation, joy, loneliness, rage, hatred, ritual, surprise, laughter, revenge, history, power, comfort, sex. ...

And food is memory. We remember a nearly infinite series of tables, receding behind us back to childhood—at home, in school, away, alone, with friends, lovers, families. Food memories, most of them forgotten or blurred, are a mystical heritage, long since digested and gone, but still lingering in our souls. Personal food, ethnic food, family food, the food of the culture in which we grew up, the food our mothers gave us—this is eating that determines who we are, what we love, what disgusts us, what makes us feel better.

Food is so tangled into every human emotion from our very beginnings that eating must inevitably become an expression of our personalities. We eat in ways that are idiosyncratic, subjective, and irrational.

Our bodies are full of connections, in fact and in psyche, from top to bottom in a curved and sensuous line. The sex life of food doesn't mean that the strawberries have fallen in love with the oatmeal; rather, it is the food connections that count, from the shape of food to its image in our souls, from cooking as an act of love to food as it travels through our bodies, from the food in fairy tales to what politicians eat, from the food that comforts us to our manners at the table, from food used as power to food that becomes a problem. And there's always sex, and the link between the table and the bed. "Sex is like having dinner," Woody Allen said a long time ago. "Sometimes you joke about the dishes, sometimes you take the meal seriously." And sometimes cooking is foreplay, eating is making love, and doing the dishes is the morning after.

After my bacon, lettuce, and tomato sandwich, I decided I wanted to explore all of this—how we eat (Favorite food first or last? Slowly or quickly? Big bites or little ones?), why we choose the foods we do (crabs yes, spiders no; cows yes, horses no), how food defines us, and all the things that are mixed into the taste of food.

Food is the pleasure of now. Food is what keeps us alive. We're better off not taking it for granted.

Part One

FILLING THE GAPS

One can only eat three times a day.
And in between are the gaps.

—Hercule Poirot in *Mrs. McGinty's Dead,*
by Agatha Christie

Chapter 1

....

EATING SECRETS

My definition of Man is, "a Cooking Animal." The beasts have
memory, judgment, and all the faculties and passions of our mind,
in a certain degree; but no beast is a cook.... Man alone can dress
a good dish; and every man whatever is more or less a cook, in
seasoning what he himself eats.— Your definition is good, said Mr.
Burke, and I now see the full force of the common proverb, "There
is reason in the roasting of eggs."
> —*The Journal of a Tour to the Hebrides with Samuel Johnson, LL.D.,*
> by James Boswell

The first meal is a simple one. Eve's was just a bite of apple; a baby's is
just a bit of milk.

Some babies try to eat even before the first meal: There are infants born
with tiny calluses on their thumbs from sucking in utero, already working
at filling the void. Once delivered, eating is the first continuing encounter
the hungry babe has with the rest of humanity. Food is our first comfort,
our first reward. Hunger is our first frustration.

Simple as it is, that small sip of milk, the first meal is the beginning of a complexity of food and emotion that is mirrored over and over again in a pattern that never stops. When we begin to eat as babies, we fall in love. We discover pleasure, we make friends, we learn to smile. We sup with darker things, too—loneliness and fear, anger, even pain—and relief, after having waited so long, empty, for the next meal.

No wonder, then, that grown up, when we open our mouths to eat, our souls fly out. We are too thin or too fat. We go on food binges, secret eaters alone with the refrigerator in the middle of the night. We eat too little, and are afraid that too little is too much. We eat too fast and develop heart-burn. We work our mouths constantly: We chew gum, we make a fashion of cigars, we drop in for a cup of coffee, we suck on candy, we smoke cigarettes, we talk too much, we drink too much.

In one way and another, we've been worrying about food since the apes moved down from the trees when the fruit ran out. We've been so busy chewing that we haven't sat down and thought about the missing link between our dinner and our selves, between the *way* we eat and *what* we eat and *who* we are—*why* we eat in the ways that we do.

Eating is not a rational process. It is enmeshed in our childhoods, our families, our own personalities. If we were rational, we would eat spiders—juicy tarantulas!—as well as lobsters. We'd eat mice and rats, as well as frogs, snails, and crabs. What we actually do eat is chickens, but not blue jays, rabbits and sheep, but not cats and hamsters. We eat honey, and name it after flowers and ponder the merits of its various flavors. The idea of eating anything produced by a mosquito—or any secretion of any insect—is disgusting to us. But what is honey if it isn't the secretion of an insect?

Supposedly, human beings eat what is available. But for those of us fortunate enough to live in the lands of plenty, food choices are not limited by the local flora and fauna.* Seasons certainly don't matter anymore: We eat strawberries in December and asparagus year-round. With affluence comes choice. Milk and honey are just the basics. Milk comes in all sorts of ways,

---

*Poverty changes the equation. Without money, people do have to make do with what's available. Sometimes, with ingenuity and invention, what's available can be made to taste very good, and then other people want it too; soon it becomes pricey and only the affluent can afford it. Peasant bread isn't for peasants anymore; packaged white bread is the bread of affliction.

most of which are far removed from a cow: You can buy skim milk, homogenized milk, skim milk with milk solids added, lactose-free milk, chocolate milk, organic milk, milk with bacteria taken out, and milk with bacteria put back in. And heavy cream and half-and-half. Ultrapasteurized, sweet, or sour. Honey is available at the corner deli in every flavor, from Greek thyme to killer bee; orange blossom honey is ubiquitous, even though oranges only blossom in warm places. It doesn't matter what grows around here— the peanut butter tree grows everywhere.

Eating is a very complicated business. Taste is not only a question of what happens to the surface of the tongue when you eat or the number of taste buds that you were born with. It is a cumulative question of judgment, history, and personality jumbled up with smell, texture, sound, sight— and, yes, of course, taste. We think of taste when we think of food, but we forget how important all of our other senses are to our sense of taste (which is the one sense, in many ways, we know the least about).

Separating taste from everything it is tangled up with is not easy. Texture, for one, is not really taste, but it is certainly related. Crunchiness (the mouth word for noise) can go a long way toward replacing flavor. Crispness is not an attribute of taste; snap, crackle, and pop have no taste at all. Crunchy food makes a lot of noise as we chew it, and taste gets lost in the uproar. Crunch replaces flavor and we are left with nothing but the sound and the fury.

Sound is also a part of texture, and texture is the feeling of food in the mouth—hard crackers and chewy meats, soft puddings and purees, crisp vegetables, melting chocolate, crunchy nuts. Outer sounds aren't taste, but they are a source of eating pleasure. Think of bacon sizzling and a stew making small bubbling noises as it simmers. These all have to do with expectations of taste and they enhance taste.

What we see affects what we taste even more than what we hear. In one memorable experiment, a researcher served a panel of tasters six flavors of sherbet. Each serving was normally flavored, but each was without any color. The tasters had a hard time tasting: Flavor is linked to color, both visually and in terms of expectations. Purple tastes grape; lemon tastes yellow.

It is a cookbook basic that the way food looks affects the way it tastes. Vary the menu, we are told, so that food appeals to the eye before it ever reaches the mouth. Don't serve chicken with cauliflower and mashed pota-toes. Too white! Think of cranberry sauce and turkey. They *look* right.

Merchandisers have long since adjusted their products to our visual in-volvement with food. Margarine didn't become a food staple until it was colored yellow. (Somewhere along the line, we stopped calling it *oleo* except in crossword puzzles. *Oleo* sounds greasy and cheap; *margarine* has more dignity.) Even butter often has yellow coloring added to it because butter's natural shade is, to many people, unappetizingly pale.

Orange juice doesn't seem to taste good unless it's bright orange. Tests have shown that most people don't want to drink yellow orange juice; orange juice with an off taste is all right—even preferred—if it's a nice bright orange. That's how it's *supposed* to be.

In 1981, Tropicana donated 26,000 quarts of grapefruit juice to a Florida food bank. The juice had been discolored by an error during production—it wasn't spoiled, or bad; it was just brown and Tropicana knew it would be hard to sell. But even as a give-away, brown grapefruit juice didn't work. "Everybody that drank it said it was good," said a local minister whose church ended up with a thousand cases of the stuff, "but the color was icky." The church was left with the problem of where to dump it.

We trust hot dogs that have been colored red and Jell-O that is equally tinted, though we've been told the red coloring probably causes cancer. Cancer is a relatively impersonal threat compared with a grayish brown hot dog that we are actually expected to swallow. Same for the nitrites in corned beef, salami, ham—all the cold cuts and preserved meats. Better to deal with cancer tomorrow and have a reddish brown slice of bologna to-day. Eating is not a rational business.

Food companies are very aware of the niceties of food color, even on the outside of what they're selling. Packaging colors are most often red and yellow—colors that are cheerful and warm. Black, of course, is pretty much out. White is good, but as we eat—and buy—more natural and organic foods, green and brown are used more often.

There isn't any difference in taste or nutrition between brown eggs and white ones. Yet people have strong preferences between the two, often with a geographic link. In some parts of America, shoppers prefer brown eggs; in others, white. In recent years, consumers have been buying more brown eggs than they used to, probably as part of the national movement toward eating healthier food. Brown eggs look more natural, and the thinking goes that if they look more natural, they're probably better for you. Before our organic era, in the days when cleanliness was next to godliness, buyers preferred white eggs because they seemed "cleaner," not as much as if they might actually have passed through the body of a chicken.

All of our senses—sight, sound, smell, and, when we're very young, touch—affect the sense of taste, but more than any of the senses except perhaps smell, taste is affected by relative intangibles—our childhoods, our moods, our personalities, our expectations, even our heritage. Some food is ethnic and reminds us of home and Mother, from pasta to sauerbraten, from pastrami to enchiladas. Food can be male, like sausage, or female, like eggs, or simply get tangled up in our feelings about sex because food and sex are so inextricably linked. Food can be painful and hot, like curry or chili, or soothing and sweet, like custard or turkey in cream sauce. Food can be maternal, like rice pudding, or sexy, like chocolate mousse. Food can be decisive, like broccoli, or just a little vague, like plain mashed potatoes.

Preferring asparagus to creamed spinach is more than a matter of taste. Asparagus is finger food, and it's biting food, too. Creamed spinach is mushy, very plainly baby food, whether we spoon it in ourselves or have Mommy to help. Spinach is good for you—look at Popeye, another echo of childhood. Asparagus is more sophisticated; you have to *know* how to eat it. They're both green, but creamed spinach can have a messy, dark look to it; properly cooked asparagus is bright green. Asparagus is a little crisp in the mouth; creamed spinach is smooth and—by definition—creamy. And then there's shape. Creamed spinach has none. Asparagus has plenty; it's the very definition—well, almost—of phallic. Asparagus and spinach are both delicious. Our choice speaks of our mood, our associations, and our memories as well as our taste buds and the rest of today's menu.

In the years since World War II, the U.S. Army has commissioned three studies of the food likes and dislikes of its soldiers with the goal of giving them what they want. While there have been changes in the results over the years—food tastes have become more adventurous and more ethnic, as the soldiers themselves have—the foods at the top and bottom of the list have been consistent. No one likes stewed prunes. Everyone likes lasagna.

In the first two studies, clear correlations emerged between the food preferences and education levels of military men and women. In one, soldiers with higher degrees of education put mushrooms, hot tea, grapefruit, crisp relishes, and maple syrup toward the top of the list of foods that they liked. Less well-educated soldiers steered away from *all* of those choices. The more education a GI had, the less that soldier liked corn flakes, cherry drink, and instant coffee—all of which were *preferred* by less well-educated GIs.

To consider these choices in order:

Mushrooms: Mushrooms are one of the most obviously phallic of foods—fine for soldiers, masculine by image, as are soldiers, even in a coed army. But mushrooms are also a little weird. They grow in dark places. The wrong ones are poisonous. Children often don't like mushrooms—they look odd and their texture is strange. They have a mystical air—fairies and elves sit on them. If it follows that better-educated soldiers are also more sophisticated, it makes sense that they would like mushrooms more than less well-educated GIs do.

Hot tea: In America, hot tea traditionally has more class than coffee. Ladies drink tea.* The English, who have those posh English accents, drink tea. Coffee is strong and direct; tea is refined. Coffee is potent; tea is romantic. Coffee is noisy and obstreperous; tea is quiet and subtle. Coffee is nouveau riche; tea is old money. Hot chocolate completes the caffeine trilogy, and is in a class by itself.

Coffee comes in bottomless cups. If you want more tea, you pay for an extra tea bag or you get hot water poured over the limp one you've already used. It's not that coffee is more plentiful than tea, or less expensive. It's that coffee is the expectation, even in this era of herbal teas and caffeine awareness (Red Bull notwithstanding). Tea in America, for all the popularity of its iced version, is still up the social scale from coffee. Starbucks is on every street corner; can you imagine tearooms right and left? Not yet. Chai seems to be an effort to bridge the gap between caffe latte and the tea bag,

---

*Iced tea operates under a different psychology from that of hot tea. It's unisex, for one thing. Lipton, for instance, advertised its iced tea in a Super Bowl spot some years back. "This ain't no sipping tea," the ad said. You can "gulp, guzzle, and chug it." No testosterone shortage there!

but herbal tea is in a whole different category. Coffee is for the working man; tea is what you drink with your pinkie sticking out.

Grapefruit: In the same way, grapefruit is up the line from an orange. Oranges aren't content to rest on their breakfast laurels. They're also lunchbox food—easy to peel and eat out of hand. Grapefruits are equally easy to peel—easier, perhaps, because they're bigger—but they're not what the guys on the I beams might eat. Order grapefruit at the local eatery and you get a half precut for you, with a cherry stuck in the middle. Still, grapefruit is on the diner's breakfast page, while oranges are so plebian that no one would dream of putting one on a menu. What shall we have for dessert, dear? How about half an orange? No? You'd rather have crème brûlée? (In Japanese and Chinese restaurants, orange slices often arrive unordered after the main course, and they are, by themselves, works of art. But they aren't on the menu.)

Crisp relishes: Radishes, celery, and carrot sticks are aggressive foods, food for biters, good for soldiers. They're healthy high-energy foods, but you have to be willing to deal with them. Are they just rabbit food to the less well-educated GI? Still tea-roomy after all these years? Or for ladies—not women—on a diet?

Maple syrup: Maple syrup is a complicated kind of sweet; dark and sophisticated when it's real, and oversimplified in the artificially flavored version. Either way, it's an intense taste, preferred by the better-educated soldier.

Corn flakes, cherry drink, and instant coffee: These are all processed food, make-believe tastes. *Corn flakes* have the life taken out of them; they're steamed and rolled and flattened and when they're all done, squashed remnants of the healthy corn kernels they started as, they're sprayed with vitamins. Cherry drink isn't big on cherries. Instant coffee is distantly related to real coffee—but not close enough to worry about genetic defects in their offspring should they decide to marry. Not bad, maybe, but not coffee. Like canned peas, they're good, if you're not expecting real (fresh) green peas. Better-educated soldiers probably expect real green peas.

Other researchers have seen many similar correlations. Someone has even studied the members of Elvis Presley fan clubs. They tend to be white women in their forties and fifties, and for the most part they haven't continued their education beyond high school. They love Elvis, and they also love canned meat, malt liquor, menthol cigarettes, white bread, Velveeta cheese, and frozen dinners. (We seem to have a stereotype here.)

For years, before yogurt was sold as it is today, mixed with sugar and fruit, marketers knew that people with college educations ate more yogurt than those who stopped at high school. Yogurt is milk, all grown up and just a little sour. The popularity of yogurt today has much to do with all the sugar that has been added to it. (There's also the virtue: It has all those good bacteria, and anything slightly sour has to be healthy. All the bacteria die when we freeze it, but that's another story.)

All these foods are more than token indicators of education levels. Read middle class for better educated, and working class for having stopped at (or before) high school. But the military studies made another connection beyond education levels and that is a link with age. The younger the soldier, the fewer foods he liked—and the sweeter he liked them.

Children, given half a chance, prefer sweets. The famous experiment, once cited by Dr. Spock, which seemed to prove that children, on their own, will select a healthy, well-rounded diet, has long since been discredited. Children simply prefer sweet food. They come by their taste for sweet food naturally. Babies begin life with sweetness—breast milk is sweet, and so is formula. The sweet taste reinforces the sucking instinct. A researcher in Jerusalem noted that almost all babies, after tasting something sweet, had facial expressions of "relaxation" and "satisfaction," even a slight smile; sometimes they licked their upper lips. On the other hand, some infants, poor things, were fed a solution that was slightly bitter. Their tiny faces showed "dislike and disgust"; they spit out the solution, refusing to swallow it, and looked as if they were feeling nauseated.

Babies also develop likings for the foods that their mothers ate while they were pregnant. A study in *Pediatrics Journal* showed that infants whose mothers drank carrot juice while they were pregnant liked their cereal mixed with carrot juice; babies whose mothers didn't drink carrot juice didn't respond to it. The conclusion was that flavors cross from the mother's blood into the amniotic fluid. By the third trimester, fetuses have functioning taste buds and olfactory cells. Thus does soul food begin.

But there is more to sweetness than what our mothers ate before we were born. Sweets are the reward foods of childhood. Eat your vegetables; *then* you can have dessert. When we're bigger, if we're good—or at our birthday party—we're given ice cream and cake. When you've hurt your-self, a kiss and a cookie—either helps, both work miracles—will make it well. We learn as we go through life that the kiss and the sweet can substi-tute for each other in all kinds of situations. We'd like them both, but you can't always have your cake and eat it, too. Still, cookies, candy, ice cream, cake: These are for comfort and for being good and for finishing our veg-etables. They're the least we deserve, poor darlings.

It's a sweet that is one of the world's single most popular foods, right up there with a Big Mac. Coca-Cola bubbles away in a universal language, the truly global soft drink. Coke complicates its sweetness with a tart, ex-citing taste. It does exactly the same thing to the bloodstream. Coke pro-vides a lift, a snort of sugar and caffeine, a food fix.

Soldiers prefer sugar too. One of the army's earlier surveys of food tastes resulted in a list of nearly four hundred foods in order of preference. Among the top ten, four were sweet: ice cream, milk shakes, strawberry shortcake, and orange juice.

Plain milk is consistently high on the lists of military favorites—not as high as milk shakes (sweet), but still right up there. Absolute rock bottom on the lists is buttermilk. Close to last: skim milk. Both buttermilk and skim milk speak of betrayal, of sweet milk gone bad, of promises made and not kept, of disappointment and trickery. Buttermilk is sourish; if you're not used to its fresh, clean taste, it tastes almost on the verge of being spoiled. Skim milk is thin, watery, almost blue. All the cream is gone.

Men and women in uniform dislike some obvious foods. Down at the bottom of their most recent food list were such dishes as braised liver, chicken à la king, lima beans, stewed tomatoes, brussels sprouts, and har-vard beets. Some things on earlier survey lists just dropped right off the most recent study: fried parsnips, mashed rutabagas, canned figs, and boiled pigs feet, among others. Not a surprising list, and probably one that most contemporary Americans would agree with. In 2003, *Bon Appétit* magazine surveyed its readers about a number of food subjects, including likes and dislikes. High on their "Yuck" list: turnips and figs.

Some of the yuck-factor foods can be explained by aural, textural, and contextual signals more than by taste. Parsnips, for instance. Properly sautéed in butter, they are sweet, tender, and absolutely delicious. But their name makes them sound weird. Parsnippity. A parsnip by any other name would smell much sweeter. Rutabagas, too. Weird word; good food.

In or out of uniform, most Americans dislike the same foods, from buttermilk to brains. Our aversions are not a matter of logic or of taste any more than are our preferences. We eat cows and sheep but we wouldn't dream of eating dogs and cats. But in many parts of the world, dogs are raised for food, just as we raise cows, lambs, and pigs. There are restaurants in China with cages of live dogs near the front door—exactly the way we keep tanks of fish or lobster—so that diners can be sure that the meat they order is fresh.

We consider veal (baby cow), suckling pig (baby hog), and spring lamb (baby sheep) to be delicacies. Roast puppy (simply baby dog) was once thought to be the same.* There are still many places in the world where if you say that you love dogs, you could be just as easily be talking about your dinner as your pets. When the Olympics were held in Seoul in 1988, the government, aware of the way Europeans and Americans feel about dogs as food for people, tried, unsuccessfully, to ban it from restaurant menus. "The French eat horses, but we give horses a decent burial," said one Korean, savoring his dog stew in a local restaurant. "... Koreans are not lecturing other cultures on how to live, so please tell them to leave us alone."

Dog as food for people even has a pedigree: Aztec Indians bred a hairless dog to supplement their meager supply of protein; Native Americans also ate dog, as did white explorers and trappers. Members of the Lewis and Clark expedition ate dog as their chief meat after they had gone beyond the bison range of the Great Plains. In his journal, Clark wrote that his men had come to prefer dog flesh to local game. They traded for all the dogs they could get from local Indians. In *The Newfoundland Journal of*

---

*Most English words for farm animals are derived from the Anglo-Saxon: cow, pig, sheep. But once we're talking about food (and not farming), words for the *same* animals come from the medieval French—the language that the Norman lords spoke when they conquered England in 1066. Veal, beef, pork, mutton ... all French derived. The aversion to speaking of our domestic animals as food is a long-standing one. So is snobbery on the menu.

Aaron Thomas, written in 1794, we read that "One of these Newfoundland Dogs, after he had been constantly worked in the woods during the winter, then slain, is not bad eating. The hams, salted and smoked with juniper Berrys and branches of Rasberrys and their tea, in point of flavor, is superior to the celebrated Hams of Bayonne in Gascony. Dog hams are a new article in the Epicure's catalogue."

Anthropologists believe that Europeans and Americans today don't eat dog meat because dogs remind us too much of ourselves. Eating dog would be a kind of cannibalism. Dogs are man's best friend. Dogs (and horses) are used for domestic service (man's best friend can still qualify for domestic service), and they are strongly identified with humanity and its needs.

Dick Gregory noted during the Vietnam War that American moms and dads who were proud to send their sons off to defend their country would have been horrified and outraged if anybody had tried to draft their dogs.

Rabbits, too, are too much like us—too anthropomorphized, in cartoons and Easter traditions—to be terribly popular at the dining-room table. Chickens, on the other hand, are too silly to be much good as people symbols (even the other chickens wouldn't listen to Chicken Little when it started to rain), so we eat them with impunity. And how many other chickens do you know with names?

When we eat lamb chops and steak, we hover between an unconscious refusal to see these animals on the hoof, and the simultaneous safety of thinking of them purely as animals rather than as friends. Linda McCartney said that she and Paul became vegetarians when, at lunch one day, eating roast leg of lamb, they looked out the window and saw their pet sheep grazing on the lawn.

There are foods, such as dog, which seem to be almost taboo to us, so bizarre is the idea of eating them. Americans don't eat snakes (though sometimes in the American Southwest they are offered and eaten as a novelty—almost as proof of frontier toughness and manhood) and we don't eat snake eggs, though we eat fish (including eels) and fish eggs (for which we are willing to pay a great price). We don't eat rats, though there are forty-two countries where the rodents are considered quite edible. Swans and peacocks have provided happy meals in other times and other places, but not here and not today. Horse meat is quite acceptable in Europe and

South America, where dried strips of horse meat are popular nibbles. It is not on the list of edibles in North America. Horse meat used to be available in American supermarkets packaged as frozen pet food; not anymore—our kittens and puppies have been forced to share our aversions.

The thing is that protein is protein. And there are many protein sources that other people find delicious. The idea of eating insects, to Americans, is either a joke—novelty shops sometimes feature cans of chocolate-covered grasshoppers and ants—or something on an episode of *Fear Factor*. But most insects are healthy vegetarians, nibbling on fine green leaves and grasses. We scorn them. Other people are not so delicate. In some parts of Africa, where meat is scarce, grasshoppers are a nutritious staple. Grilled, they are said to taste like peanuts. Burmese eat termites, which are supposed to taste like almonds. Termite queens—about two inches long—became a fashionable food in Singapore recently. Residents flocked to a nearby Malaysian town (and paid about seven dollars for each queen) to eat the bugs live, dipped in alcohol, or preserved in rice wine. According to a local newspaper, they are hard and firm on the outside and cool and creamy on the inside. Indians once made flour from ground roast locusts. Aztecs ate cactus worms and made a kind of caviar from mosquito eggs, which float on still waters.

Billions of cicadas emerge from the ground every seventeen years—most recently in 2004. They're high-protein, low-fat, and they have no carbs. They spend their time, in between appearances, sucking sap from tree roots, and so they have a green flavor, something like asparagus, especially, notes one scientist, when they're eaten raw or boiled. Onondaga Indians in upstate New York eat the seventeen-year locusts when they appear between the season of the strawberry and the season of the blackberry. They're stir-fried with butter and salt, or panfried with honey, sugar, and cloves. "They're like flying vitamin capsules," says a local enthusiast. America Online featured cicada recipes in the spring of 2004—cicada pesto, cicada scampi, and Texas cicada popcorn were just three of the recipes. The question of whether they should be accompanied by red wine or white was raised, but not answered.

Cicadas, like all insects, belong to the same biological phylum (arthropods) as do crawfish, lobster, crab, and shrimp. Eating the latter but not the former is nothing more than cultural squeamishness; we've learned it, we weren't born with it. There are probably more countries where insects are eaten than there are where they are not. A water bug that's big enough to eat small fish is on menus in Thailand and Burma; a Mexican restaurant features black-ant larvae soup. Movie theaters in Colombia offer roasted leaf-cutter abdomens instead of popcorn.

Even roaches are edible. They have been used for food in Australia, Japan, New Guinea, China, and Thailand. American prisoners held by the Japanese during World War II found that eating roaches—which they ground into a paste and mixed with their rice—prevented death from malnutrition. American Captain Scott O'Grady survived for six days after being shot down over Bosnia by eating insects and grasses, just as his survival-kit pamphlet recommended. It notes that the hard portions of grasshoppers and crickets—like their legs—should be removed. The rest is edible, and full of protein. It suggests cooking grasshopper-size insects.

The American Explorers Club holds an annual black-tie banquet, with appetizers from the far-flung lands visited by the club's members. In 1907, moose marrow soup was on the menu. In 1960, members ate iguana and Macao monkey. For the 100th-anniversary dinner in 2004, the chef ordered tarantulas and rattlesnakes as well as raccoons and nutrias. A particularly tasty morsel: mealworms in vol-au-vent pastry with roasted scorpions hidden inside, the whole thing covered with escargot butter.

Milk—one of our most basic staples—need not come from cows, though we're most used to it that way. There are people who drink milk from water buffalo, yak, and reindeer. Mongolian koumiss is a sweet, fermented, slightly intoxicating drink made from the milk of horses. In Kazakhstan, the favored drink is fermented camel's milk. Some tribes in East Africa milk their cows and also cut a vein in the cow's neck and bleed it. The blood is either drunk fresh, allowed to clot, or mixed with milk. One man's milk is another man's poison.

There are those who dine on half-digested grass taken from the stomachs of freshly killed antelope. In Iceland, rotted shark meat was long considered a delicacy. Even crocodiles—and their eggs—have made it into the dining room on a plate. Calf testicles are not unusual fare in the Rocky Mountain states; Kentuckians prize squirrel brains, though they've been warned away from eating them because squirrel brains can transmit a fatal variant of mad cow disease. (Mad squirrel disease?)

Alexandre Dumas offered a recipe for bear paws, noting that front paws were preferable. The medieval Catholic Church advised that beaver's tails, since they remain submerged in the water while the beaver builds his dam, were suitable for days when eating meat was forbidden. Elephants were eaten until the end of the nineteenth century; one of Baron Rothschild's chefs said best of all was the foot of a young elephant. Henry David Thoreau ate moose nose, and if someone else got the nose first, his second choice was the tongue. Baffin Islanders prize a sauce made with seal meat, chopped and mixed with fat, blood, and ptarmigan intestines. Also eaten at ceremonial dinners is a dip made with the contents of caribou stomach, after grass, leaves, and lichen have been removed. Squeamishness depends on what you're used to.

In India, where cows are sacred and endowed with privilege, the idea of eating beefsteak is disgusting, and, in many places, illegal. In the United States for a large part of this century, beef in one form or another, from hamburger to T-bone steak, was the all-American meal. (Even in this day of low-fat dining and mad cow disease, you can still find steak topped with fried eggs on some hearty breakfast menus.) But beef didn't become a staple of the American menu until relatively recently in our history. Until the development of refrigerated railroad cars in the 1870s, it was impossible to market beef on any kind of mass basis. For the popular taste, it didn't take to preserving with salt, as pork did.

Salt pork was America's main-dish meat for generations; it flavored just about everything on the table except dessert (though lard-based crusts for pies are also pig-descended). Cincinnati, commanding the river trade, was the nation's salt-pork capital. It was upstaged and up-rivered later by Chicago's railroad tracks and stockyards, and by Mr. Armour and Mr. Swift. Until then, cows were kept not for steak, but for milk. It was later that beef became a symbol of prestige, and then one that was increasingly available, not only to the upper classes, but to the rest of us as well. Now, the idea of a well-marbled steak is triply questionable: It raises nutritional eyebrows, has become politically and morally suspect, and with thoughts of mad cow disease, another level of qualm is added to the red meat dilemma.

It was not that long ago when beef was considered essential for a healthy diet. It would have taken a mad cowboy to believe in mad cow disease.

We still choose our dinner on something of a moral basis—today, it's steak and hamburgers that are "bad" foods. Virtue is whole wheat bread, broccoli, mangoes (Kramer, on *Seinfeld,* told us that mangoes restore potency), wild salmon, flax seed. If you're on a diet and have a piece of cake, your self-judgment is simple: "I was bad." Fat is immoral.

Self-denial is an important part of the way we eat, just as binge eating is, on the other end of the scale. Something that is "sinfully" rich—full of butter and sugar and eggs and maybe even chocolate—can hardly be good for your soul. Somebody has said that the only food to be eaten without guilt is a raw carrot. Now, the Atkins Diet has given even that crunchy pleasure moral question marks.

The virtue of self-denial, of course, is only valid when there's more than enough to eat. Anorexia is a disease of plenty. It isn't healthy to be fat, obviously. But losing and gaining, which is what most of us do repeatedly, isn't good for you either. On a less physical level, we speak of fatness—obesity—as something vaguely repellent, even though so many of us are overweight. "Fat" is a nasty adjective; if there's anything worse than being a pig, it's being a fat pig. And that's part of the problem: Fat means piggishness, overeating, gluttony, lack of self-control, greed, laziness, self-indulgence. Actually, very often it's unhappiness made visible. It also owes something to the abundance of cheap junk food in poor communities as well as to ever-growing portion size, more time spent at desks, and suburbs without sidewalks. A group of overweight people marched in Washington, D.C., in 2004 to protest negative attitudes about weight. "Fat is not a four-letter word," one of their signs read. But what fat is is a four-letter word that has been on a diet.

We're ashamed of ourselves when we're fat. During World War I, some popular writers pointed out that fat was unpatriotic. If you ate too much during a time of food shortages, you could hardly think well of yourself, and if the result showed on your body, nobody else would think well of you either. The war ended, but the attitudes remained. Fat was once the symbol of aristocracy. Louis XIV padded himself to look more imposing. Large was power. Came the French Revolution, one of the rallying cries was "the people against the fat." Really.

More recently, in a study of food choices, a group of college students compared two versions of written profiles of the same fictitious people—all in good shape—runners, say, or tennis players—of average height and weight. The only difference between the two sets of profiles was preferred foods. Those who ate "good" foods were judged to be good people, while those who loved doughnuts and hot fudge sundaes were bad.

Food taboos and tastes are unique to each country or culture but universal in defying the belief that one eats what is available. They're also almost always about meat. (Meat is a much more potent substance than vegetables or fruit. Meat has a power that lettuce lacks.) Chicken is often a taboo food, sometimes forbidden expressly to women, sometimes to everyone, sometimes only to members of certain age groups or social classes. Pork is one of the most common taboos. Many African tribes will not eat pork. Religious Jews and Muslims alike refuse to eat it. The Old Testament forbids the eating of pigs. For Jews, pork is not kosher. For Muslims, who follow Mosaic law, it's not halal. Muslims who are Arabs share food preferences with Jews as well as taboos. Falafel—fried chickpea flour balls—are a Mediterranean staple, as are eggplants, garlic, lemons, olive oil, sesame seeds, and various herbs. Jews and Arabs quarrel in the same brotherly fashion—like Cain and Abel—when their meals are over.

As children, we eat what we are given. Grown up, we close the circle by preferring the food that reminds us, in one way or another, by choice or by denial, by safety or by daring, by comfort or by courage, of home.

Ethnic food, the food of our homeland's kitchens, is as individual as the culture from which it originates. The same ingredients magically change form as the globe spins—wonton to ravioli to dumplings to kreplach—the world round, it's filled pockets of dough poached in liquid. For each of us, the food we grew up with is the original, correct form. It is a symbol of our parents, our homes, our beginnings, ourselves. It's what was—or what we wish it was. Ethnic food is the nostalgia of the table.

Some ethnic foods are so powerful that they achieve potency on a mass level. Chicken soup is Jewish penicillin, but everybody, Jewish and otherwise, takes it without prescription. The trouble with Puerto Rico, said a resident who had gone home again after living in New York City for a while, is that you can't get good pizza there.

In *The Raw and the Cooked,* and various other books and papers, French anthropologist Claude Lévi-Strauss has written extensively about the cultural importance of food. He writes that the way in which a natural substance— a meat, for instance—is transformed into food goes across cultural lines. The food remains the same but has different shapes (as ravioli, kreplach, dumplings, and wonton). Ingredients can be the same or very similar, but the whole in each case is different from the sum of its parts, and from the other wholes.

Methods of cooking are also the same across cultural lines—boiling and roasting, for example, are processes that exist everywhere. Lévi-Strauss believes that roasts are status meals in every culture because roasting is such a wasteful way to cook food. When meat roasts, it shrinks—and some of its juices are lost. Boiling or stewing or braising or poaching preserve the juices so that they remain part of the meal. Stewing is plebian—peasants eat stew—and roasting is aristocratic. If you can afford to waste it, you must have more than enough; this is wealth; this is status.

Animals choose their food more simply. Even domesticated pets eat on a universal basis. There is no true ethnic food difference between a cat in the south and one in the west, or between a Maltese and a Manx. They all catch mice or eat cat chow. But people eat differently, depending on where they are and where they come from. In Georgia, grits are on the menu for breakfast and for dinner and in California they're a joke. Manhattan clam chowder—with tomatoes—is blasphemy in Boston, where clam chowder is made with milk or cream. Does chili come with beans or without, with tomatoes or without? All this variation, within one nation's borders. In Italy, the debate is between olive oil in the south and butter in the north; in France, the geographical fat of choice is either goose fat, olive oil, or butter. Culture shapes food, as a theme with variations.

Even the texture of food is affected by culture. Where bread is a staple food—the backbone of the diet and not just a wrapping for a sandwich— it is hard and dense, chewy, substantial. When bread becomes a dietary af-terthought, not much more than a pusher or a sop, it becomes fluff, as is packaged white bread.

The same principle applies to rice. In countries where it's a mainstay food, it is substantial and glutinous. When it's just another side dish, not the main event, or the basic filling substance of the meal, rice becomes light and airy. The land of plenty polishes its rice along with its nails and bleaches both its flour and its hair.

America used to be called a melting pot—a place where the cultures of its immigrants merged and blended into a brand-new mix: American. But until fairly recently—in the historical scale of things—Americans melted more outside the kitchen than in. At home, we ate what our grandparents ate. The best products of the American kitchen were thus international: Italian, German, Russian, Irish, "Czech and double check" American. Something like Spanish rice was considered a bit exotic to most non-Spanish Americans a mere fifty years ago; Chinese food was limited to chow mein and chop suey in Chinese restaurants; and gazpacho was simply unheard of.

World War II was the impetus toward the international menu. Pizza, for one, was hard to find in America before GIs returned home from the beaches and mountains of Italy. After the war, the new prosperity meant that international travel was possible for more people than ever before, and some of their food discoveries followed them back home. More than anything else, though, television has been the great assimilator for American food, just as it has been for everything else. We watch the same shows from coast to coast and the media has become the mother of us all.

Television advertising created the true melting pot kitchen, something that all of our cookbooks and magazines were never able to do. A chicken in every pot was a political promise; the recipe was left up to the voter. Now, fast-food hamburgers, canned biscuits, potato flakes, instant coffee, and take-out food have almost replaced sponge cake, ricotta pie, sauerbraten, and borscht. Ethnic food is something we've come back to—because we had left it behind.

Media food is sold with a media message. On television, a mother-in-law watches a bride open a jar of spaghetti sauce, tastes, and—amazed—approves. That's Italian! Media food is rarely sold as a convenience—though that is all it is. What is pushed at us is its moral goodness. It's just like Mother used to make.

Merchandisers are cheating the next generation of adults of their memories when they sell instant cocoa (with dried marshmallows on top) and instant soup. Images—like a politician and his promises—may be enough for election day or for the first time around in the supermarket. But images are not filling when you're hungry. What kind of love is it that offers only boiling water or a five-second timer? When we think of Mother making cocoa on a snowy day, we feel warm and comforted. We'll come in from the cold, our fingers icy, chilled to the very heart, and in the kitchen—the warm, steamy kitchen, filled with the thick smells of dinner, of cake baking and meat roasting—we'll drink our warm, sweet milk, dark with chocolate, and it will sustain us until we are hungry again. Microwaves just can't do that. They're an echo, not a source.

Instant food is sold with images of comfort and love: On the packages there are pictures of steaming bowls of hearty soup, and inside there are plastic mugs filled with cardboard noodles, which spring to some kind of rubbery life when they are dipped in hot water or microwaved for microseconds. Instant love could be the same, and last just as long and be just as real. And if food is sex, will today's children grow up to be as satisfied with fast sex as they are with fast food, instant intercourse, wham bam, thank you ma'am, and know only a half-perception, a faded promise, of something ineffably better? Instead of intimacy, they will have a cardboard sort of passion that passes away quickly and leaves all concerned hungry again.

Eating is intimate behavior. We've learned, with civilization, to keep our most intimate selves secret. Only our bed partners know how—or if—we make love. We keep the bathroom door closed. We pick our noses in private.

But we eat with friends and colleagues and strangers. We eat too with memories—good or bad—of mother and father, of home, of childhood.

Hunger is just the first of the reasons why we eat, and very often when we eat we aren't even really hungry. When we eat without hunger, taste has nothing to do with what happens in our mouths. When we're lonely or bored or anxious or angry, we turn for relief to the refrigerator. Couch potatoes have a food name. Most of us stuff or starve ourselves when we're stressed. Falling in love makes some innocent souls lose their appetites. But most of the time, we nibble and suck and chew, as we did when we were little babies. We snack almost continuously, sip and sup, feeling safe as a baby at the breast just as long as our jaws keep moving up and down.

We live again our anger, our needs, our love, three times a day. Between meals, we still keep our mouths busy, one way or another. There aren't as many smokers as there used to be, making jokes about adult pacifiers—inhaling and exhaling great clouds of smoke, ready to die as they were born, sucking. In vast numbers, we keep drinking too much alcohol, surrendering ourselves passively to liquid voluptuousness as infants do, and designating a stand-in mom or dad to drive us home.

The compulsive eater—but isn't everybody by nature?—uses food and mouth to fill the gap, whatever that unhappy abyss may really be.

Chapter 2

··

THE SEX LIFE OF FOOD

Now live splendidly together.
Free from adversity.
Pick figs.
May his be large and hard,
May hers be sweet.
    —*The Peace,*
        by Aristophanes

The most obvious association—among the many—between sex and food is the shape of the dish in question. Even in elementary school, we knew about bananas. And sausage. There were awful jokes in the cafeteria on the days when knockwurst was on the menu.

Sausage is masculine because it looks so phallic. Oysters are feminine because they look like the vulva. Sort of. Language says it for us, all around the world: In English, a hot dog is a show-off and a wiener is a prick; in French, *le champignon,* the mushroom, is more of the same. In several languages, the word for oyster is a slang word for female genitalia. Venus, after all, was born on the half shell.

Most vegetables are obviously masculine. Think of root vegetables—carrots and beets and turnips and parsnips. The shape's the thing. The American colonists, puritans all, regarded parsnips as "an incentive to venery." In Rome, Catullus wrote a poem about a Roman wife who left her husband because his "equipment dangled like a limp-leaved beet." In Victorian England, a sexier period than its image generally admits, carrots were a not uncommon masturbatory device. The word for carrot is also a slang word for penis in several languages. A seventeenth-century poem describes a dinner served at a famous inn:

> A dish of carrots, each of them as long
> As tool that to fair countess did belong
> Which her small pillow could no so well hide
> But visitors his flaming head espied.

We think of carrots more obliquely today. Of all the vegetables in Dr. Freud's garden, the carrot that Bugs Bunny nibbles on is our most popular image. Think of that potent rabbit in phallic terms: Bugs holds the carrot with its pointed tip upward (like the soldiers who once went into battle carrying an erect wood phallus, a flag of aggression which was proof of their power—their manhood). The carrot is Bugs Bunny's testosterone logo. He knows we're watching him—he's looking at us looking at him—voyeurs all. He takes a bite. He chews for a minute, big front teeth working, and you know that he's laughing at us. And then, still holding the carrot in its frontal position, phallus erectus, comes the famous line, so full of friendly arrogance and contempt: "Awwwwwwwwr . . . what's up, doc?"

Like carrots and mushrooms, asparagus are genital-shaped vegetable perfection. To say they are phallic is to belabor the obvious. Have you ever seen asparagus growing in the early spring? Their tender green shoots thrust out of the ground, dark dense tips poking up like verdant caps above the virile green stalks. Mushrooms and asparagus are supposed to be potent aphrodisiacs, and their shape is certainly inspiring. Celery also belongs in the roster of frankly phallic veggies. The Greeks awarded stalks of celery to the winners of nude athletic contests.

If vegetables are mostly male, fruits are female, with only an exception or two. Swelling out of sweet blossoms, drooping from heavy branches, fruit is suggestively womanly in shape and image. The most obvious exception is the banana, phallic in shape, to be sure, but with a taste—creamy and sweet—that is female.

Apples, the fruit of Eve, are the most female of fruits.* They're a breast symbol and a symbol of mystery, carnal knowledge, and sophistication as opposed to innocence. Melons and pumpkins are both often compared to breasts. Thomas Wolfe described cantaloupes as "musty, fragrant, deep-ribbed...in all their pink-fleshed taste and ripeness." Could they be anything but female?

Kiwis are one of the exceptions on the Freudian menu of food. They remind me of a boy I knew in high school—just too precious, we all thought, for sex. Not that a kiwi is asexual, exactly, just unsexy, like Billy. The kiwi is puckery, yes, and full of fiber. They're very pretty, and they have a faded kind of popularity, like a movie star that was, but they're not womanly, even with all those seeds, and they are certainly never macho. Kiwis are more hermaphroditic than anything else—or like eunuchs, desexed, here to serve.

Grapes and cherries and all the other little berries are female. Raspberries and strawberries are like little eggs all covered with seeds. But gooseberries are something else again. They're hard and green and look like tiny testicles. Very sour are gooseberries—not tart, *sour*—unlike the other sweet berries. Cranberries are sour, too, and hard; maybe these three—goose and cran and kiwi—are simply bisexual berries.

But berries are just the beginning of the fruits. A virgin loses her cherry. Women are peaches—oh, you peach!—and their complexions are like peaches and cream. The Chinese say that the sweet juices of the peach are like the syrups of the vagina, and both Chinese and Arabs, among many others, consider the deep, furry cleft of the peach to be a symbol of female

---

*There's a lot to say about apples. See Chapters 9 ("Fairy-Tale Food"), 11 ("Comfort Me With Apples"), and 18 ("The Big Apple").

sexuality. "Sharing the peach" is an old Chinese euphemism for sodomy, and Arabs use the word for peach in many expressions having to do with oral sex. The French say *pêche* frequently to talk about sex, from the missionary position to sodomy; in England, a "peach house" used to be a working phrase for a whorehouse—what we call, with less poetry and zest, a cathouse. There's even a porno film called *Pretty Peaches.*

Figs—like apples—are a potently erotic food, from their mention in the first pages of Genesis to the present day. The leaves which Adam and Eve sewed together to make little screening aprons are themselves verdant genitalia, a reproduction in silhouette of a hanging penis between two testicles—Adam might just as well have worn a sign: Penis Here! Like a medieval codpiece, like blacked out genitalia or breasts on TV news, the fig leaf focuses attention on what lies beneath. Rather than symbolizing modesty and making us think about things other than sex, they themselves become the symbol of sex, almost the sex itself. They fascinate the eye.

But figs, like bananas, are problematic symbols. They are clearly masculine in design but sweetly feminine in taste—and full of sex both ways. To Hindus, the fruit symbolizes both the penis and the vulva.

"Fig you" (and variations) is an obscenity in England. In Arabic, "to nibble a fig" is a euphemism for cunnilingus. In Turkey, fig means anus; in France, *faire la figue* means "to give the finger"; in India, various Latin American countries, and throughout the Mediterranean the word for fig means "fuck." It also means the finger gesture "fuck you," which is different from the American erect middle finger. It's an unmistakable penis as the thumb, tucked between the index finger and the middle finger, projects from a clenched fist.

The last gesture didn't begin as an insult. It was originally a protective device to ward off the evil eye, a "devil repellent." At one time, figs were supposed to bring good luck. And, of course, fertility.

One thinks of all the luscious fruits, peaches, plums, grapes, and even figs, their skins stretched tautly over their sweet, syrupy juices, as female. It's therefore especially strange that the gods of wine, sweet womanly liquid, are male. "How fair and how pleasant art thou, O love, for delights?" says the Song of Solomon. "This thy stature is like to a palm tree, and thy breasts to clusters of grapes. I said, I will go up to the palm tree, I will take hold of the boughs thereof: now also thy breasts shall be as clusters of the vine. . . ."

The image comes to mind of Roman orgies with bunches of purple grapes on silver platters, dishes crowded with V-shaped clusters of plump nipples, each ready to burst forth with sweet juice at the slightest, softest pressure. Yet Bacchus and Dionysus are male, and often fat, drunken, perhaps even slobbering, stained purple with excess, bits of grape leaves caught in their hair or behind their ears, or over their sticky genitals. The word *Bacchus* itself is of Sumerian descent, originally meaning "erect penis," though, in the end, one thinks of Bacchus as rather limp—or at least, exhausted. The gods of the orgy are male, consuming female fluids, almost obliterated by them, sucking them in, soaking in them, reveling in them, intoxicated by them, full of abandon within them.

The perfect orgy is the fantasy of a child—a *male* child. A female goddess of wine might well be inhibiting, like a mother. It is the male who must storm the body of the woman, penetrate it, surround himself with it. Females would be more ambivalent—toward their mothers and their mothers' milk. They are mothers themselves, and see less magic and mystery in the breast and in the vine.

Is it coincidental that the countries that drink the most wine are those that seem in many ways to be the most female? According to the *Britannica Book of the Year*, the leading wine-drinking countries, year after year, are Italy, France, Portugal, Argentina, and Spain. And where do we drink the most beer, that lusty piss-colored brew? Germany, Australia, Belgium, Luxembourg, and the former Czechoslovakia. Their names even sound male.

Our perceptions of the sex of food—from bananas to beer—have very little to do with our political or social attitudes toward men and women or their roles. Eggs are female and bacon is male, not because of stereotypical visions of male and female roles, at breakfast or at work or in the bedroom, but because of more subliminal associations—a kind of frontier psychology of the soul.

Males, in our vision of primitive life, were the hunters. The man subdued the beast—he brought home the bacon. Women, we like to think, were gatherers. Hers was the basket for collecting the eggs, the bowl which, womblike, held the seed.* His was the phallic weapon—the spear, the knife, the arrow, eventually the bullet. He was hard and tough. The male food that sustained him is in his image. She was softer, rounder. Her body still shapes itself around their infant, before its birth and after, too. The sweeter food, the more soothing, is hers.

Milk is obviously hers. Dairy products are female. After all, they exist because cows are mothers. Milk, cheese, butter, cream, yogurt: all female. Eggs, of course. Chickens and turkeys are female, even if the turkey is a tom. Their taste is maternal—calm, soothing, slightly sweet, adaptable, reassuring. (Your mother wasn't like that? But wasn't she *supposed* to be?) On second thought, turkey is probably gay, a chicken in drag. Lamb is bisexual—or maybe just a little confused, like a wolf in sheep's clothing. Mutton is masculine, but a sheep—all those wooly curls!—is feminine. Pork is like beef, but with attitude: male.

Steak is much clearer. Red meat is masculine. Milk comes from a cow, but steak comes from a steer. It's old-fashioned macho cowboys who herd cattle; did you ever hear of a rodeo for dairy farmers? Meat is solid fare, hearty, filling—you know you've eaten when you've had meat. (It's odd that "cowboy" is such a masculine word. Cows, after all, are female, and boys aren't men yet. To call a man a boy is insulting, but call a man a cowboy, and you've paid him a compliment.)

Steak houses are masculine restaurants—no peach-colored lampshades or masses of flowers on stands in the middle of the room. A steak house is a male preserve—it's where the hunters go to eat—and it's more likely to have sawdust on the floor and dark wood on the walls. The waitstaff is all male. By the same token, for years when we thought of men cooking, we thought of Dad tending steaks and hamburgers on an outdoor grill. Man the hunter, again—only now, he's back at the cave, tending the flames, cooking the macho meat.

The more rare the meat is, the more masculine it is. There are primitives who believe that the rarer the meat, the more of its power reverts to

*Women are still gatherers. Though more and more men are supermarket shoppers, making the routine day-in, day-out purchases as well as the stereotypical impulse grabs, they are still considerably outnumbered by women—women whose work is at home as well as those who shop at the end of the office day.

the eater. For them, blood is more than a symbol of life; it is life itself—life made visible, because when blood flows, life ebbs. In many tribes, warriors drink their enemies' blood in order to incorporate their enemies' strength. Bloody meat is powerful.

Raw meat, then, is the most masculine meat of all. I ordered it once, a long time ago, in a restaurant in Bonn. The waiter took the liberty of explaining to me—I was very young and obviously American and clearly did not know any better—that ladies did not enjoy eating steak tartare, because, he said patiently, it is uncooked. Perhaps I would prefer something else? Russian eggs, perhaps? In Germany, Russian eggs are hard-boiled, served with mayonnaise and caviar on top—eggs with eggs—and eggs are, after all, as feminine as you can get.

All of us, not just old-fashioned German waiters, give gender to food in various ways. Rona Jaffe has written about a male friend who accused her of being unfeminine because all she could cook was steak. He obviously thought that women should be good cooks. But if the only thing she could cook had been an omelette instead of steak, he might not have cast aspersions on her femininity. In *The Food of the Western World*, Theodora FitzGibbon describes a hearty English stew made with mutton and root vegetables (turnips, carrots, leeks, and potatoes) as a "very masculine" dish. It's meat. And the root vegetables, after all, have that visual impact which cannot be denied.

Then there are the couples: bacon and eggs, ham and cheese—still married, after all these years. A salad is often another happy marriage of male and female foods, whether it's warm slices of rare breast of duck with beet salad on radicchio, or the more plebian chef salad, with its ham and turkey, cucumbers and tomatoes, and cheese and hard-boiled eggs.

Dessert is usually female. Think of Spanish custards, the dome of flan, satiny smooth, quivering slightly on the dish, lying in a silky pool of sweet syrup. Cheesecake is what we used to call pinup photos, making subconscious associations: cream cheese, sugar, and vanilla in a soft, melting cake, sweet, delicate, delicious—directly descended from milk; clearly female in every way.

Honey as a sweetener is female. The honeybee is as busy as a housewife, a woman whose work is never done. The drones are male (they bring home the pollen), but the hive is a matriarchy and the image is female. The queen is the queen, and the honey is for her babies. The sting of a bee is male (an old French superstition has it that if you've been stung by a bee, you have been injected with a powerful aphrodisiac) but the end product of all that buzzing and beeing is certainly feminine, like everything sweet: cakes, pies, candy, cookies, ice cream, tortes, and tarts. Tart has three meanings: 1. a sweet pastry; 2. sharp in manner—either on the tongue or in behavior or language; 3. an immoral woman or a prostitute.

Candy is a confection—and an American slang word for the vulva. It's also a cute and sexy nickname for a bimbo. You'd never call a man your little lollipop, unless you were busy at something or other or you smiled when you said it.

A sweetheart is the one you love best and sweetie is a love name, and so is sugar, and so is honey, and all are more female than male. Lots of popular songs belabor the same point: "Candy, I call my sugar candy. . . ." "Ohhh sugar, honey, honey. . . ." "Sweet Sue," and dozens of others.

Chocolate is so sexy it's beyond gender, in the mystical way in which opposites—here, male and female—meet and become one. Chocolate is a universal ichor, a rich, oozing sensuousness that transcends sex. Chocolate is all in one. It's the opposite of kiwis, and they taste good together.

Traditionally, chocolate is what men give to women—a heart-shaped box of chocolates on Valentine's Day, for instance. Marketers have found that women like small bits of chocolate better than big bars: Hershey's makes Kisses (milk chocolate) and Hugs (with white chocolate) and women love them both. Their names are catchy, too.

Many food choices can be categorized by gender. Women eat more fruit than men do. They drink more herbal tea. Vanilla and chocolate ice cream are favorites of both men and women, but the premium ice-cream maker Häagen-Dazs reports that women choose offbeat flavors more often. Both Häagen-Dazs and Hershey's have found that mint is a flavor preferred by females. Campbell's introduced its Chunky line of soups with the slogan, "How to Handle a Hungry Man," but some years later found that women enjoyed it as much as men did. The slogan changed. Women like multigrain cereals more than men do; Tony the Tiger has a certain (cute) macho appeal, and men go for Frosted Flakes. Men and women don't divide over apples and bananas, no matter that apples are female and bananas are male, but women prefer cantaloupes, and men like raisins. Generalizations, of course. But marketers have come to depend on them. It took years for beer commercials to begin to appeal to women; beer is a male drink and men buy considerably more beer than women do. That's changing, just as the image of bottled water is changing—long female, now bisexual.

Eating styles have gender labels, too. Women nibble; men dig in. Women tend to eat less food when they're out with other people—it's not feminine to have a hearty appetite. Women pick; they'll just have a taste. It's a virtue for a woman to eat like a bird. Men are hearty eaters. If he eats like a bird, it's an eagle. Women talk about luncheon and dinner parties; men are more likely to say lunch and supper. Women have dessert more often than men do. Even cookies (a feminine word if ever there was one) are divided by sex: Women eat more Milano cookies—pale and delicate, a bit crisp, with a sweet almost-hidden chocolate layer. Men choose big, chewy chocolate chips, like Pepperidge Farm's Sausalitos, with chunks of chocolate and lots of nuts right out there for everyone to see.

Women talk more about food, too. They talk about recipes, and ingredients, and diets and food prices. Men are more likely to discuss how much they spent at the gas station, and how many miles they get to the gallon. (The Atkins Diet—all protein, all male—is probably the final gender leveler.) Virginia Woolf noted in *A Room of One's Own,* her marvelous essay on women and fiction, that most writers—then more often than not men—don't focus on food. "It is a curious fact that novelists have a way of making us believe that luncheon parties are invariably memorable for something very witty that was said, or for something very wise that was done. But they seldom spare a word for what was eaten."

Some food comes in couples: two by two, male and female, right on the table, going steady for life. In England, roast beef comes with Yorkshire pudding. The first, its outer layers crisp and crackling brown, its heart rare and red, oozes bloody juices: male. The pudding is soft and yielding beneath its thin crust, almost sweet, a sop for the juices, the perfect foil and partner: female. This is a marriage as perfectly sexed as Italy's pasta and tomato sauce. There are the male curries and female yogurts, the *raitas,* of India, the hot spices and sweet custards of Spain and Latin America, the steak and potatoes of the U.S.—each country's menu matings.

What follows, for fun, is my list of old married couples and perfect pairs. And isn't it interesting that one nearly always mentions the masculine half of the food marriage first? I've listed them the other way around. Just for a change.

Feminine	Masculine
Eggs	Bacon
Cheese	Ham
Poultry	Beef
Wine	Beer
Tea	Coffee
Sauce	Pasta
Peas	Carrots
Mayonnaise	Vinaigrette
Soup	Nuts
Breakfast	Dinner
Tomatoes	Lettuce
Candy	Nuts
Milk	Cereal
Jam	Toast
Dumplings	Stew
Fruit	Vegetables
Vanilla	Chocolate (male or female)
Sweet (sugar)	Sour (lemon)
Butter	Bread
Cheese	Crackers

Chapter 3

EATING STYLES

People predestined to gourmandism ... have ... bright eyes, small foreheads, short noses, full lips and rounded chins. ... The ones who are most fond of tidbits and delicacies are finer featured, with a daintier air; they are more attractive. ... People to whom Nature has denied the capacity for such enjoyment, on the other hand, have long faces, noses, and eyes. ... They have flat dark hair, and above all lack healthy weight; it is undoubtedly they who invented trousers, to hide their thin shanks.

—*The Physiology of Taste,*
by Jean Anthelme Brillat-Savarin

What is America famous for eating?

Hamburgers, hot dogs, fried chicken, corn on the cob.

This is a nation of finger-food eaters. And biters.

At the most basic level, finger food is eating the way it should be, all burbling and sloppy, full of fingers and fun, just the way it was in the high chair before proper society took notice of us and we learned that nice children don't play with their food.

The trouble is, children *want* to play with their food. Kittens push and pull at their mother's nipples while they suck. It makes the milk flow. Babies do the same thing, touching while their mouths work, exploring with their hands, making a connection between a soft breast and their warm fingers, while their mouths make a suction which is the ancient seal between mother and child.

Then, when they're a bit older, children still want to poke their food and push it, squeeze it up between their fingers and spread it around with their hands. It feels good. Food feels so good once it gets inside; why not give it a little squeeze first? (It might even be safer that way; it might seem logical to a baby to mush it around on the outside before agreeing to let it in.)

Finger foods are baby-fun for grown-ups, and they're baby-safe, too. They are democracy in action. They're easy to eat; no effete table manners need apply. Forget about whether you should use the dinner fork or the salad fork— just pick it up and go. If your chin gets greasy when you're eating corn on the cob and bits of corn stick between your teeth, if strings of melted cheese reach like primitive yardsticks from your mouth to the pizza in your outstretched hand, there's no need to worry. We all have slippery fingers now.

Fried chicken and hamburgers and hot dogs and corn on the cob—the all-American finger foods—are all also biting-food. And biting-food is a little later along on the time line than the first finger foods—teething is over and done with and now there are molars to do the work. Gumming the chicken as if it were a piece of zwieback just won't do the trick. When you're really little, the mouth by itself is relatively passive; ferocious noises come out of it, and milk goes into it, and that's more or less it. Biting is something else; it takes action. You have to reach out to bite; you have to chomp down. Biting is aggressive. Biting is taking, it's competitive. Biting is assertive: *This is mine.* Biting is no-nonsense eating.

Other countries have finger food (*pommes frites*, fish and chips, pizza, samosas, falafel in pita—street food is almost always finger food, and every country has street food). And other countries have biting food (crudités, tacos, and wurst more obviously than some, but pork pies and pizza and all the others qualify for biting as well as for fingering). But Americans have made finger and biting food into a kind of a national image. The Big Mac began here and it still means America no matter where it's sold.

Around the world, what we all seem to love is food with handles. Wraps. Pork pies. Spring rolls. Sandwiches. Tacos. Hamburgers and hot dogs. Ice-cream cones. Pizza. Buffalo wings. Fast food, street food—democratic food, plebian food. Franklin and Eleanor Roosevelt served hot dogs to King George and Queen Mary when they visited at Hyde Park, and the meal made headlines. It took a royal couple to make a hot dog news.

It isn't only the food itself that's telling. It's the choice of food, which obviously reflects on the chooser. Are Americans more democratic eaters? A chicken in every pot, and a hamburger in every hand? Are Americans more aggressive eaters? This is mine, this sandwich, and, dammit, *that* country? Perhaps. Let it also be known that Americans would rather cook Italian food—pasta—than that of any other nationality. Pasta is soft. Al dente, yes, but soft.

Researchers in England and America have come up with categories of eaters from "oral sadistic" to "infantile eaters." (Sounds bad, both ways, but it isn't really. They're just labels for the sake of labels in a magazine quiz kind of way.) According to their studies, people who like to chew a lot ("oral sadistic," and their dentists probably think very highly of them) also like foods that are strongly flavored, spicy, crunchy, sour—intense (espresso is preferred over cappuccino, and either over a glass of milk). In terms of personality, they're active and rugged types; they enjoy being alone, and they are somewhat cold and impatient. They tend to be pessimists; they're apt to be well educated.

Next, according to the researchers, are those who resemble the oral sadists, big chewers, but not quite as intense. (Swiss cheese, not goat; Brie, not Stilton.) They're readers, nonconformists but not rebels, and they're competitive.

In the middle are those who like bland and mushy food as much as spicy, crunchy food. Well-adjusted! All things are possible! But sliding toward infancy are those who prefer sweet, soft, bland food. (Coffee with cream and sugar, never black.) These folks are relatively relaxed, sociable, and somewhat optimistic. They're conventional and will go a long way to avoid confrontation.

And then there are those who eat almost nothing that isn't bland and soft. (Banana cream pie over mince or rhubarb every time.) Here, the researchers say, are people who have unresolved needs left over from childhood. They're dependent on others, sociable but desperate to fit into their group, and are often taken advantage of. And yet they are often optimists. Have another spoonful of pudding, dear, it'll be better in the morning.

Oral sadist or not, chewing is inward; biting is outward. Chewing is thoughtful—think of the cow and its eternal cud. Biting is crisp and active. Some people just don't fool around at the table. They sit with their backs to the wall, their hands in plain view next to their plates, and they attack their food. They grab it in; by God, it isn't going to get away. They eat fast and they chew hard and when the going gets tough, they swallow it anyway.

Aggressive eaters are anxious, too. They worry. And when they eat, they choose to do something about it. They reach, they take, they bite. They look their troubles right in the eye and then they pop them into their mouths and they deal with them. It's known as getting your teeth into a problem, and it's not all bad. If you do have a problem, sometimes it helps to chew it over for a while.

Overeaters often use food to smother the raging fires within. Aggressive eaters use food similarly, but they are appeasing the flames. Perhaps for that reason, aggressive eaters are often fast eaters, edging toward desperation and courting more than indigestion. There is an element of reckless hopelessness in stuffing food in, fork rushing from plate to mouth and back down again, stoking the fire—perhaps in anticipation of a critical shortage of fuel.

Fast eaters are impatient, and more. They're insecure. Is there a part of the fast eater that remembers the hungry interval between bottles, between breasts? The fast eater needs all the food—all the love—he can find, and he needs it *now*. If we remember hunger and we anticipate hunger, we need to eat quickly while we have the chance, get it all in before it's taken away, so that we can wait—full at last—in the long, lonely stretch before food comes again. Abandonment is the primal fear, and to the infant, hunger *is* abandonment. Or maybe the fast eater just wants to get it all over with. Maybe the table just isn't a comfortable place to be.

As a nation, Americans tend to be fast eaters. No two-hour lunches, followed by a nap. The international Slow Food movement started in Italy. Maybe one reason why weight is such a constant problem in America is that Americans eat too fast. The brain doesn't have a chance to do its work—the signals from the stomach that say "enough!" take twenty minutes to half an hour to kick in, and that's more than enough time for second and third helpings and just one more sliver of cake.

If America's favorite foods are finger foods—biting, aggressive foods—and its national pace is fast (American fast-food restaurants westernize the world as fast as the world can gulp down what they serve), then the statement Americans are making about themselves with their mouths, is an aggressive, anxious, insecure one. Who loves ya, baby? That was Kojak's line; big, bald, stern Telly Savalas, lollipop firmly in mouth, policing the big city, baby's dream of what it would be like to be Papa. We've left the age of innocence far behind, and languishing with it is Mom's apple pie, sweet, soft, and ever so gently spiced.

While fast eaters are gulping down the stew and biters are gnawing on their spare ribs, soft-food eaters (and they are frequently also slow eaters) are having a gentle go-around with an omelette or a soufflé. For them, food is sensual, not hard and crunchy. Conflict sits on somebody else's plate. Aggression isn't on the menu. Not today.

Soft foods are the foods of childhood, in a different way from finger food. Chocolate pudding preceded chocolate cookies. Soft food came first. Milk, cereal, mashed bananas, strained string beans, scraped apples: These are the foods of infancy, when eating a teething biscuit was an adventure in gummy gastronomy.

Baby has mashed potatoes; big Daddy has fries. Grown-ups take care of such complicated things as cracking lobster and boning shad. When we're ready to face the world as adults, we can get a grip on things in the mouth as well as in the hand. Then we'll chomp away at the roast beef and bite into the crudités. Custard is for babies. Caramel sucks.

A Chicago pastry chef correlated pies with personality types. Apple pie, of course, is exactly what you'd expect: safe and secure. It speaks of home, even if you buy it frozen at the supermarket. Middle of the road, says the chef. Sweet potato pie, he says, is family, but not specifically Mom, and it's warm, welcoming, and hospitable. Blueberry: outdoorsy and determined. Cherry: so sweet—in fact, too sweet! Not entirely trustworthy, perhaps. Chocolate: seductive, strong, suave. Lemon: bright, energetic, and with a sharp tongue. Peach: for sun worshippers. Pecan: simplicity, but looking for love. Coconut cream: needing an escape from reality. Pumpkin: sentimental but comfortable. Mincemeat: intelligent, and perhaps a bit pretentious. Banana cream: so relaxing! It's for overachievers who don't want to be in charge anymore. Rhubarb: split between truly old-fashioned types and hipsters. But come to think of it, maybe hipsters *are* old-fashioned types. And if you add strawberries to the rhubarb? Life is full of adventure.

Whatever the menu, whichever the pie, everybody likes something best. And there is always one thing that is better than best, because food is garnished with food. There are grilled mushrooms on top of the steak, a sprinkling of croutons or *lardons* in the salad, a soft whirl of creamy *schlag* nestling *ober* the Sacher torte. Do you like the lemon better than the meringue, the à la mode more than the pie? What happens to the crème de la crème, the best bite of all, the oyster of meat resting against the chicken's backbone, the fried onions that come with the calves liver, the cookie on the plate with the poached fruit?

Some people like to eat the best bite first; they begin with pleasure. Others save it as a special treat, savoring it in anticipation. The aggressive eater—ever on the attack—is prone to eat the best bit first. It's another symptom of being a worrier. That morsel has to be gotten in, fast, first. After all, there are other people watching and waiting, and they're all hungry, too. Or they can't resist the call of the whipped cream, the fried onion.... Food is seductive; Adam and Eve never made it past the apple.

Letting the last forkful of sausage stuffing dally on one side of the plate while you finish the turkey and the sweet potatoes is more than just wanting a good taste to linger after the food has gone. It's security. Obviously, you aren't worrying that someone else will grab it away and gobble it up before you can wave your arms and holler, "Stop!"

Some people eat their food as if a meal were a round-robin. They take a bite of the meat, then some of the potatoes, then a bit of the vegetable and then more of the meat. It all goes down at a regular rate, all at the same time, and nothing is really saved for last or eaten first. These are without a doubt the kind of people who take a bland, busy approach to life. They are not particularly authoritative, nor are they decisive.

The orderly (not to say compulsive) mind eats neatly: first the meat, then the potatoes. One thing at a time and a time for each thing. One suspects that they approach love in the same way. First the kiss and then the squeeze. They lack a sense of savor, and are equally lacking in spontaneity.

Then there are those who play with their food. In some ways, this is a souvenir of childhood, perhaps happily, but more likely as an expression of rebellion or discomfort which was never otherwise resolved. Some toy with their food in a more complicated fashion, pushing it around, messing it up, arranging it and rearranging it between bites. They seem to be creating chaos out of order and then creating order once again in an endless circle that stops only when the plate is bare.

Even before the first bite is taken, there are differences in eating patterns. Bare-plate children—"Take as much as you want, but eat as much as you take!"—grow up to greet full plates with a sinking sense of horror. They see before them a mountain of food that can't just be tunneled through. It has to vanish completely. It weighs them down.

Others feel best the other way around, when their plates are heaped. A full plate, for them, is a visible token of love; it's security incarnate. For them, the proof of the pudding is not in the eating; it's in the prospect.

Salad bars and dessert buffets trade on our subliminal wish to be given plenty. There seems to be a kind of love among the bowls of pickled beets and three bean salad, the small squares of cake and the blobs of chocolate mousse. No one has to wait for anybody to dish it out. Serve yourself! As much as you want! And we're greedy. Finally, enough whipped cream! Chickpeas, no holds barred! It's only later, after the salad dish has been heaped with raw broccoli and sliced onion and sweet pickles and grated Parmesan and Russian dressing, that it all begins to seem a bit tawdry, like casual sex, perhaps a little drunken, on the morning after. The salad bar, the dessert table—they're nothing more than a one-night stand. Worse. It's love that had to be paid for. And it's not quite what it seemed at first. The lettuce is limp around the edges, the dressing is gooey, and the cucumbers are bitter. The mousse was made from a mix. We've been tricked and betrayed—again.

Fussy eaters are more careful. They worry about what they eat. They look it over very carefully before they agree to incorporate it. Fussy eaters seem nervous, but way down deep, they are really rebellious types. They learned early that rejecting food is a power ploy. Saying "No!" to dinner is simultaneously a "No!" to Mama and Papa. It's a nice rebellion for nervous types, because it's a safe one. "I just don't want any" is ever so much easier to hear than "I don't want what you want me to want," even though, as rebellions go, it's a fairly hungry one.

Children are often fussy eaters—many a child has grown to maturity, or at least adolescence, on peanut butter and jelly sandwiches. Children eat on trust. Food is what children are given by the people with whom they are the most profoundly involved. If those people aren't worth trusting, neither is their food. And if the food doesn't taste good, or if it's followed by a stomachache (from nerves or dinner), there is a great deal to wonder about. There may be no reason not to bite the hand that feeds. It's self-defense.

Children who worry about food go in circles, sometimes: If they don't trust Mommy and Daddy, they don't trust food, and if they don't trust food, they don't trust people. The child who is consistently suspicious of strangers will grow up to distrust food that is different from the usual fare. If you don't like foreigners, chances are you won't like foreign food either, and vice versa.

Eating between meals can also take us back to the time of the child. There are sensible, small meals, meant to sustain us in a healthy way, and then there are the snacks which are another way of keeping our mouths busy, or diverting ourselves from the world, or comforting ourselves in a munchy sort of way. So many of us don't recognize hunger because it has never had a chance to arrive. Hunger has nothing to do with why we eat— the bag of chips, the candy bar, and even the apple fill another sort of need.

The bedtime snack is another, a sweeter harkening back to childhood. Some of us hate to go to bed on an empty stomach. That vast space beneath the heart is a terrible burden when there's nothing in it. The night is long and dark, and a hollow stomach is not reassuring. How warm is the memory of mother, straightening the blankets, smoothing the hair, kissing the cheek. Food at bedtime is like mother; a comfort. The full stomach tucks us in under the warm winter quilt, all snug and safe, ready to drift into dreams and be strong until breakfast.

Part Two

SEX IN THE KITCHEN

A book of Verse underneath the Bough,
A Flask of Wine, a Loaf of Bread—and Thou,
Beside me singing in the Wilderness—
Oh, Wilderness were paradise enow!

—*The Rubaiyat of Omar Khayyam,*
by Edward FitzGerald

Chapter 4

SEX IN THE KITCHEN

Sugar glistened on his lips and raspberry jam trickled down his chin.
"Lovely," he said. "I sometimes think I'd as lief have a doughnut as a
woman. One bang's like any other, but every time you sink your
teeth into a doughnut's like the very first time."
—*Bones and Silence,*
by Reginald Hill

Back in the days of our innocence, before we divided things up into
hard- and soft-core, there was a classic pinup pose. It was a male cooking fantasy—not of mother, rather more like kitchen pornography instead.
It might have been drawn by Vargas, who did the *Esquire* Girl. It was
kitchen pose—long-legged, long-haired, and all yours, always ready, always
willing. As I recall it, she (The Girl) is wearing nothing but black fishnet
stockings and a tiny curved apron that is tied around her waist. We see her
in three-quarter profile, from the rear. She's bending over the oven, her legs

43

straight and her bottom all round and curvy. She's looking back at us and smiling, and she's taking something out of the oven, or putting something in—either way, it's delicious.

It's a warm, loving, unselfconscious, sexy fantasy—something like what used to spring to mind when Sophia Loren in her prime wrote a cookbook and talked about how much she loved to cook pasta. "Everything you see," Loren said, "I owe to spaghetti."

That's kitchen sex: steamy and lusty and joyful and for all that, still somewhat innocent. It's based on the recognition that food and sex satisfy twin appetites—hungers that began before we were born.

Dr. Freud said that a kitchen is the most female room in the house. (According to the doctor, rooms are, symbolically speaking, generally female—the hollow space, enclosed.) Following that Freudian theory, cooking is the essence of womanliness.

Toss Freud out the kitchen window and cooking is still stereotypically female. The giving of food is the first task of motherhood. For nine months, there's no choice; in that interval, mothers *are* food. They are kitchens with feet, ambulatory efficiency units.

After the nine months are up, women do have choices to make and one of the first is whether or not to breast-feed. Like the other choices women have today, simply *having* a choice is liberating. Before bottles could be sterilized or formula bought at the local supermarket, women remained the food source for a long time after a baby had been born. Only a woman—wet nurse or mother—could keep an infant alive, nourish it, and give it its first knowledge, that love is food and food is pleasure.

And also, until relatively recently on the time line, once the infant had been weaned it still depended on women, not baby food jars, to make its meals palatable. Some anthropologists believe that cooking had benefits for women as well as the people for whom they cooked. Women stayed home with the children while the men were out hunting; they were the keepers of the family flame—and the cooking pot. One scholar, anthropologist Dr. Sonia Ragir, calls this "the nibbling theory of human evolution." Their greater access to food before the men came back and it had to be divided up, meant that women, in the leap from australopithecine to Homo erectus, grew 60 percent taller and bigger than her female ancestors—about

44

the same difference in height as that between a modern ten-year-old girl and her mother. (Men, making the same evolutionary leap, became only a tiny bit bigger than australopithecine males.) For those early housewives, this meant greater fertility, stronger infants, and probably healthier lives as well.

We've come a long way, and not only from the cave. Marriage roles are changing from what we once considered those of the traditional family, but expectations and stereotypes are slow to catch up with reality. Do men feel guilty when they haven't prepared a hot meal from scratch? Women are *relieved* when they phone out for food; men just look forward to dinner.

In the families in which most of us grew up, the woman's moment at the stove, wooden spoon firmly in hand, was a moment of control, subtle but no less strong for that. Before take-out food and home delivery of dinner, women had to learn to use that moment for all it was worth.

Sex in the kitchen is part of that moment, whether the food is home-grown or arrives at the front door in under a half hour. Sex in the kitchen doesn't mean only something like Kevin Costner and Susan Sarandon doing it among the cornflakes on the breakfast table (in *Bull Durham*). We're talking symbols here. Allegory. Metaphor. Fantasy. Psychology. (Anyway, if she'd known he was going to end up hearing voices in an Iowa cornfield, she probably would have felt differently about him in his *first* baseball movie.) Sex in the kitchen is two things: what you cook and how you cook it.

Sex in the kitchen is nothing new. It has been going on for centuries. About two thousand years ago, a story in *The Golden Ass of Apuleius* tells us, a man named Lucius wandered into the kitchen of a Roman household where he was a guest. He watched a slave named Fotis prepare pork rissoles for dinner. "As she alternately stirred the casserole and shaped the rissoles with her pretty hands, the twisting and turning made her whole body quiver seductively. The sight had so powerful an effect on me that for a while I stood rooted in admiration; and so did something else."

"Dear Fotis," he finally said, "how . . . charmingly you stir that casserole. . . . What a wonderful cook you are! The man whom you allow to poke his finger into your little casserole is the luckiest fellow alive."

"A wonderful cook, am I? Yes, I certainly know how to tickle a man's . . . well, his palate, if you care to call it that, and how to keep things nicely on the boil. . . ."

After dinner, Lucius and Fotis moved from the kitchen to the bedroom. The bedside table was covered with "little dishes of tasty food," some leftover rissoles, and cups of wine. "It was as though," says Lucius, "the apple-bough of love had bent down over me and I was gorging myself with the fruit until I could gorge no more." But he and Fotis drank more wine and nibbled a rissole and, revived, began again.

Cooking, as Fotis well knew, can be an act of seduction. You don't even have to wiggle as you stir; you can stand still, eyes modestly downcast, and let the food do the work for you. I don't mean aphrodisiacs (which are discussed in chapter 5) as much as I do food that is subtle, well spiced, not overwhelming or heavy or rich, and not meant to sate and dull the appetites. To seduce with food, M.F.K. Fisher composed a classically perfect meal as well as one with exactly the opposite intention. The latter is anaphrodisiac cooking, meant to turn off, rather than on, the flames of desire.

There is indeed cooking that is meant to control rather than to delight, to be selfish rather than giving, to be a substitute for sex rather than an adjunct. There is cooking that gives the cook a smug kind of pleasure, an almost unisexual satisfaction, making him or her as hermaphroditic as a hydra. This cook nibbles while stirring, tasting this and sipping that and comes to the table sated and satisfied, too full to take another bite. Pleasure has been standing alone by the stove, joining mouth to spoon in solitude.

Cooking can overwhelm eating if it becomes an easier or safer mode in which to take pleasure. Then, like the ladies who chose to masturbate with carrots and parsnips (before there were vibrators), the cook picks the menu to pleasure the cook.

In the detective novel *E is for Evidence*, Sue Grafton wrote about two women sharing a meal of steamed clams. "She speared a tender button of clam flesh and placed it on her tongue, her eyes closing in a near-swoon as she swallowed.... As she bit into it, she made a little sound low in her throat like something out of an X-rated video...." Kinsey, Grafton's detective, teases the clam eater about her food, and she replies, "Someone asked me once which I'd rather have—sex or a warm chocolate chip cookie. I still can't decide." For Kinsey, it's no contest. "Go for the cookies," she says. "You can bake 'em yourself."

There's another kind of cooking, based on a conscious, calculated recognition, a kind of refrigerated bargain. Marabel Morgan, antifeminist author of *The Total Woman,* wrote that in order to be happy, a wife must learn that her husband's happiness *precedes* her own; he will love her if he appreciates what she does for him and how she makes him feel—if she fulfills his needs and wishes and even his fantasies. If she does all this, he'll be happy, and then, oh, then, and only then, *she* will be happy. (It's codependent heaven!)

"When a man's got butter in the refrigerator at home," Ms. Morgan said, "he won't go out in the street for margarine." The relationship thus oozes along, greased by condescension and carefully planned spontaneity. A husband won't be bored, she told a generation of women, if every so often he's met at the front door by his wife, wearing nothing but a cold martini.

It wasn't that Marabel Morgan didn't believe in sex. "Physically, the climax during intercourse is the greatest pleasure on Earth.... Emotionally, a woman's climax, coupled with the joy she receives giving herself to her husband, completes her...." And her kitchen did have sex left in it—butter in the refrigerator is food in a hollow place, which meets the Freudian guidelines for symbols—but it's kind of cold in there in the fridge. Unlike the fantasy of the luscious lady bending over by the oven—sweet-smelling, bubbly fun, an after-school snack all grown up and turned into an afternoon delight—this one is as cold and calculating and self-conscious as a glossy mirror carefully positioned over the bed.

Better than Marabel Morgan's butter—better than her naked housewife at the front door—is the image of Sophia Loren in the kitchen with a plate of pasta, carried at breast level, wisps of steam curling into her hair, full of joy, giving herself because that's what she wants to do, not because the pasta and the body are part of a careful bargain. That kind of cooking is free and spontaneous, Sophia Loren as mother of Julia Roberts and mystical pizza.

Offering food, after all, is offering love. Cooking, at its best, is an act of love as well as a seduction. Lea Bidault, one of the celebrated *Mères Lyonnaises* whose cooking as professional chefs has been responsible for several great restaurants in Lyons, said that "cooking and making love are the same. They both stem from the desire to give pleasure."

The *Mères,* women who cook professionally, were unusual because for so long paid cooks were only male. Once in a while, if a woman needed money and if she made really good pie, she opened a little restaurant. (Never play cards with a man named Doc, and never eat at a place called Mom's, said writer Nelson Algren. There don't seem to be many places called Dad's.)

What's happened in our time is that there are female chefs, OK, but the male chefs are the hot ones, in both senses of the word. "Women who've lived the fantasy report that having an affair with a chef offers the same risks and rewards as scoring a table at a buzz-inflated restaurant," writes a contributor to *Food and Wine* magazine. "It's thrilling, when it isn't maddening. The food and sex connection, of course, is right up front." The article goes on to quote a woman now married to a star chef. "All the chefs I've met have a passion for food that definitely translates into other areas. When I met [my husband] on a blind date, his hands were greenish from chopping herbs, and he had all these little cuts and burns. I thought it was *so* sexy.... When I saw him in his whites, I thought, Eating this amazing food cooked by this very, very cool guy—oh my God, it's foreplay!"

Cooking *is* a kind of foreplay to the intercourse of the mouth. It is a giving of the self, of the senses, a direct predecessor to the moment of penetration. In *A Married Feminist*, Angela Barron McBride writes that in parts of Africa, language about cooking is explicit. "To put fuel in the fire and to blow is to cohabit; the hearthstones are the posteriors; the cooking pot is the vagina; the pot ladle is the penis."

The same symbols are present in the most sophisticated kitchen, self-cleaning oven and all. We, too, speak of the heat of passion, of hot women and hot men, and blow jobs. And from the fire in the cave to the convection oven, it has ever been thus. "Coynte it was the porridge pot," wrote Bobbie Burns in "Merry Muses of Caledonia," "and penis was the ladle; / Buttocks were the serving men / that waited at the table."

Even children understand. Iona and Peter Opie, collectors of children's songs and rhymes and chants, quote the poem "Jemmy Dawson" in their *Oxford Nursery Rhyme Book*—

> Brave news is come to town,
> Brave news is carried;

Brave news is come to town,
Jemmy Dawson's married.

First he got a porridge-pot,
Then he got a ladle;
Then he got a wife and child,
And then he bought a cradle.

Cooking has never been more popular than it is in our sexy times—despite the take-out meal and the microwaved dinner. There's almost an inverse relationship between the interest in cooking and the things that make cooking less necessary. Cooking schools abound; cooking magazines flourish; cookware catalogs are issued monthly, it sometimes seems. Emeril has become a television star (whose audiences, for inexplicable reasons, applaud whenever he uses the word *garlic*), and the Food Network is right up there with Discovery and Comedy Central and CNN. Cookbooks are published in greater and greater numbers—and at the same time, in a survey asking what was inside America's refrigerators, 93 percent of the respondents said leftover take-out food. You'd never guess that in another survey, conducted by Dr. Mihaly Csikszentmihalyi, a professor of psychology at the University of Chicago, a study of daily logs kept over a twenty-year period showed that cooking was the seventh most common daily activity. Lovemaking was number one. (Numbers two to six were socializing, talking, eating, sports, and shopping. Cooking outranked watching television and reading.)

Maybe part of what's happening is that as cooking becomes less of a female-dominated activity belonging almost solely to mothers and wives, it becomes more available (and less threatening). As chefs become sexier—the rock stars of the kitchen—what they actually *do* at work becomes sexier, too. The idea of cooking is sexy and appealing and wonderful; a dream. The prep work is what happens when you wake up.

It used to be that it was embarrassing to talk about cooking. Sitting by themselves, women might chatter about a recipe and its secret (ooooooh!) ingredients, but the subject of cooking certainly wasn't a topic for mixed company. It wasn't only that preparing food was women's work and was thus automatically boring and low status (like child care), it's also that there was a pronounced tendency not to admit to any of the things that give the most pleasure. Both sex and food "have some aspects of voyeur appeal," says Susan Friedland, an important and successful cookbook editor, in a *New York Times* article about cookbooks. (Maybe that's why it's often as much fun, if not more, to read about cooking than it is to get down and cook.)

At the same time, women have become aware that cooking is a vital part of their history, and scholars readily agree. Food history is a valid study now; anthropology includes food as an integral part of culture. The culinary arts are considered a serious academic study, and not just as part of women's studies. Understanding what we eat means understanding who we are; studying how and what we cook tells us how we got to where we are. Hansel and Gretel left a trail of bread crumbs in the forest so they could get home again, and so has humanity.

We've also come to understand that cooking is a kind of therapy—it certainly reflects our problems and our neuroses, and it also helps to heal them. Maybe not while you're rushing to feed four different people with four different tastes and four different allergies and four different schedules and you've just come home from work and you're tired, too—but certainly when there's time to savor the preparation before you get to enjoy the product. "I can lose myself making a Bolognese sauce, finely chopping the onions, the carrots, three kinds of meat, and the slow, slow simmering," says psychology professor Dr. Csikszentmihalyi. "There is a sense of order and control and something so wholesome and tactile about cooking."

Many home cooks agree. You have to concentrate when you're cooking; chopping and slicing are idiot work, but they are idiot work done with a sharp knife in your hand. Cooking is rhythmic and engrossing; it's orderly and has predetermined limits. You can't think about the usual stresses and strains while you're whisking and stirring. And cooking can be done in groups or with friends, but mostly it's solitary and it's sensuous; everything needs handling, and the best cooks work with their fingers. Cooking demands concentration, and concentration is healthy. It lowers blood pressure and settles the heart as well as the mind.

More than one psychologist has written a cookbook. In *Cooking as Therapy*—a book of recipes, the cooking of which can influence your mood

(but it's really your mood that influences what you cook, and how)—
psychiatrist Louis Parrish explores a variety of emotions in a kitchen setting. (He also discusses the seduction and anti-seduction dinners, with
somewhat less refinement than M.F.K. Fisher, but from a related point of
view. After a big dinner, Parrish, too, wants to go to bed, "only the last thing
I want to do is make love! I want to go to sleep!")

His book was based on the premise that cooking can satisfy all of the
emotions, not only the overtly sexual ones. There is much to be said for letting it all hang out in the batter, the soup, the potatoes, the stew. With perfect freedom—it's what you're *supposed* to do—the cook can pummel the
dough, slash the carrots, gentle the sauce, and fondle the fruit.

The copy on the back cover of the paperback version of Dr. Parrish's
book makes it all explicit. "Mince onions," we are advised, "not words."
"Tension—Make it work for you, by pounding an inexpensive cut into
meat as tender as filet mignon." "Depression—Don't take medication. Take
magic cake." And on it goes, with a recipe for every mood. "The Angry
Cook" is chapter 3 and "Sex in the Kitchen" doesn't begin until chapter 9.
In reality, sex in the kitchen is what it's all about.

Chapter 5

BEDTIME SNACKS

> I don't buy sugar,
> You just have to touch my cup.
> You're my sugar,
> It's sweet when you stir it up.
> When I'm takin' sips
> From your tasty lips
> Then the honey fairly drips.
> You're confection, goodness knows,
> Honeysuckle Rose.
> —"Honeysuckle Rose,"
> by Fats Waller and Andy Razaf

The simplest life, a single cell, fills its tiny days in only two ways. It eats, and it divides in half. That's all there is to it, in the beginning—food and reproduction. The amoeba wraps itself around its dinner and then halves itself and eats twice as much. Life starts with basics, food and sex, to be and to be again.

Food is the first sex object. Baby boys offer ample proof, their tiny

53

penises rising to meet the world as their stomachs swell and their bodies are filled with sensual comfort and warmth. When we grow up we complicate things. We make cream sauces out of milk, and we cover the bed with designer sheets, but our twin appetites, food and sex, remain.

In dreams, Freud said, the mouth symbolizes the vagina, as does any hollow place—a cup, a box, a cave, a kitchen. And we—we are symbols incarnate: Our bodies contain a series of hollow organs surrounded by flesh.

The mouth begins and genitals end. The connection between them is more than neighborliness of the body, more even than symbolism. Mouth and genitals are linked in physical and psychic identity. Food is love, and food is also sex; cooking is foreplay, and eating is fucking.

Our love words are food words, from sweetie to hottie. You can be a dish, in America; in France, *un petit chou* (a little cabbage); in England, a bit of crumpet (a flat griddle cake dripping butter). Teenagers used to "chew face." She's delicious; he looks good enough to eat. There's a tart, a cookie—candy, I call my sugar candy. Rosemary Clooney's early hit "Come On-A My House" was a catalog of sexy food (and sexy euphemisms—figs, dates, grapes, cakes, candy). We don't confuse food and sex; we recognize that they are the same. And they're sweet and dripping, fleshy mouthfuls.

Inevitably, there's a connection between the way we eat and the way we make love. German psychologist Alfred Gebert talked to women about what their men were like as lovers, and then correlated those findings with the way each man ate. "There were amazing similarities," Gebert said. He added that a woman looking for a certain kind of lover could make fairly accurate predictions by watching the way a man eats—then she'd know "whether to make an excuse and leave—or accept the invitation home for a cup of coffee."

His findings: If you're looking for a strong man, one who takes control, avoid men who mash their food up and eat several things together. If they eat in that mushy way they tend to lack new ideas in bed, the doctor said. A man who eats his vegetables before the meat is self-absorbed; better to avoid him. Men who play with their food, making patterns with it on the plate, are probably good company, sympathetic, and generous—they even have the potential to be good fathers. Avoid men who season their food without even tasting it. "Men like that are bossy and controlling," said

Gebert. "They are traditional and like men to be men, and they like their women in the kitchen."

In *Booty Food: A Date-by-Date, Course-by-Course, Nibble-by-Nibble Guide to Cultivating Love and Passion Through Food,* Jacqui Malouf decodes food choices (rather than styles of eating) as early as the first date. If he orders oysters, he's a "premature ejaculator or will rush you down the aisle." Caviar means he's "overzealous; will stalk you." Watch out if he wants a cup of coffee before you've even finished eating: "Will please himself then instantly roll over."

Several years ago, a London psychologist studying obesity accidentally found a clinical correlation between the way people eat and the way they make love. Maurice Yaffe, on the staff of Guy's Hospital, noticed that many of the obese people he was seeing also had a variety of sexual difficulties. Might there also be a link between food and sex even in people *without* weight problems? Yaffe began a study of couples with sexual, rather than weight, problems, and found the link going from sex to food, rather than the other way around.

Yaffe divided the people he studied into four overall groups, based on their eating styles: fast and slow eaters, plus food savorers and those not particularly interested in food. He then related each group to their attitudes about sex.

The first group—slow eaters who savor food—were sensualists. They focused on what they were eating, its tastes and textures. They were interested in how it was prepared. As lovers, they were equally sensuous and caring.

Slow eaters in the second group weren't particularly interested in what they were eating. They didn't care much about how it was prepared, or combined, or where it came from. They reported that they often had problems in bed.

The other two groups were the opposites: fast eaters who enjoy food, and fast eaters who don't care about what they're eating. People who enjoyed food and were somewhat knowledgeable about it but who ate quickly turned out to be anxious in bed. This group seemed to be self-conscious; people in it worried about how others perceived them, but took no great interest in their own sensuousness. Women reported that men in this category found it difficult to relax in bed.

Now things get more complicated. The final group, fast eaters who were not interested in food, subdivided into four separate categories.

The first subgroup was called "presexual" because they found it difficult to have any kind of sexual relationship. Many were virgins.

The second subgroup had a low sex drive; they were not very interested in making love.

The third subgroup was the largest. People in this group used food as a substitute for sex. They were particularly likely to be overweight, and if their sexual difficulties were resolved, they lost weight easily.

Finally, for the fourth subgroup, sex was a mechanical act. They avoided intimacy or any kind of real emotional involvement. They didn't get excited about a perfectly made sauce, and they maintained the same detachment in bed.

Bedtime and dinnertime. Fast eaters, fast lovers. If they race through the hors d'oeuvres, chances are they don't care much about the foreplay, either. Wham, bam, thank you, ma'am; eat and run. This nation of aggressive, fast eaters has a lot to answer for in bed: It's no accident that McDonald's happened here first and so did Masters and Johnson.

It makes sense that slow eaters have it better in bed, and not only because longevity counts. They are the sensualists at every turn, between the sheets and savoring the sauce. Love, like food, should linger on the tongue.

For those who are not terribly interested in food—it fills an empty stomach, and that takes care of that—sex fills another need, probably just as routinely. They forget that our senses need commitment; food tastes better when you know how to cook it and even how to eat it; that works for love-making, too.

Some people eat instead of making love. Perhaps eating is easier for them—it's acceptable in polite society; it's available all the time; and it doesn't involve anybody else. For them, eating is a secret thrill, a self-indulgence as lonely as masturbation.

Then there are people—men and women—who treat food as if eating were a kind of rape. They grab at their food; they stuff mouthfuls into their cheeks; they chew and drink and swallow, and watching them, it seems as if they hardly have time to taste. Eating for them seems violent. What are they like in bed? Sex for them must be at best fast and simple, and they probably fall asleep as soon as it's over.

Poet Gabriele D'Annunzio used the relationship between eating and making love for his own practical purposes. "I always determine the sexual capabilities of a woman by the way she eats fruit," he said. "When testing a potential bedmate, I offer her an apple or pear to see how she eats it. Small mincing bites—the ladylike kind—they are not good. But if she crunches the fruit, salivates with pleasure and crinkles her nose in enjoyment, this girl, my friend, should prove to be a redoubtable love partner." In *Reading Lolita in Tehran*, Azor Nafisi wrote about women who could be expelled from the university because of the way they eat a peach.

Describing the memorable dinner scene in his novel *Tom Jones*, Henry Fielding wrote that "love frequently preserves [us] from the attacks of hunger, [and] so may hunger possibly, in some cases, defend us against love." In the movie,* as Albert Finney and Joyce Redman made radiantly clear, hunger and love—eating and intercourse—can be almost one and the same.

Margaret Mead found a similar basis for comparison, between the way South Pacific babies are fed and the way they have sex as adults. In *Male and Female,* she describes Arapesh mothers who carry their babies in soft bags suspended beneath their breasts. The babies curl up there just as they did in the womb, and when the baby is hungry, it is fed, quickly, carefully and gently. The children are passive, Mead writes. As adults, girls have fewer problems in store for them than boys. "To transfer an attitude of pleasant expectancy from mouth to vulva, of soft, optimistic retentiveness, requires very little shift in attitude." But the boys grow up to be men who distrust active, well-sexed women.

Itamul headhunters also fed their babies tenderly. Immediately after birth, before the mother has her own milk, the infant is fed by a wet nurse,

---

* Tom Jones offers one of numerous movie meals. A partial listing: *Like Water for Chocolate; Eat Drink Man Woman; Babette's Feast; La Grande Bouffe; The Cook, the Thief, His Wife and Her Lover;* and a host of others. Food is just as important on Broadway—or at least, the table on which it's eaten is. From *Death of a Salesman* and *Long Day's Journey into Night* to *The Dining Room,* the table (whether home or restaurant) is a focal point, an underlining, and a metaphor.

but "with a touch of the gesture with which mothers later stop their babies' temper tantrums by thrusting their nipples into their mouths like corks into soda-water bottles." Children are expected to have wills of their own, and to *demand* food when they're hungry. When the Itamul child is only a few weeks old, the mother keeps it at a distance from her body, and it has to cry before it's fed. The baby teethes on pieces of ornaments made from hard shell that the mother wears as a necklace. "The sense of the mouth is built up as an assertive, demanding organ, taking what it can from a world that is, however, not unduly unwilling to give it." As they grow, boys develop an especially active picture of what they imagine the female's role in sex to be.

The Mundugumor went about their lives quite differently. Babies are carried in rough baskets which scratch their skin; later, they're placed "high on their mothers' shoulders, well away from the breast." Mothers stand up to nurse, and they push their babies away "as soon as they are the least bit satisfied. . . . In later life, love-making is conducted like the first round of a prize-fight, and biting and scratching are important parts of foreplay."

The formal groupings of Yaffe and Mead exemplify the emotional and symbolic links between food and sex, between eating and making love. There are other ties, too. Physically, there are similarities between the mouth and the genitals. Lips, tongue, and genitals all have the same neural receptors, known as Krause's end bulbs. Lips, tongue, and genitals are all sensitive, charged, and highly responsive. The line that connects them is an intense thread that winds through our bodies, from lips to labia, from tongue to penis. Mouth and genitals are the most sensitive parts of our bodies; the lips rank with the clitoris, the penis, and the tongue as the body's most sensitive, and therefore most sensual, skin. The word *labia* is Latin for lips; the labia are the external folds of the vulva, the lips of the vagina, pink and pursed around a deep, moist hollow.

Desmond Morris, in *Intimate Behavior* and *The Naked Ape,* noted that most animals don't have the kind of lips that people do, "inside out" clearly defined fleshy folds. Most animal mouths are not much more than a simple line. According to Morris, human lips evolved as a kind of genital signal substitute because we needed a way to display interest in sex. We don't puff out our feathers or ruffle our neck fur when we're ready for a little adventure.

Morris writes that lips are darker than surrounding skin because they are imitating genital behavior. When a woman is sexually aroused, the labia are flushed with blood and change from their delicate pink color to a deep red. Lipstick, says Morris, is an emphasized genital signal. "... The colours vary from fad to fad, [but] they always return before long to something in the pink-red range, thereby copying the flushing of the labia during the advanced stages of sexual arousal."

If there is ever a "Miss Genital Signal Substitute" contest, Marilyn Monroe ought to be awarded first prize posthumously. At the same time sacrificed virgin and high priestess of sexuality, the body both knowing and pure, Marilyn offered the ultimate invitation and her own surrender to sex in all the photographs of her with her full, red lips pursed and her mouth slightly open, sometimes showing her small tongue in its sweet, dark, pink, juicy hole.

Writers and poets have always been fascinated by the mouth, which can probably claim more erotic literature in its own right than any other single part of the body. The language of love is filled with images of the mouth, of food and of eating, beginning with the Bible. "Thy lips, O my spouse," says the Song of Solomon, "drop as the honeycomb: honey and milk are under thy tongue.... Let my beloved come into his garden, and eat his pleasant fruits." Can hard-core pornography be far behind?

The identification of mouth and genital is Freudian; it is poetic, it is pornographic, and it is also somewhat mystical. The mouth and the vagina, these two glorious holes, are two doorways to the psyche, full of words and secrets, the twin beginnings of the passage to that hidden place we point to when we say "me."

Deep kissing is the final tie between mouth and genital. It is the missing link between infant hunger and adult sex. Like the baby's supper, the kiss refers the pleasures of the mouth to the receptive genitals. The mouth feels good while the lips and the tongue explore tastes and textures—the smooth teeth of a lover, the hard or slippery tongue, the wetness, the warmth, the taste of somebody else's mouth—and blood rushes to the genitals. "Let him kiss me with the kisses of his mouth," says the Song of Solomon, "For thy love is better than wine."

Kissing isn't quite universal. There are tribes in Finland who bathe together naked but consider kissing to be indecent. In African tribes where the lips are stretched and decorated, there is no kissing. But nearly everywhere else there is some kind of kiss. The greeting kiss is face-to-face—sometimes mouth-to-mouth, sometimes mouth to cheek, sometimes nose to nose. Kissing may have begun as a smelling ritual, first a smell recognition and then a way of scenting another person's mood and well-being. In the Bible, when Isaac grew old and blind, he called his son Esau to come and kiss him and receive his blessing. But Jacob put on his brother's clothes so that he would smell like Esau. Isaac recognized the smell, kissed him, and believing Jacob to be Esau, gave him his blessing. All that Esau was left with was an empty bowl of potage.

Kissing often remains potent as a blessing. We kiss dice before we throw them, we kiss our good luck charms, we kiss the godfather's hand and the bishop's ring, we kiss a religious icon, we kiss the ground our heroes walk on, we kiss the flag, we kiss a child's hurt finger, and we kiss our own fingers to throw a kiss when we say good-bye. "Kiss my ass" is a phrase of contempt—the kiss, perverted.

The lipsticked kiss-print on the back of an envelope is related to the row of kisses—*XXXX*—at the bottom of a loving letter. In the Middle Ages, when so many people couldn't write their own names, a cross—*X*—was accepted as a signature on legal documents, as it sometimes still is today. The cross stood for St. Andrew's mark, and it meant that the person making that mark was vowing to be honest, swearing on St. Andrew's name. As part of the pledge, they kissed the *X* after they had drawn it. Eventually, the *X* came to be the sign of a kiss.

Kissing is fairly universal among animals as well as people. Animals often kiss to pass food from parent to child, and adult animals often say hello with a mouth-to-mouth greeting. If the gesture is descended from infant feeding, the memory of food is long gone. The touch may rekindle the good feelings the food originally brought, and it certainly results in a social kiss, not unlike the juxtaposition of cheeks which is called a kiss in our own social jungle. Insects touch one another's antennae; birds caress one another's bills; cats and dogs lick one another, and even give one another gentle love bites. Mother cats purr while they clean their kittens. Mouth to mouth, mouth at work: It feels good.

From the feeding kiss of parent for child through the species and the aeons, to the love kiss of man and woman may be a slow-motion leap through evolution, but the similarity—the memory of sensation—is still there. Somewhere, we remember the pleasure of infancy, the sensitivity of baby lips and the warm touch of the mother's nipple, or the sweet flowing of milk from the bottle.

Freud writes of "kissing epicures," who as adults are as turned on by sensations of the mouth as they were when they were little hungry babies. They are avid for pleasures of the mouth, and they retain, says the doctor, the erogenous significance of the lip zone long past the time in infancy when that significance ought to move to other parts of the body. Sometimes, he adds, the epicure becomes a pervert, a mouth monomaniac, with "a tendency to perverse kissing...." He writes that such kissing perverts sometimes also show a strong desire for drinking and smoking. (Freud himself smoked cigars. But of course sometimes a cigar is just a cigar.)

Mouth-to-mouth kissing, perverted or epicurean, is just the beginning. Casanova wrote of placing oysters on the lips of his love and sipping their broth together with her own. Oysters are slippery, and perhaps a few escaped from his lover's lips and slid to her dishy mounds just below. Any mouth worth its salt starts moving around after a while. There are other sweet spots. The ear is just a cheek away and then there is the neck and the breasts and the navel and...

Oral sex has been around for at least as long as oysters. Animals, who lick and nibble one another freely, enjoy oral sex. Orgiastic sex, from man's first frenzied fertility rites, embraced fellatio and cunnilingus. Pre-Incan pottery, decorated with erotic drawings, has been excavated from Mochica and Chimu grave sites in Peru. Fellatio is clearly depicted. Many of the unearthed jars are made so that the drinking spout is in the form of a vulva or an erect penis. Greek and Roman vessels were often formed into genitals or breasts; sometimes the food itself was shaped in the same way, completing the psychic circle: infant mouth to maternal breast, adult mouth to aroused genital, hungry mouth to erotic food. Two hundred years ago, a woman was said to be "milking" her lover when she kissed his penis—her sucking made his milk flow. (*Milking* can also mean masturbation. In dreams, masturbation is sometimes represented by squeezing fruit or pouring water. Some psychiatrists relate premature ejaculation to infant morality; they call it spilling the milk before it reaches the lips.)

Kissing opens our bodies to another human being. That which was separate and alone is together; the seal is joined; passion has begun. We drink of each other's bodies and we fill ourselves with the food of love and sex. Wherever they kiss, lovers do so with suckings and bitings, licks and squeezes, for all the world like babes at breast. The tongue and the lips are nearly as busy in lovemaking as they are in eating. Kissing comes close to fulfilling the search for our most imperious needs—food and sex, again and again—at the same time.

I have a friend who has a friend who is always in one of two conditions: either on a diet or off it. These two, my friend and his friend, who was on a diet, were walking in New York City (the Big Apple, and still one of the most erotic of cities), the second friend hoping to burn off extra calories and accelerate weight loss, when they happened to pass one of his favorite bakeries. People on diets have favorite bakeries on many streets, but this was a really good one, famous for a particular cake: dense, moist layers of rich chocolate separated by whipped cream, each layer of cream covered by sliced, sweetened, ripe strawberries, and each layer of chocolate, strawberries, and cream covered in turn by more chocolate and cream and strawberries until the top.

They stood at the window, and finally my friend's friend gave up. "I have to go in," he said, and inside he bought not one but two of the chocolate fantasies.

"Why two?" my friend asked.

"Because," he answered, "I want one to eat and one to fuck." Without any doubt, he ate them both, diets being states of deprivation between indulgences. If he didn't, he's still way ahead of Philip Roth's Portnoy, who used raw liver.

Chapter 6

DINNER IN BED

One cannot think well,
love well, sleep well,
if one has not dined well.
—Virginia Woolf

Many a teenager bakes brownies for her boyfriend. Chocolate chip cookies left the Toll House Inn behind and achieved national fame when they were sent by the pound to absent husbands and boyfriends during World War II. (Why is it that females need to *transform* chocolate for males? Traditionally, men simply send chocolates. Women bake.) These days, there are countless thriving food businesses, selling everything from fruitcake to mustard, to do the cooking for us. It's all based on the simple awareness that an offering of food is a gift of the self and a statement of love. (And if we order something for ourselves, it's still nice—maybe even especially so—to know that we care. It could be the beginning, as Oscar Wilde said about self-love, of a lifelong romance.)

Ranked against statements of love, chocolate is a keynote speech. In his *Memoirs*, Casanova mentions chocolate as a stimulant for love more often than any other food except champagne (which shouldn't count because it acts directly on inhibitions, while chocolate simply suggests).

A box of chocolates in the shape of a heart, with a throbbingly red cover, is a favorite old-fashioned gift for one's sweetheart on Valentine's Day. Harkening back to the days of the Romans and the Greeks, when food was often made into erotic shapes, some fancy candy stores sell nudes in classic pinup poses, some made of dark chocolate and some made of white. *Cosmopolitan* magazine lists chocolate as one of the top ten aphrodisiacs.

Chocolate has always had a reputation. The Mayans used cacao beans to pay for the use of women in their whorehouses—eight to ten beans was the going price for one woman, one time. When chocolate reached Spain, clergymen denounced it as "immoral and provocative of immorality." During chocolate's early years in Europe, it was used to cure a host of illnesses and discomforts—among them anemia, gout, kidney stones, burns, bowel dysfunction, and loss of sexual desire.

The power of chocolate is partly chemical. There are all sorts of good things in chocolate: antioxidants (which can block damage to our cells and arteries) and stearic acid (a saturated vegetable fat that acts like the monounsaturated fat in olive and canola oils and has a neutral effect on cholesterol—cocoa butter is a vegetable fat, and is without cholesterol). Chocolate's antioxidants work the same way as those in red wine, protecting against heart disease and possibly even cancer. And there's more: Chocolate's antioxidants are flavanols—like the ones found in tea, red wine, and some fruits and vegetables, and are positively good for you. (Milk chocolate has less of the good guys than dark chocolate does, and flavanols are removed to make cocoa powder and chocolate syrup when they're processed with alkali.)

There are also low levels of anandamide inside chocolate, which stimulates the same brain cell receptors that respond to THC, the psychoactive substance in marijuana.* Two other chocolate chemicals work to prolong the effect of the anandamide; one is phenylethylamine, a chemical your brain produces naturally when you fall in love, and when you fall in love it feels awfully good. Euphoric, in fact.

Add to all of this the combination of caffeine and sugar for quick energy, a stimulating high. But it's what chocolate does on the tongue that really counts. On the menu, chocolates are a kind of hors d'oeuvres, or, for dessert (or between meals) a suggestive and sensuous bonbon. More serious and more self-conscious is the seduction supper—the brownies all grown up and ready to play house, the chocolate chip cookies come home to roost. No matter what stage of the sexual revolution we are in (postwar? cold war?), the seduction supper is a meal which still happens. Its contents change from cook to cook as do the roles of the sexes involved, but its form is a constant. It intends to please, and then to seduce.

"Considered solely in connection with the pleasures of the table," M.F.K. Fisher writes, "a wanton woman is one who with cunning and deliberation prepares a meal which will draw another person to her.... Her basic acknowledgment that sexual play can be a sure aftermath of gastronomical bliss dictates the game, from the first invitation to the final mouthful of ginger omelet." Men who cook seduction suppers are equally wanton. And seduction suppers work even for those who have already been seduced.

The meal Mrs. Fisher cunningly and deliberately suggests is light and good humored. Its spices are subtle, and at its finish no one will be left feeling sodden or heavy. She proposes first a well-made drink, good scotch for him and a very dry martini for herself. Dinner then begins with a hot soup made of equal parts of clam juice, chicken broth, and dry white wine. It proceeds to a "light curry of shrimps or crayfish tails. The fish must be peeled raw, soaked in rich milk, and drained, and the sauce must be made of this milk, and the fish poached for at best six minutes in the delicately flavored liquid." There is rice to go with the curry and a "bland green salad," made with considerably more oil than vinegar. For dessert, chilled

---

*The National Institute of Mental Health estimates that a person weighing 130 pounds would have to eat twenty-five pounds of chocolate in one sitting to feel anything like the effect of marijuana. Undoubtedly, they'd feel sick first. Still, Alice B. Toklas's marijuana brownies deserve extra credit for good chemistry.

poached fruits, "with a seemingly innocent sauce" made of honey, cinnamon, and brandy. To drink with dinner there is a moderately dry champagne. Afterward, Mrs. Fisher serves "coffee in great moderation, to put it bluntly, lest it dampen the fire with cold reason."

Mrs. Fisher's seduction supper is meant to lead to resting violate. Her emphasis is on seafood and spices: This is classic aphrodisiac food.

Greeks, Romans, French, Italians, Spanish—all the best lovers swore by oysters and eels and salmon and lobsters. "The pot snaps shut, the stout eel wriggles," writes Rabelais, "Lord! what juicy framble friggles! / Marriage? Marriage is my oyster! Harder, deeper, lower, moister."

Chemically, seafood is rich in phosphorus, which has an irritant and excitant effect. Poetically, Aphrodite, the Greek goddess of love and beauty (from whom comes the word *aphrodisiac*), was born rising from a seashell in all her loveliness. Even the aroma of seafood, reminiscent of the scent of the genitals, can be erotic.

Spices—the curry for Mrs. Fisher's shrimp, the cinnamon to stir her honey—are equally renowned as aphrodisiacs. They heat the body with their warmth and awaken the senses with their aroma. The Puritans took all this so seriously that they barred spices from their tables on the belief that their use "excited passion."

There are many aromas which are indeed erotically appealing—flowers, musks, perfumes, reminiscent of the heady, earthy scents of the body itself. "How much better," says the Song of Solomon, "is the smell of thine ointments than all spices!"

The scent of the body is intimate, the smell of the genitalia is—how could it be otherwise?—sexy. A James Jones heroine could arouse her lover in a restaurant by returning from the ladies' room with the scent of her vagina on her fingertips, which she held for a second under his nose.

With intimacy the smell of a lover becomes a personal, secret knowing of the flesh, a particular blend of the bottled and the body. Silvio Venturi, an Italian psychiatrist in the late nineteenth century, described the odor of the body as a secondary sex characteristic. Indeed, sweat isn't smelly until puberty, when the apocrine glands develop. They're located in the armpits, breasts, and anal and genital areas and are activated by hormones. They are considered part of the secondary sex system.

The smell of food is sexy, too. According to *Prevention* magazine, men get excited about smells—but not the ones you would expect. *Prevention* reported that tests at the Smell and Taste Treatment and Research Foundation in Chicago showed that certain smells induced blood flow to the penis. At the top of the sexy smell chart for the men tested was pumpkin pie combined with (strangely enough) lavender. Other winners were a mixture of doughnuts and black licorice, followed by pumpkin pie combined with doughnut, and then oranges alone. Forget Estée Lauder and Chanel No. 5; dab a bit of pumpkin pie behind your ear. The food smells given in the test were originally meant to be controls—scents that wouldn't have any effect at all on the men being tested. "But lo and behold, we found that baked cinnamon buns had a greater effect than all the perfumes put together," said the study leader. And pumpkin pie put cinnamon buns in the shade.

Freud wrote that scent once had a primary role in the human reproductive process, as it does still for animals. Dogs and cats can detect a mate in heat several streets away. When humans went from loping on all fours to standing erect, our genitals were no longer hidden and were suddenly open, visible, and vulnerable. When man leapt upward, winning his first battle against gravity, sex was no longer a sometime thing, concealed, and therefore needing to be sniffed out. It was right there to be looked at and to be seen.

And so to fig leaves and to shame, while the sense of smell, no longer necessary for the survival of the species, is for the most part an adjunct to the sense of taste. Brillat-Savarin called the nose the chimney of the laboratory which is the mouth, or "to speak more exactly . . . one serves for the tasting of the actual bodies and the other for the savoring of their gasses." Without the nose to sniff and smell and almost pretaste food, everything tastes dull, lifeless, similar. Eating is no fun when you have a cold and your nose isn't working; children recognize the mutuality of nose and mouth when they hold their noses while they take their medicine.

Today, we are dependent on factories for our body smells—deodorants to suppress them, and perfumes to replace them. We massage our bodies with perfumes and oils and lotions, each made of its secret formula of myrrh and frankincense, and we hope they will be as powerful as the best love philters. "All our successful perfumes," said Paris perfumer Jean-Paul

Guerlain, "have two notes—vanilla* and an animal scent. In short, they are aphrodisiacs." The chairman of International Flavors and Fragrances (a multimillion dollar company) agrees. "Our business," he has said, "is basically sex and hunger."

The word *aphrodisiac*, with its memory of Aphrodite, seems so exotic, yet aphrodisiacs can be found on supermarket shelves everywhere. Bread, beans, pears, pineapples, chestnuts, cabbages, and onions—even garlic, chives, leeks, and shallots—have all, at one time or another, been considered powerful aphrodisiacs, as have oranges and eggplants and strawberries and artichokes. Even spinach, which Popeye said made him "good to the finich." It's easier to think of things that *aren't* aphrodisiacs, in one way or another; there are fewer of them. "An aphrodisiac," says sex therapist Dr. Ruth Westheimer, "is anything you think it is."

Over the years, people have thought that everything from powdered rhinoceros horn to gallbladder of bear would do the trick. Does it look like a penis? Try it! Carrots, cucumbers, ginseng... or, on the other hand, oysters, pomegranates, avocados. Then there's sea swallow nest soup, crocodile dung (is it worth it?), and the famous Spanish fly. Also on the list, perhaps more practically: celery seeds, which contain adrostenone, a biochemical cousin of testosterone. Asparagus, full of vitamins A and C. Bananas, which contain bufotenine, a mood improver and lots of B vitamins, important in the manufacturing of sex hormones. Cocoa and chocolate, as we've already seen. Garlic—as long as both eat it—improves blood circulation, and also stimulates the production of nitric oxide synthase, responsible for the mechanics of erection. Ginger increases the blood flow to the genitals. Viagra does it all, in one little pill.

There have been aphrodisiac cookbooks, many written by fine writers and excellent cooks and—who knows?—superior lovers. (*Venus in the Kitchen, or Love's Cookery Book*, for one, was "edited by" Norman Douglas, with an introduction by Graham Greene.) Sometimes these cookbooks of love have been the handbooks of courtesans and sometimes of wives. Sometimes they have been given—spotted with the stains of innumerable dinners—by mother to daughter to daughter again. In the 1958 movie

*The word *vanilla* originally meant "little vagina."

Gigi, Gigi's mother, in passing along her secrets, even taught her daughter how to light a gentleman's after-dinner cigar. Courtesans, like madams, have always been schooled in the foods of love. Aphrodisiacs are their life work.

But the classic line about aphrodisiacs, after everything has been considered, is that there are really only two: the presence of a beautiful woman, and her absence. (Classically, aphrodisiacs are for men.) Beauty is in the eye of the lover, thank goodness, and so we are all beautiful when we are well loved and even more so when we are also well fed.

French gourmet and food writer Grimod de la Reyniere once said that the only essentials for a love nest are a stove and a mattress. He was the publisher of *Almanach des Gourmands,* the first magazine for gourmets—it appeared in 1804—and he was a practical man. Surely then, if he had been forced to make a choice in his love nest, he would have given up the mattress, spreading his cloak on the floor, letting the stove emerge as the single essential, for he also said that "there are many occasions where a lover would be far below best form if the culinary art did not come to the aid of nature."

Aphrodisiacs may indeed arouse the jaded or tired lover, or the one who believes most firmly in the powers of phosphorus and ginseng and vitamin E. But the young lover, the innocent, the passionate one, he or she who is new to love, will have no need to be inflamed by spices and fishes, soft fruits or sweet wine.

Aphrodisiacs titillate, as does pornography, but reality is both less boring and more erotic. If we link certain foods and smells with better lovemaking, it tells more about us than about the food. Food excites because of the psyche, not the soma, because food and sex are inexorably, subliminally, paired from our very beginnings.

Chapter 7

LOVE AND BREAD AND WEDDING CAKES

Italians, love bread, heart of the home, savor of the repast, joy of health; Respect bread, sweat of the brow, pride of labor, poem of sacrifice; Honor bread, glory of the fields, fragrance of the earth, feast of life; Do not waste bread, richness of the father-land, sweetest gift of God, most holy reward of human toil.

> —Benito Mussolini,
> April 1928

Fortunately the Italian people is not yet accustomed to eating several times per day.

> —Benito Mussolini,
> December 1930

Eating is *The Joy of Sex* transformed into *The Joy of Cooking*. It's a sensual pleasure from the very first, when we are little more than roaring digestive systems, needing oceans of warm, sweet milk to fill our hungry void. Grown up, we remember our beginnings. We talk about food when we talk about love: "You're delicious," we say, and "I love you so much I could eat you right up!" And we proceed to prove it. Not too long ago, a sexy woman was called a tomato. A girl is a chick; even the heart is sweet and we call our sweethearts food-love names: honey, sweetie pie, lamb chop. Breasts are like melons; lips are like strawberries. Love is intoxicating, love is delectable. "If you don't like my peaches," says the blues lyric, "don't shake my tree." "It must be jelly," sings another, "'cause jam don't shake like that." A. J. Liebling described Lillian Russell, a luscious woman from a time when more was better—she weighed over two hundred pounds—as "a butterscotch sundae of a woman as beautiful as a tulip of beer with a high white colar...." That's a delicious woman, a peach, obviously full of her juices. We salivate for dinner, full of juice ourselves, and afterward, with any luck, we salivate for sex. Food and sex are inextricably linked, from our beginnings to our bottoms, and food and love are linked in just the same simple, basic way.

The process of falling in love has its own rhythms. From the first time on, every time, this love is the best one, the right one, the one that will last. Later—when your life passes before your eyes, maybe—they're all the same. There is a repetitive pattern, a progression, a logic that is consistent each time and always leaves room for the overwhelming feeling that it is all marvelous and exhilarating and brand-new.

Love has its seasons. There is a time for laughter and a time for absent-mindedness. There is a need to say the other's name out loud, to give love presence by speaking its magic word. There is a moment for first sharing the same spoon and there is also a time for discovering shared memories of food. She loves canned corn. Fantastic! So does he. How incredible love is and how perfect their own if as children neither could find anything better to eat than a piece of lettuce rolled up around a blob of ketchup. What joy! Obviously, they were predestined to find each other, two souls in this whirling world whose passion remains coffee ice cream with chocolate sauce. The mouths of lovers, they learn, match as mysteriously as the rest of their bodies, like the marvelous way that his goes up and hers goes in.

In a world in which sophistication can be measured by what books one keeps in the bathroom or the brand of water that is sipped with lunch, lovers bring the greatest innocence to the discovery that they share the same lusts, not only for each other but also for food.

There is—sometimes sadly and sometimes not—also a time when love cools. Then it is all a different story. This is the opposite of that delicious moment when lovers discover their shared longing for pizza with onion.

When she begins to hate the way he chews, she loves him less. She sees—the light is so much brighter now that the candles have been blown out and the lamp turned on—that he really eats like a pig. She sits across the table, fascinated, but no longer enchanted. Rather, she is repelled by the way his jaws move. He, on the other side of the lamp, can't stand listening to the sound the vegetables make in her mouth—a damp kind of crispness, much too sloppy—wet, really. Oh, God, do her teeth click?

Before, eating was full of sex: bodies moving, phallic tongues tasting and sipping, the sucking of breasts. Now, it is simply audible humanity. It's chewing, that's all it is, and it's much too loud.

When love is best, lovers are safe with each other and desire each other totally. They want to devour their love with love, to consume each other with their passion. They want to eat each other up, to become each other, to possess each other, to *be* each other. Later, when love turns to dismay, such thoughts are altogether horrifying. When love is over, lovers are each relieved to be whole again, to be themselves again. The possibility of being consumed, devoured, eaten alive, is disgusting. It makes them angry.

When we stop loving, eating together is no joy, and when we no longer love to eat together, we no longer love so well either.

When we find a love we hope will last, we mark it with a marriage, and marriages begin with rituals established by law and religion. Their first consummation is with a feast. Whether the courtship began with glasses of wine or with beer and pretzels, marriage in a variety of cultures is baptized with a wedding cake.

Wedding cakes go far back in the history of nuptial celebrations. Wheat has always been a symbol of love and fertility. ("That's why we throw rice as the joyous couple leaves the wedding celebration and heads toward the marriage bed," writes Jeffrey Steingarten in *It Must've Been Something I Ate,* "and one reason a special bread or cake and not a special meatloaf has been central to our wedding rituals at least since the Greeks and Romans.")

Greek brides baked cakes to give to their grooms. Later, Roman couples offered wheat cakes to Jupiter. The priest who served the god burned the cake over a flame, and this sacrifice symbolized that the woman was now under the jurisdiction and protection of her husband; it demonstrated that the wedding was both legal and sacred. At Roman weddings, the bride carried wheat as a good luck charm. She and her groom ate cakes made of flour, salt, and water, more like bread—or biscuits or matzo—than cake, but even so a forerunner of today's five-tier extravaganza. At medieval weddings, grains of wheat were thrown at the happy couple with exactly the same wishes—luck, love, fertility—as today's rice and confetti. The Anglo-Saxons crumbled small cakes (again, like bread, or oatcakes) over the heads of brides, a shower of wheaty crumbs that was meant to foretell fertility to follow.

The Romans eventually took to making their flour and water wedding cakes a little more festive and easier to swallow—and there was less sacrificing of the cake and more sharing of it with the wedding company. Spices and flavorings were added and before long the cakes were topped with white sugar and bitter almonds, chosen to represent the pleasures and pains that would inevitably follow.

In France, at the time of Louis XIV, newlyweds ate cakes that had been soaked in alcohol—and thus the rum cake!—in order to give themselves a little extra zing for the long night ahead. Medieval English bakers flavored their cakes with spices and dried fruits. Sugar was added when it became available, and then nuts, and soon the Banbury cake—the dark English fruitcake—was the conventional wedding cake. (Steingarten says that the poet Robert Herrick coined the expression "wedding cake" in 1648, but that nobody used it until the nineteenth century. He also says that "bridal" comes from the Old English "bride-ale," for the ale which was the beverage of choice at wedding feasts.) In 1769, Elizabeth Raffald published a cookbook with a recipe for icing with ground almonds in it (instead of the French royal icing, made with sugar and egg whites, which becomes rock hard when it's dry), and soon Banbury cakes were covered with her white icing—so virginal!

Today, the wedding cake is resplendent. Its fragrant heart is covered with swirls of innocent white icing. On top: tiny replicas of the bride and groom or, more modestly, a bed of flowers or a host of curlicues and dots. It is, to the last crumb, a delicious psychological symbol.

When they cut the cake, the bride and groom join their hands, just as they have together pledged their futures, to make the first slice. The bride holds the knife; it is shining and silver, and it is pointed and hard and phallic. The cake, into which it cuts, is virginal, soft, round, and sweet. The ritual is a symbolized intercourse and at the same time a vision of a good, sweet, and fruitful future.

Like the wedding cake that was first made of flour and water, bread is another simple link between food and sex. As old as the history of man, the story of bread is the making of civilization. Civilization began when we tamed our food and, staying in one place, began to grow it—thus, agriculture—instead of just finding it, eating it, and wandering until we could find it again.

The metamorphosis from wheat to flour marks our advances, one by one. Grinding began with variations of a pestle and mortar, then with two stones rubbing against each other, turned first by waterpower, then wind power, and, along the way, by animals and by slaves. Wild yeast, floating through the air, gave us leavening, and then we learned to save a bit of each batch of dough in order to raise the next batch, as we do with sourdough bread. The first ovens were flat stones heating in the fire, and then we covered the stones with an overturned pot, and then we built separate ovens—like beehives or igloos, self-contained, with a fire burning at the bottoms, outside.

The baking of bread was a community endeavor. There was often a village miller, and a village baker to save heat and building materials. Our word, *companion*, identifies those who eat bread together—as does *company*, both from the Latin *panis*, bread, and *com*, with.

Bread and water was the only food for those in the community who broke the law, or who were doing religious penance. When the water changed to broth, with a thick slice of bread at the bottom of a bowl, the result was first a *suppa*, then *sop*—English, to soak—and eventually, soup. Bread and soup is a fine meal, unrelated except through words, to the sparse, sad food of remorse.

A gift of bread means fertility and abundance to a new home or a new neighbor; and breaking bread together is the sign of trust and the beginning of friendship. Slang words for money include both bread and dough, and bread is a generic term for food. Our words *lord* and *lady* are bread derived: *Lord* comes from the Old English *hlafward*, which meant loaf guardian—keeper of the loaf. *Lady* is from *hlaefdige*, or kneader of the loaf. She cooked it; he watched it. Even their baby, the smallest peer of the realm, was bread-marked, connected to its mother through the placenta, a Latin-derived word originally meaning "intending to please." The Roman word for a flat cake, thin sheets of dough made with cheese and honey, was *placenta*, and it is the placenta, in that same shape, that nourishes the unborn child.

In church, bread and wine are the symbols of the body and the spirit of Christ. Yeast creates both alcohol and bread; bakers used to buy their yeast from brewers, and the word "bread" is derived from the same root as the word "brew."

Inevitably, brothels were long associated with bakeries. Fornax was the Roman goddess of the oven, and *fornus* was the Latin word for oven, while *fornix* was the word for a brothel, and fornicate is our word for what they did there. Roman prostitutes baked special breads and cakes in the shape of male and female genitals, to be dedicated to the phallic guardian of fertility. After the baking was done, when the ovens had cooled down enough, the girls and their customers crawled in where the bread had been and heated the ovens back up again.

In Germany in the Middle Ages, a girl who lusted after a fellow who wasn't lusting her back might have been advised to try this dusty trick: When the wheat was ready for the miller's, she was to take off all her clothes, lie down in the wheat and writhe about, rolling her body in the seeds. Afterward, when the miller's work was done and the wheat was flour, she was to bake bread with it and give it to the man she wanted. He was supposed to be passion-struck the moment he swallowed it.

In the thirteenth century, the Bishop of Worms felt it necessary to warn his congregation about playing thusly with the dough. "Have you done what certain women are in the habit of doing? They prostrate themselves face downward, rump upward and uncovered, and have a loaf of bread kneaded upon their nude nates; when it has been baked, they invite their husbands to come and eat it; this they do in order to inflame their men with a greater love for them." His directions are almost a recipe in their precision. Nevertheless, certain questions are left unanswered. Especially one. Who kneaded the loaf on the nude nate? It is a process, one imagines, which might further fan the fires of the lady. As for the baker, busy back there squeezing and pushing and pinching, it might do a little something for him as well. How nice that it could all be done for one's husband! A virtue, surely.

The power of bread, like the wheat itself, flows more to the miller than the baker; the miller is the man who grinds. There's a Norse saga about a prince named Amlodhi who owned a mill on the edge of the world. It was operated by nine goddesses who took turns grinding meal for Amlodhi, grasping, each in her turn, the "twisting or boring stick" that turned the millstone.

There is sensual satisfaction in all cooking, arousal in the blending and brewing, in the textures and smells of simmering and roasting, but the baking of bread—whether on nude nates or a marble slab—has it all. It is sensual, from the mixing of the dough and the kneading, pushing and pulling, to its earthy redolence, the primal aroma of yeast and flour, part of the primitive harvest smells of the soil, to the final loaf, shaped like a phallus, the stiff staff of life.

It is, after all, for bread that we plea for first in our prayers: "Our father, Who art in Heaven...Give us this day our daily bread...." and, after we have eaten, forgive us our sins.

Chapter 8

··

A BUN IN THE OVEN

Nothin' says lovin'
like something from the oven.
—Pillsbury flour

Food is loving, cooking is foreplay, and eating is making love. What are the logical results nine months later? What is it you said little girls are made of? Oh yes, sugar and spice....

For children, the fantasy of oral impregnation is perfectly logical, just as reasonable (and certainly more palatable) than the unlikely truth. If the baby comes out at the bottom, it must go in at the top. All you have to do is look at a pregnant woman and you can see how big her stomach has grown. So the mommy ate the seed, and it grew into a baby.

Throughout history, we have had trouble associating coitus with pregnancy. It is a sequence of events not particularly obvious in its linkage. There's a long gap, after all, between the moment of love and the moment of birth. Even for the sophisticate, a scientific leap of faith is required in order to imagine the sperm swimming upstream, against the current of gravity, to meet its mate. Some peoples once thought that the sun fathered earth's children; after all, it is the sun's warmth which impregnates seeds in the soil in the light of day. Others believed different spirits were involved; many thought a specific food could engender life.

There have been beliefs, too, about certain foods making it possible to have the risky production of a particular sex of child be more certain. Even less scientifically, many women fantasize during fellatio that they will become pregnant if they swallow semen; others worry, on a subliminal level, that the semen will pass through their bodies and emerge at the vagina, where they will then, in time, grow a penis, a different sort of mouth–baby connection.

Anthropologist Claude Lévi-Strauss wrote about the natives of southern Brazil whose language includes a verb meaning both "to eat" and "to copulate." By the same token, he noted that Pueblo women gave birth over a heap of hot sand in order to transform the unborn child into a "cooked person."

Being pregnant is "having something in the oven." The baby is cooked in our vernacular just as Lévi-Strauss's tribes "cook" the newly born infant. "A natural creature is at one and the same time cooked and socialized."

These are the traditional female roles: cooking the daily meal, transforming a lump of raw dough into a loaf of crusty bread or a sweet cake, taking the raw seed, the unborn bit of life and letting it emerge from the night kitchen nine months later, all cooked, but alive and kicking. Once done, babies begin the circle all over again: They are born hungry and sensuous.

Hunger and love, babies and cookbooks: The message is the same. We eat, and we are. We love, and we are again.

Part Three

GROWING UP

The Grizzly Bear is huge and wild;
He has devoured the infant child.
The infant child is not aware
It has been eaten by the bear.

—"Infant Innocence,"
by A. E. Housman

Chapter 9

FAIRY-TALE FOOD

I one my mother.
I two my mother.
I three my mother.
I four my mother.
I five my mother.
I six my mother.
I seven my mother.
I ate my mother.
—Children's chant

The images in fairy tales are repeated over and over: angry giants, powerful kings, wicked witches, nasty stepmothers, three brothers, three wishes, beautiful princesses, and strange, small, supernatural creatures with endless patience. And food. Fairy tales are stuffed with food. There are gingerbread houses and poisoned apples, golden eggs and magic seeds, even porridge that comes in three sizes and three temperatures.

But with a few exceptions, most modern writers of books for children don't deal with food as a symbol. Maurice Sendak is the most obvious exception; his books are dream tales, about symbols and unconscious meanings, as much as they are about stories and the children in them.

His *In the Night Kitchen* is a perfect food and sex dream, beginning with the inexplicable noises that children hear in the night. It's about the transformation of food in the night into a different substance—a bun in the oven—and the fierce joy of mastering food: "I'm in the milk and the milk's in me," Mickey sings. "God bless milk and God bless me!" It's a book full of a child's desire to be immersed in food, to have endless amounts of it, to be part of it—and to understand exactly what it is that might be happening in the magical, mysterious, and very important night kitchen.

Many of today's children's books have plainly moral food messages, right out there for any fool—or any five-year-old—to see: If all you ever eat is bread and jam, you're missing a lot of good things. If you give a mouse a cookie, he'll want a lot of other things, too. And Sam-I-Am likes green eggs and ham! But few deal with the enormous power that food has for children, and the reason why Frances likes only bread and jam, and the great bravery—not the foolishness—of Sam's appetite.

Winnie the Pooh believes in food. Pooh is one of our first encounters with the happy fat guy. But happy or not, Pooh teaches us what happens when you overeat. (You get stuck in a rabbit hole.) Pooh is young yet. His food arrives on schedule (elevenish); he always eats the same thing; when he's worried, he gets hungry, and when he's hungry, he gets worried. He's silly—silly old Pooh!—but we love him, and his sweet, round, tender tummy is adorable. One wants to pat it, to reassure ourselves maybe more than to reassure him. It's like the sweet tummy of a kitten, or a baby.

In the old stories, though, the fairy tales, Grimm and grimmer, food is as potent a part of life as it is in reality for children. Food is all. Food is dangerous. Food is the barrier between existence and extinction. If the stories children love best often include thoughts of food, not as sustenance but as promise or threat, as problem or as solution, it is because their fantasies and fears are more likely to be confused with reality. They haven't grown as far away as their parents have from the subconscious soil in which their roots are planted.

Fairy tales can be interpreted in many ways. Goldilocks is an imperialist warmonger and a colonial power; Snow White's wicked stepmother is convicted on circumstantial evidence —and besides, they played the dwarf card. The big bad wolf speaks for himself—huffily; the three little pigs provide practical lessons from the school of hard knocks.

Third Reich propagandists in Nazi Germany said that Little Red Riding Hood represented the German people, endangered by the Jewish wolf. At the end of World War II, the Allies banned publication of Grimm's fairy tales in Germany, saying that they had contributed to Nazi savagery.

The tales have been twisted any number of ways; they've been gentled and changed, rewritten and retold from a variety of points of view. In one version of Cinderella, our heroine organizes a labor union for local maids. The king arrests her, agitator that she is, and in the end she emigrates to America, where there are no kings and queens, though there are plenty of glass slippers.

Cinderella has universal appeal. It dates back as far as ninth-century China; it has so many variants that folklorists call it "The Cinderella Cycle." All the world round, it's a perfect story. No more siblings! No more step-mother! And we, sitting by the fire with ashes on our cheeks—at last, we'll be beautiful and loved, and we'll end up in the castle, where we belonged all along, with a prince who adores us. Even for adults, the story of the un-appealing woman turned into a beauty has endless appeal—from *Pretty Woman* to *My Fair Lady* and *The Princess Diaries*. The dream is ours.

Fairy tales can be stories of redemption, amazing grace, or of paradise lost, sought, and regained. They can be feminist tracts, or reviled as sexist and patriarchal. The prince is almost always a hero. (The king can be evil, but not the prince—and he'll be king someday; what a transformation! from baby to a higher father.) And the princess can be clever or good or kind, but most often she's helpless and passive. She's always beautiful, of course, just as we are, underneath it all.

Most of all, fairy tales appeal to us because they tell a good story. They are also a piece of the universal unconscious, a dream we have all dreamt, a nightmare which ends happily ever after. These are stories told and retold, generation after generation, and they have a magic shape to fit each and every one who listens. They have assumed a form which encompasses the fears and wishes, the dreams common to us all, the ones that go so far back that we have forgotten that they ever existed.

Hansel and Gretel, Little Red Riding Hood, Jack and the Beanstalk, Snow White—Hansel's trail of bread crumbs, the gingerbread house, the basket of goodies, the hungry wolf, the ogre's kitchen, his wife's oven, the fatal apple—these stories use food as a secret language, to whisper scary, important things into the ears of children so that they can fill a child's soul without anyone too large knowing they are there. Its language, like any other, can be translated. Its vocabulary is like a tourist's guide to the unconscious.

Children speak the language without need of an interpreter, without knowing that they are hearing something we adults either don't understand or often find too grim. In some tellings, the old fairy tales have been polished and their grisly, rough edges smoothed over or left out altogether, but the polish is strictly for nervous parents. For children, fairy-tale language is simple. They live right on the line between dreams and reality—what they pretend is what *is*, while they're pretending it.

Fairy tales, just as Sendak's *The Wild Things* does, take the fears of children and reshapes them, recasts them, takes them from the dark, tangled places of the mind into the daylight, where they can be tamed and given names and dealt with. Fairy tales make the fears of childhood more real and less real, giving them a story line, a beginning, a middle, and an end—and a solution. And that's one of the keys. Fairy tales end right; the wicked are punished and the good live happily ever after.

In his Pulitzer Prize–winning book, *The Uses of Enchantment*, Bruno Bettelheim wrote about fairy tales in this way, as a psychological path through childhood. That path, winding through the stories, is as clear as the trail of bread crumbs in *Hansel and Gretel* before the birds find it.

Why *does* Hansel leave bread crumbs? Because, says Bettelheim, bread is the single most basic food, next to milk, that children eat, and Hansel still believes, as does the squalling baby and the hungry toddler, that a full stomach is what one needs to be happy. Food solves the most pressing problems.

His real mother doesn't refuse to feed him; only a stand-in, a pretender, a stepmother, would do that. A real mother would never be so wicked and cruel. A real mother always has food for a hungry child. Alas, stepmothers of the world. What's in a name? But this is the framework of the story—and in the end, the mother is very real, step or otherwise; she just wanted her babies to grow up.

The wicked stepmother has no food for Hansel and Gretel; there simply isn't enough, and they will have to find their own. That's their only real task in this story: They must give up the easy life. Cast out from their cribs, they can't be passive babies anymore, dependent, helpless, happy when it's lunchtime but not doing anything much about it. Think!, the story says. And then: do!

When Hansel and Gretel find the magic gingerbread house in the woods, they want to eat it. They never stop to think that if they do, it won't be there anymore. There won't be any shelter from the dark and the cold, and—once again—there won't be any food. They'll be hungry again. They don't forage in the woods, these country children, no dandelion roots for them; they don't try to find food. They simply wander around, poor hungry babes in the woods, until food arrives. It's given to them, as if by magic. As if by Mama. That's the way it's always been.

The gingerbread house is a dilemma, the first dilemma of infancy. There is the wish to eat, to fill up all the clamoring spaces, to eat until there is no more, to eat everything. But: *then what?*

When there is no more, the mother is gone. The baby—who thinks with its mouth—would love to eat its mother, because the mother is food, all food. Food comes from her body—her breast or her hand—so her body seems to *be* food. In dreams, houses symbolize the body, usually the mother's body. How wonderful to hear a story about a house made of gingerbread, all sweet and spicy! Just like a baby's mother, whose body is made of milk, warm and sweet and soft.

But Hansel and Gretel try and eat that marvelous house all up. Greedy children! Surely they should be punished! We all know, somehow, that they should be punished. And then, look—before they can eat up the house, it turns out there's a witch inside, and *she's* going to eat *them* all up!

If the baby wants to eat the mother up, to suck and suck until what's outside is inside, then, in that scheme of things, mightn't the mother also think about eating the baby? That's a reasonable sort of baby logic. It's all quite possible when you stop and think about it. "I love you so much," Mama says, "I could eat you up!" "What a delicious baby!"

Hansel and Gretel are just like helpless babies now, stuck away in a crib-cage, while someone comes and feeds them and they eat and grow fat.

Things look pretty desperate. They need a plan. In fact, they have to do something about all this. They have to act, take things into their own hands, figure out what to do.

They've learned the first lesson: Food doesn't solve every problem. The birds ate the bread crumbs; food isn't always the answer, food didn't work, you can't go home again. They need something on a higher order to get out of this jam.

Still, it's the boy who wants to stay at the breast a little longer. Gretel has been following along after Hansel in a helpless, frightened little girl sort of way. Now she's the one who thinks of what to do. Gretel is the witch's kitchen servant—girls work in the kitchen—and Hansel is going to be eaten—first, at least—unless Gretel is able to save him.

How little credit she gets for her imagination, her bravery! Hansel's name comes first whenever we think of them both, and Hansel always seems smarter, stronger, the leader. Gretel is just the woman behind the man. The fact that there wouldn't have been any man at all if it hadn't been for the woman is lost to us all. Fairy tales teach on that level, too.

Hansel and Gretel solve their problem. (No, Gretel solves their problem.) They find their own way out of the mess, and they don't use food to do it. They punish the witch for her evil wishes. After all, they only nibbled at her house. The witch's house is a symbol of food, not the real thing—but the witch—was going to eat them, not a symbol of them, but *them*, and you don't get any more real than that.

Gretel pushes her into the fire, and her gingerbread turns into jewels (no more food; they're growing up now—but they're still consumers). They find their way home to their mother and father, and all rejoice—even the mother, which just doesn't make any sense if you read it straight; it was the mother who tried to get rid of them in the first place. Hansel and Gretel have begun to take command of their own lives. They have begun to learn how to live happily ever after.

Jack travels something of the same route, but by way of a bean stalk. First, he finds food answers to his problems: The cow his mother sends him to market to trade is the family's source of milk, and the seeds, which he accepts so trustingly in trade for the cow, are the source of growing food. It's a weaning, to be sure, but it's still about food—from liquid to solid.

Then the strange story of Jack's magical, phallic bean stalk goes off in other directions, upward in the story, downward in a Freudian way. Says Freud: The child is able to give up his or her oral dependency if there is sufficient belief in the power of one's own body to give pleasure and to sustain life. In other words, the genital phase comes after the oral.

One moves out of the oral phase—when it is the mouth that has power and gives pleasure—quite simply by becoming independent, accepting separation. Beginning to grow up. That independence involves sexual as well as social development. Now Jack has to face another problem: oedipal.

Jack and his mother live alone. No father! All they have is each other—and the cow. Jack's mother gives him food, and when there isn't any left, he himself finds more in a magic place he reaches through the strong vine that grows out of his magic seeds. The place he finds, though, is not his own: It's a palace and it belongs to an ogre; it is the ogre's private preserve. Here are the most marvelous riches, but they all belong to somebody else, an incredibly grouchy big-daddy ogre who doesn't want Jack to trespass.

Oh, Papa! You live with Mommy in that other room, and you keep the best part of her secret and all for yourself. Talk about greedy!

Jack needs help. And the ogre's wife is there to provide it. She gives him food. She hides him in her stove (just as a mother hides a baby inside her body). The ogre, with a keen sense of smell—little boys must have a particularly distinct odor—suspects Jack of trying to steal what's his. He's angry! And he wants to catch Jack, and take all his goodies back. Just like the witch, he would eat Jack right up. He's a jealous ogre, and he punishes children who try to take what belongs to him.

Jack is little, to be sure, but he's quick and clever and sweet, and remember: He has his *own* magic bean stalk. It's strong and grows so fast that it can support him and, in the end, the bean stalk and his own quick thinking make it possible for Jack to escape and carry his new riches back home in triumph.

He has made it! He can find food and treasures beyond milk, and he has the most wonderful, magical, beautiful stalk that grows right up whenever he wants it. And look what he can give his mother! (The wife at the top of the bean stalk did all the helping and took all the risks, and the mother at the bottom gets all the treasure!) Then his mother sort of recedes into the background, as she should—and we know she'll be busy now, too, with Jack up and around and able to get into all sorts of things.

Snow White takes another look at all of this from a little girl's point of view. First, she has a jealous stepmother. Children know perfectly well that real mothers—good mothers—love their children; that's how it should be. So mean mothers can't be real mothers. It's not that a stepmother is Daddy's second wife; it's much more simple: Real mothers love you. The fairy-tale stepmother is just a dream image of a birth mother. It's safer if it's the step-mother who has her mean moments, and who doesn't really want her children. The evil jealousies and murderous wishes that frighten children within themselves are much more frightening if they exist in other people as well. They can more safely be recognized in wicked witches and wolves and stepmothers and ogres than they ever can be in Mommy and Daddy.

Snow White's real mother wished for her, wanted her so much, painted such a lovely picture of what her child should be. But her mother was weak, and died. The real mother is gone; the real father doesn't seem to be around; the stepmother is powerful and magical. It is these two, mother and daughter, who are locked in a painful, terrifying struggle.

Snow White is successful at first. She's separate; she's safe. But the evil Queen has much on her side, real power *and* magic power—a talking mirror, and poisoned combs, and deadly apples. Snow White is beautiful and lucky and hard to get rid of, but the Queen finally finds the perfect way to finish her off, once and for all. (The poison—the comb, the apple—never actually kills Snow White; it simply immobilizes her, neutralizes her, takes her out of the competition.)

Snow White's apple is like the one that Eve ate: It is the symbol of the line that divides knowledge from innocence, sexuality from childhood. The apple is itself divided: The Queen bites into the half which is as pure as Snow White, but Snow White—now that she believes the apple to be safe—is fatally tempted by the half which is as red as blood. The Queen's half is asexual; Snow White's is colored with eroticism, with woman's blood.

Snow White has bitten into maturity: sexuality, menstruation, desire. Though she chokes on it, she can't give it up. The poor little dwarfs, not men, not women, just like little children, like good friends, cannot revive her. She has gone beyond their power to help. They watch as the child who was Snow White dies.

When Snow White triumphs over the Queen, she rises again, born anew, but no longer innocent—she has been kissed!—ready to live, with all the others, happily ever after.

Even so, Snow White's passivity has always bothered me. Her triumph is not based on her own ability or maturity or independence. She's always seemed a little dense to me, too easily distracted by little vanities, too easily turned by trivia. Don't eat that apple! I wanted to shout at her when I was a child: Don't be so silly—put down that comb! But that's because I believed in Snow White and wanted to save her—the way I now want to shout at Romeo: Wait! Juliet isn't *really* dead! Don't drink that poison!

Worst of all, Snow White has nothing to do with her own salvation. She just lies there, looking good. She's saved mostly because she's beautiful. The handsome prince comes along and looks at her and falls in love (just as we always wished he would, I suppose, look right through us, through our glass boxes, and see how lovely we are inside and what it is we need). He picks her up, moves her passive body, and there goes that chewed up piece of apple. Ick!

He saves Snow White; he keeps her safe; he punishes the evil Queen. When he gallops off into the sunset, Snow White sort of goes along for the ride. I think of her as slung over the saddle, not even sitting behind him.

After they get married and have a baby of their own, Snow White won't have too much to think about. I can see her now, approaching forty, staring into the mirror, counting the wrinkles, and beginning to worry. The prince will be out, as usual, saving things, and the baby will be growing up very fast. Mirror, mirror, on the wall. . . .

And so it goes, indeed, forever.

Chapter 10

I SAY IT'S SPINACH

Food Eccentricities and Problems

> ...His distinction between Me and Us
> Is a matter of taste; his seasons are Dry and Wet;
> He thinks as his mouth does.
> —"Mundus et Infans,"
> by W. H. Auden

A whole list of phobias circle around the dining room, from the amusing and the odd to the downright dangerous. For instance, at one end of the scale: triskaidekaphobia—the fear of thirteen at the table ("to be dreaded," said Grimod de la Reynière, a nineteenth-century French gourmet and food writer, "only when there is food enough just for twelve"). Most serious is cibophobia, the fear of food. In between there are carnophobia, fear of meat; dipsophobia, fear of drinking; potophobia, fear of drink (which is different from drinking); and phagophobia, fear of swallowing.

There are food eccentricities that are not formal phobias. One of them is a focus on the color of food,* most often an avoidance of red food (so bloody!), less often *only* eating white food. Ruth Reichl, editor in chief of *Gourmet* magazine, has written about her son. "For years, I carried a couple of raw eggs along each time I was invited out for dinner. They were for my son, Nick, who steadfastly refused the hot dogs, pizza, and chocolate cake routinely served to children. In fact, with the exception of five foods, all white, he refused to eat anything. Given my profession, my friends all found this highly entertaining." She doesn't say what the five foods were, but to survive, they could have been chicken or turkey, potatoes, white bread (with mayonnaise, for a chicken sandwich), milk, and, for dessert, a peeled apple. For the rest, one assumes, pills.

This kind of food eccentricity is much more common in children than in grown-ups. Rare is the adult who would want to survive on only white food, but one of note was producer Leland Hayward, whose daughter Brooke described his food tastes in her book, *Haywire*. "He had very dogmatic eating habits, which we children were delighted by, never touching anything remotely tinged with color: this eliminated most vegetables except potatoes from his diet, and for that matter fruit, except for strawberries (in spite of their color and his allergy to them); as for meat, he ate only chicken, lamb chops or steak, and no more than an arbitrary two bites from the entire serving, but he consumed with passion what we alluded to as 'white food'—scrambled eggs, custard, vanilla ice cream and the Beverly Hills Hotel chicken hash."

Without knowing the true reason for Hayward's chosen diet of white food, one can speculate at will. White food is clean. It can be eaten without fear of making one's insides any dirtier than they are already. White food

---

*When Isak Dinesen, Carson McCullers, and Marilyn Monroe had lunch together in McCullers's Nyack, New York, home, McCullers served a white meal—oysters, a soufflé, champagne, and grapes—presented on a white marble table. After lunch, the three women—longtime mutual admirers—climbed up on the table and danced.

denies appetite—denies the *animality* of eating, denies the need to eat in order to survive. White food is innocent. Original sin was red. Milk is white,
and eating only white food is like never growing up, always being pure, guilt-
less, and taken care of. Whatever one wishes for—violence, perhaps, which
is bloody red—or deserves, white food keeps the slate clean.

Avoiding meat is similar. Its concept is as violent as its color. Chewing
meat is an oral act of aggression. Eggs, custard, ice cream—they slip right
in and slide right down. They're soft and yielding—psychologically female
food, nursery food, mommy food for baby. Meat is masculine: broiled or
grilled, rare or well-done. Meat is also more directly related to excretion.
Early vegetarians used to talk about the way that meat decays in our bodies, just as if other food did not decay after it has been digested, too. Nothing is forever, not even crunch.

In a sophisticated and successful man such as Leland Hayward (one of
Pamela Harriman's early husbands), such food tastes are somewhat
amusing. They are also an expression of the psyche, although it's truly
impossible to take one's speculations too seriously. After all, it's possible
(anything is possible) he just didn't like red meat or yellow bananas. At
least he continued to eat.

In someone less debonair, such eccentricities are less charming and
more worrisome. Beyond eccentricity, problems with food are a classic
symptom of deeper and more disturbing problems.

Jean Stafford wrote about the immediate effect of a week's menu on
Lizzie Borden, who with an ax gave her parents all those whacks. It was a
very hot summer in Massachusetts that year, and the Borden family had
been eating roast mutton leftovers all week. Every day, for breakfast, for
lunch, and for dinner: mutton. On the fatal day, another scorcher, hot mutton was served for breakfast again, this time with johnnycakes, bread, coffee, cookies, and hot mutton soup. Lizzie didn't eat. "... Lizzie may have
foregone breakfast," Miss Stafford writes, "because she was fed up. She
may indeed have been repelled by her family's provender for all of her 32
years, and this meal (hot mutton soup on a scorching day!) was the last
straw that caused her to pick up the ax and dispatch her messmates to
kingdom come. Her acquittal never surprised me."

If it wasn't the mutton that caused Lizzie to snap, her lack of appetite was still a warning signal. We eat less—or more—when we're under stress, and sometimes our perceptions of food change completely. "I can't taste food," says a character in Neil Simon's *The Last of the Red Hot Lovers,* after she discovers that her husband is having an affair with another woman. Linus, one of the sweetest of Charles Schulz's "Peanuts" gang, once said something similar. "Ever since Lucy buried my blanket, I've felt sort of dizzy ... I can't even eat ... Everything tastes sour." It's funny because it's recognizable.

From the very beginnings of our lives, food is used as a way of dealing with our problems (or, worse, food *is* the problem), and eating and digestive disorders are often an infant's statement that something is going wrong someplace else. Like Eve, children have learned how much depends on dinner.

Babies suck, eat, and drink while they're still in utero. By the third month after conception, the unborn baby has lips and the sucking muscles of its cheeks have filled out. Taste buds have appeared and there are working digestive glands in the stomach and saliva glands in the mouth. The three-month-old fetus has begun to swallow amniotic fluid and the fluid is utilized by the growing body. The baby urinates—a few sterile drops—from time to time. The baby is born, and food preferences begin. Many babies have a taste for sweetness—mother's milk is sweet, and babies often choose sugar water over plain water. Sometimes a baby whose mother had a severe problem with morning sickness will have a taste for salt—one that lasts, after infancy, through pretzels, potato chips, and popcorn. Some babies have an immediate liking for the foods their mothers ate during pregnancy. Some babies are natural super tasters—they seem to have the ability to taste flavors that other people don't recognize. And many children develop food aversions—sometimes to strong tastes (spinach), sometimes to new textures (mushrooms), and sometimes for reasons best known to themselves.

For a baby, hunger is painful and eating feels good. If it doesn't feel good, babies have only limited ways in which to react. They can cry, refuse to eat, spit up what they've eaten, or they can swallow their discomfort, as we learn later to swallow our anger, and eat anyway.*

---

*Some Chinese call the endurance of hardship "eating bitterness," and tell their children to cope with frustration by "putting it in your stomach."

Sometimes, the method a baby happens to use to deal with unwanted food is successful and it's repeated for years. When she was about five years old, Peggy Guggenheim was served her meals at a large Louis Quinze table in the upstairs library. She writes that she was fed by "a maid whose sole duty . . . was to see that I ate. [But] I never had any appetite. When my tears were of no avail, I protested by vomiting, and the feeding came to an end."

Lois Gould wrote similarly in both her memoir, *Mommy Dressing*, and her novel, *Such Good Friends*. In the memoir Gould writes that her governess saved her dinner plate, night after night, until either the food had been eaten or it had spoiled. In the novel, she writes about being forced to stay at breakfast until the lunch hour arrived, while she sat, staring at the cold bowl of Farina. "The single spoonful I'd taken was always wedged solid in a corner of my mouth. I was not allowed to get up . . . till I'd finished breakfast."

Woody Allen remembers back to infancy—he was, he used to say in his stand-up act, "breast-fed on falsies."

No wonder so many of us grow up troubled at the table, eating too much or too little, or eating what we shouldn't. The triumph is that we survived infancy—and childhood—and adolescence. And that our children will as well.

So many things can go wrong. The passive baby endures for as long as it can and then stops eating. The active baby screams or holds its breath until it turns blue, or stretches its tiny body until it is rigid with anger, arms and legs stiff, back arched. Some babies eat, but their bodies refuse to digest the food they have swallowed.

Babies in institutional settings, if there's a low ratio of staff to infants (or if there's a high turnover of staff so that there are constantly new faces), are deprived of the simplest ingredients of the love they need: familiarity, cuddling, trust. Such babies may refuse to eat, or they eat too little to prosper. Their hunger strike has severe consequences. They become listless and withdrawn; they don't grow properly. Their motor skills develop poorly and late. Sometimes they don't learn to speak. Sometimes they don't survive.

The baby who refuses food is taking the most drastic action possible in order to deal with whatever problem exists, inside or outside of its body. Eventually, taken to its logical extreme, this solution—which has the power of rejection—will leave the baby totally powerless, just as it does depressed old people, who die of malnutrition because they've lost all interest in life and simply stop eating.

Kafka's "The Hunger Artist" stopped eating—people came to watch him as he starved. The story is a metaphor; "If I had found the food I liked," the Hunger Artist says, "I would have made no fuss and stuffed myself like you or anyone else." This is dying, Joyce Carol Oates said in a *New York Times* article about food and literature, to spite the very instinct to live. She also quotes Emily Dickinson:

> It would have starved a Gnat
> To live so small as I—
> And yet I was a living Child—
> With Food's necessity
> Upon me—like a Claw—

Whatever its form, prose or poetry, real or imagined, to whatever degree it is carried out, the childhood (or adult) hunger strike says one thing clearly: Something is wrong. We tend to think of gastric problems as being emotionally caused—not always true, but surely sometimes. Children are not guaranteed immunity from the same symptoms adults have because they are young. Upset stomachs are the classic symptoms of kindergartenitis, but they are not as cute as they sound. Pediatricians say that stress-related stomach problems are among the most prevalent of childhood disorders.

Children aren't safe from stress, and they also suffer from despair and depression, loneliness and hopelessness, anger and hurt. Children as young as six, and even younger, have managed to take their own lives, though their deaths are often recorded as accidents. Researchers have found that many poisonings, usually thought to be tragic accidents, are in fact suicides. This is death by mouth, by taking in rather than by rejecting. A life that has been poisoned poisons itself.

A study by the University of California, which included 23,000 childhood injuries (636 of them fatal) over a two-year period from 1996 to 1998, found that the main source of injury for children between the ages of nine and eleven months was swallowing of nonfood objects, and from twelve to seventeen months it was swallowing hot liquid or vapors.

For adolescents, suicide is the second leading cause of death, behind only car accidents—some of which are suicidal in themselves. In a 1999 national poll of teenagers, ages thirteen to seventeen, 46 percent knew someone who had committed suicide. (Girls attempt suicide more often than boys, but boys are often more successful than girls.) In 2002, according to reports from the Centers for Disease Control and Prevention, nearly 125,000 young people attempted suicide.

More and more, depression is recognized as an illness of early childhood just as it is of adolescence and adulthood. The American Academy of Child and Adolescent Psychiatry estimates that 5 percent of children and adolescents are seriously depressed—not counting those who are dealing with stress, loss, or learning or attention disorders. The Food and Drug Administration estimates that 7 percent of antidepressant prescriptions are for children between the ages of one and seventeen.

The use of psychoactive drugs (for depression and for attention deficit and hyperactivity disorders) has risen by 15 percent in the last three years—faster than any other medicine for children. Studies have shown that some children taking antidepressants have increased suicidal thoughts, yet it's legal to prescribe them because they've been approved for use by adults. In Britain, the only drug in this category that has been approved for use specifically with children is Prozac. It is also the only drug in America that has been approved by the FDA for use with depressed children from the ages of seven to seventeen; it's believed that its benefits outweigh its risks. Primary risk is suicide, and the FDA has ruled that all antidepressants must carry a "black box" warning linking them to increased suicidal thoughts and behavior in teenage patients.

A universal symptom of suicidal thoughts—among many others—is a drastic change of appetite or eating patterns, either eating much more than usual, or much less. Way back in 1932, in *The Psychoanalysis of Children*, Melanie Klein listed some of the symptoms of marked neurosis in children: eating extremely slowly, not chewing properly, lack of appetite, bad table manners. (Like any other symptom, each—or all—can also exist in a normal and happy child.)

Bad table manners in particular, if not part of a neurotic syndrome, still offer one of the traditional battlegrounds between parent and child. Chewing with your mouth open is a terrific way of expressing hostility—all your teeth show! Bad manners are defiant as well as hostile. Bad manners are an active, positive frustration of parental control. The child who talks with his mouth full of food or eats with a perpetually greasy chin may not be very nice to look at—or to eat with—but he is at least retaining pleasure both in eating and in revenge.

More negative, more of a whiner, is the fussy eater. All children are fussy sometimes and about some things. But picking at this and that, shoving bits of food around the plate, poking at the potatoes and the string beans, the truly fussy eater allows much less pleasure to remain within his or her own sphere. The fussy eater is also more passive. That child is so busy not eating that there can't be much pleasure left to enjoy—certainly eating, or more to the point, *not* eating, is no fun. The battle over the spinach is just a beginning: The child is saying "No! I won't!" to mother and father, but the child is deprived as well.

The power to reject breakfast, lunch, or dinner is an enormous one indeed. It can throw parents into a tizzy of anxiety, guilt, and pacification. Children learn fast. "The child," wrote Bertrand Russell, "since he has very little power, is dominated by the desire to have more." What a marvelous amount of attention a child can get just by refusing to eat!

There is a difference between the child who resists food because it's a way of resisting the power of parents, the child who just isn't terribly interested in food, and the child who has another, deeper reason for not wanting to eat. In countries where food is abundant, children are notoriously picky eaters. And then, food often tastes different to children—green vegetables may be more bitter, for instance, than they are to adults. Taste buds change as we grow older. There are genetic taste differences, and many children are especially sensitive to food textures—mushrooms are simply slimy to them. It isn't neurotic to dislike broccoli, George Bush the Elder notwith-standing. It *is* neurotic to dislike *everything*.

Yes, many a child—including one of my own—has managed to achieve adolescence on a diet of peanut butter and milk, or orange juice and ham-burgers, and an occasional slice of pizza.* (My son, at Chinese restaurants, would have a portion of rice and a Coke.) These are the safe, easy, reassur-ingly familiar foods, and some children worry about anything different. It is, after all, going to end up inside them. There are children who eat the same foods over and over—and nothing else—in the same spirit that they insist on wearing the same clothes over and over and, while they love buy-ing new sneakers, can't bear to actually wear them. Children like the familiar—they know it's safe. A child who loves peaches might be willing to try a nectarine; liking salmon by no means indicates a willingness to taste squid.

It's when the kitchen table turns into a battleground—"Eat your carrots, damn it!" "You're eating too fast!" "Stop playing with your food!" "Eat!" "I say it's spinach and I say the hell with it!"—that food becomes a weapon in the war between parent and child. Most often, the issue at stake is control.

The parent who wins the battle gains control of the child's body, what goes into it as well as what comes out, but loses the war because the mind cannot be so easily controlled. The child who wins cannot win, for the re-jection of food is a rejection of love and, finally, a rejection of life.

Babies and children have food problems. Sometimes, mothers and fathers do, too. There are parents who feed their children too much, or at the wrong times, or for the wrong reasons. They use food as a cure-all. A cookie heals a skinned knee and a disappointment is sweetened with a candy bar. Hunger has nothing to do with it. By the same token, food can be a reward—a spe-cial treat for a good mark on the piano lesson, dessert for eating all the veg-etables.

Parents who take pride in children's capacity for food, and ultimately in

---

*According to *The New England Journal of Medicine*, researchers have found that children take in the calories they need each day, even though they may eat next to nothing at one meal and a lot at another. Moral: Left to their own devices, and offered enough food at every meal, chil-dren will get enough to eat. Parents needn't force them to clean their plates. That club doesn't need any new members.

their weight, might be measuring out love in ounces and pounds. Look, the scale says, how much they love what I cooked. They must love me, too. Look, Mama or Papa says, how well I feed them. I must love them a lot. What a good parent I am! The parental ego is fed on the child's food.

Children can also be overfed by hostile parents, who stuff their children's throats to quiet their mouths (the way some children may suck their thumbs to plug up the opening into their bodies—preventing both entrance and egress). Hunger is a ferocious arouser of emotions and food is just as potent at stilling them. Early man offered the gods food to placate them. Even lions like to take a nap after dinner.

Other parents dole out food, bit by bit—instead of a cookie for each hand, there's one for now and another for tomorrow. *If you're good.* Or they keep one eye on the scale and another on dinner—so that each forkful carries a load of disapproval and guilt. Fat is ugly; food makes fat; food is ugly. And you're bad for wanting it. Researchers have found that there can be a correlation between a mother's focus on her daughter's body image and weight and a food disorder in the girl. Mothers in the study were more critical of their daughters' weight than they were of their own, and rated their daughters as "significantly less attractive" than the daughters rated themselves.

Parents can also give food at the wrong times, in the wrong way, and for the wrong reasons. They can focus on particular foods, battling over the orange juice or the milk. It's quite possible never to provide someone's favorite food—it's too expensive, it's too fattening, it's out of season. Dinner can be consistently undercooked, over-salted, or way past well-done. I have a friend who says his mother cooked everything until she was sure the flavor was gone; then she knew it was done.

Parents can be too indulgent. Or they can refuse to care at all about what their children eat—witness, the school lunch bag that contains a jelly sandwich, a bag of potato chips, and a candy bar. Or the total lack of a school lunch bag, which has absolutely nothing to do with whether or not the parents can afford to provide one.

A hostile—or passive-aggressive—cook can stuff food down the throats of the diners in the sweetest, kindest way, as if it weren't secretly wished that they choke on every morsel, every bite. And if the victims resist, they must dine on guilt instead, for they have refused the fruits of what they are told (and told and told) is a loving labor. Nobody says "I've been slaving over a hot stove all day" anymore. We have better insulation these days; stoves don't heat up quite so much, and there are convenience foods and microwave ovens. But the feeling remains radiant: Eat! Eat! Eat! I did it all for you. And may you choke on it all! May it stick in your throat! There is no way to win, for if you don't eat, the message goes, you don't love. Either way, you lose.

An unhappy parent can make children feel ugly and greedy while they eat—"Don't eat so much, you're too fat already!" One mother can make the table the testing ground of her family's love for her and what she has produced. Another can turn into her family's victim, poor tired soul, shuffling around the kitchen in search of an ice cube for brother, more salt for Daddy, a glass of milk for sis.

Meals can be battlegrounds, or races against the clock, or silent marathons accompanied by a television set and the day's grim news. Meals can be lonely, isolated and isolating, grudging, or angry. Tasteless is the least of it.

Parents (and later, in their turn, children) can turn the dining table into an arena where every caged emotion is released. Family therapists often focus on the kitchen not because it's the heart of the home, but because it's the *mouth* of the home—the place where problems surface most clearly. There are those who say that the refrigerator door—covered with magnets and happy, childish drawings, or blank and clean and sterile—is a window into the soul of the family. Even the magnets themselves have a message.

Novelist Anne Tyler has written about food in many of her books—from food shopping, storing, and preparation to dinners around the family table. "I'm amazed," she says, "at the number of times someone says, describing how some crisis began, 'Well, we were just sitting around the supper table.' Surely it can't all be coincidence. And people's attitudes toward food reveal so much about them. Are they feeders or hoarders? Enjoyers or self-deniers? Food is a very handy tool for any writer interested in character."

A. R. Gurney's play *The Dining Room*, focuses on the now-neglected room that was once the center of family life. Writing later for *The New*

York Times, Gurney said, "The odds are, more and more, that everyone in the family arrives home tired, angry and hungry, to a dark house and a cold stove at the same late hour, and the age-old ritual of communal regeneration becomes a series of squabbles about whose turn it is to do what . . . everyone wants something different to eat. . . . soup can be complicated and dessert threatening. So normally after 10 or 15 minutes at the table, plates are clattering into the dishwasher, the telephone is ringing, the television is droning away and dinner, such as it was, is over."

A character in a story by Ludwig Bemelmans describes the meals he remembered eating at home and in restaurants. "Meals with the family," he said, "were always a disaster. Toward the end of my father's life, they became terrifying, silent sessions. Nobody spoke, for every word somehow provoked my father to outbursts. In ordering meals, as in everything else in his life, he decided on what was to be eaten. He . . . consulted no one's wishes."

There are endless examples—in fiction, film, theater, and, of course, life—of the dinner table as the family disaster area. But in the whole parental kitchen arsenal, there is one weapon which is, all by itself, the most potent: withholding food. Saying to a child that it may not go to the bathroom or to sleep would be considered by most people to be a kind of child abuse—torture if it were done to an adult. Yet eating is as basic a function as eliminating or sleeping, and depriving children of food is a fairly routine form of discipline. The child recognizes, without any doubt, that food is love, and so does the parent. You are bad, the parent is saying, and so I no longer love you and therefore I will not feed you.

If a naughty child is sent to his or her room, the punishment serves several purposes. Parents are given a few minutes of peace, depending on the duration of the sentence, and the child has a chance to express his or her emotions in private and then to recover in peace and pride. Your behavior was bad, the message is, but in time it will be forgiven, and after you have thought about it, you may regret having done it. Dignity remains undamaged; he may have been removed from the battleground, but he was honorably discharged. And besides, nobody said he couldn't read or play with his toys or rearrange his penguin collection.

But being sent to your room *without dinner* is something else altogether.

It is a deprivation—of food, and therefore of love. Hunger reinforces anger. The hungry child will repent out of need—dignity flies out the window when hunger comes in the door—but another grievance will have been added to the injuries which sustained the anger, and this one is the original one: You didn't give me what I needed; you didn't love me; you didn't care about me.

Using food as part of a system of rewards and punishment is dangerous. It breeds resentment, anger, a feeling of powerlessness, and a need for revenge. The deprived child will be angry as well as gloomy, greedy, and sad. The infant who feels anxiety when he eats, wrote Dr. Joyce Brothers (probably America's first popular psychologist) "may . . . tend to withdraw, rather than opening himself to the world. Too great frustration at this period can lead to distrust, anxiety, pessimism, selfishness and an insatiable craving for love while being unable to give any love himself."

All told, the child who is suspicious of food may be exercising a sensible caution. Or have a digestive problem. Perhaps, though, the problem is more serious. The child may already have learned that the love he is offered is suspect and cannot be trusted.

Maybe it shouldn't be eaten.

....

Chapter 11

COMFORT ME WITH APPLES
Comfort Food

What is Patriotism
but the love of the good things
we ate in our childhood?
—Lin Yutang

A pples were the first power food, as the story of the fall has taught us. Their power then was external and objective. Subjectively, apples retain their power as a symbol—of the breast, sexuality, fertility, eroticism, knowledge, eternal life—but they have lost their potency as a food. We are long since fallen. Innocence is fading in the front of the book while we approach The End.

We have met the apple, and we have mastered it. Apples have been cooked, sweetened, and mashed. They've been turned into applesauce, which is a synonym for baloney. They've been sliced up into apple pie, which goes with God, country, Mom, and a chunk of cheese. A raw apple remembers its original power in its juicy crunch, fresh and full of afternoon sunshine, straight from Eden. But cooked, apples are nursery food: soft, sweet, and soothing, and another story altogether.

Nursery foods are easy to eat. You can use spoons to eat them if you want—knives are never needed. Nursery foods are soft, like mashed potatoes, or ground, like hamburger. They're sweet and milky, like custard and ice cream. They fill the mouth; they ease the body. Some of them grow up to achieve a kind of immortality of the stomach, and then they become comfort foods.

Comfort foods do more than simply relieve hunger. In fact, most often hunger has nothing to do with why we eat comfort foods. The thing about comfort foods is simple: They make us feel better. They make the hurt go away. It's comfort food that appeals in the middle of the night when everyone else is asleep. It's comfort food we want when we're tired, or when we're anxious, or far from home. Comfort food, on one level or another, reminds us of the kitchen table the way it was—or the way we wanted it to be, bright and happy and full of love. Comfort food is what Mama cooked when she loved us the most.

Or what we wished she had cooked, if only she had been the mother we wished she had been.

Comfort foods can be almost anything. They change as our taste migrates through the seasons of the mouth. A glass of milk might do the trick for a while after you've first left home. Later, fried eggs and cold stuffing might be just the thing when the chips are down. Pot roast has its moment, in middle age. Cold cereal revitalizes when you're old, as does hard candy.

Some foods comfort only at certain times, but these times are all their own. Fruitcake and eggnog may be good for the soul at Christmas, or matzo brie at Passover. Other times, they taste wrong. They have no magic. Conversely, a holiday without a holiday meal defines loneliness. Eating holiday food is a physical incorporation of the holiday. It simply isn't *really* Thanksgiving—no matter how you try—if you don't eat turkey. In a letter to *The New York Times* published on December 25, 1996, defending turkey, CBS anchorman Dan Rather wrote, "Turkey is a symbol of plenty, of festivity, of family—and of love. Turkey says home, no matter where we are. There are memories in that bird. . . ." In a University of New Hampshire survey of American eating habits, researchers found five basic categories of eaters: meat-and-potato types, who eat what their parents ate; child-oriented parents, who eat the things their children like; seniors concerned about health; natural-food enthusiasts of all ages; and sophisticates, who are young, urban, and affluent. The food that unites all five groups? Turkey at Thanksgiving and Christmas.

Turkey makes the transition to the rest of the year's meals without trouble. So do most main-course meats—roast beef isn't just for Christmas, nor are ham or lamb confined to Easter. It's the trimmings and the special desserts and the combinations of food that define holiday feasts.

Some foods comfort best on their native lands. Turnip greens belong to the South, as firmly rooted as a peanut vine. Creamy clam chowder tastes best in New England. Food can be exactly reproduced in a faraway kitchen, but chances are it just won't taste the same, any more than a Christmas carol will sound the same in July as it does in December. It isn't only a matter of methods or of ingredients, though that certainly counts: French flour isn't the same as that of other countries; water doesn't taste the same everywhere you go; milk and butter are different from place to place because cows eat different grass, grown on different soil. Even beyond these obvious differences, there is magic in connections to the earth, and it matters where you are when you cook dinner and when you eat it.

Comfort foods keep us safe. More accurately, we believe that they do. A January 2004 article about SUVs in *The New Yorker* quoted cultural anthropologist G. Clotaire Rapaille, who studies the unconscious motivations of consumers. Speaking about automobile safety, Rapaille says, "The No. 1 feeling is that everything surrounding you should be round and soft, and should give." Thus, air bags. "Then there's the notion that you need to be up high," despite, he notes, the fact that SUVs have higher chances of rollovers. At the deepest level, he says, car buyers "think that if I am bigger and taller I'm safer. . . ." Finally, "What was the key element of safety when you were a child? It was that your mother fed you, and there was warm liquid. That's why cupholders are absolutely crucial for safety. If there is a car that has no cupholder, it is not safe. If I can put my coffee there, if I can have my food, if everything is round, if it's soft, and if I'm high, then I feel safe. It's amazing that intelligent, educated women will look at a car and the first thing they will look at is how many cupholders it has." It isn't just to be nice that fast-food restaurants have drive-up windows. A huge percentage of meals sold by restaurants are eaten in cars.

Some comfort foods *do* travel, and not only by car. When people move, their foods tend to move with them, though they may not stay exactly the same. Italian food became Italian-American food, with the hyphen, when Italians found that their original ingredients weren't available here. Adaptations had to be made. The same holds true for Chinese food—all those years of chop suey, and chow mein! Bagels have traveled from coast to coast, though New Yorkers may shudder at the very idea of cinnamon-raisin bagels. With lox??? Food writers Michael and Jane Stern have specialized in writing about the kinds of wonderful foods available on a purely local basis, in diners and clam shacks and roadside barbecue stands. "A bagel," says Michael Stern, "tastes better if it's gotten from the bagel bin by a guy who kvetches."

Some comfort foods can be packed or crated, mailed or carried. Americans abroad wait for visits from home as eagerly for the goodies in the suitcase as for the friendly faces. Everybody has particular favorites, but some of the most often requested imports are maple syrup—the imitation kind, not the real thing—and Oreos, Hellman's mayonnaise, and peanut butter. Travel writer Jan Morris writes that the English miss "decent eggs and bacon" when they travel abroad (not to mention Marmite and salad cream); Germans miss local beer; and, she says, Americans crave cornflakes. Obviously, there are substitutes for some of these foods, but a substitute is not the real thing. Comfort needs the real thing.

Comfort foods are, by their nature, idiosyncratic. Comfort foods are always personal and often inexplicable. They may be liquid, like soup, or solid, like hard-boiled eggs. Acid foods, like tomato juice or lemonade, are a little hard to swallow in times of stress. The best comfort foods—the most satisfying as well as the most universal—are slightly sweet (but not necessarily sweetened; chicken is excellent comfort food) and a little bland. They soothe rather than excite. Comfort food may be pedestrian—boiled potatoes—or posh—caviar—but its whole point is the essence of simplicity. It makes us feel better.

Almost everybody, from poets to presidents' wives, has a favorite comfort food, and most of us take our comfort food very seriously. When she lived in the White House, Nancy Reagan told Barbara Walters on coast-to-coast TV, she ate bananas in the middle of the night, when she couldn't sleep. "No crunch, crunch," she said. She meant that her bananas wouldn't wake the president.

Poet W. H. Auden kept a bowl of cold potatoes by his bedside at night. James Beard used to find comfort in marshmallows. "I don't like them toasted," he said, "and I don't like those nasty little ones. I like the large, puffy ones, and I eat them right out of the bag."

"My whole childhood," said Hungarian cookbook writer and restaurateur George Lang, "is brought back with goose liver. My mother spread golden red 'paprikaed' goose fat from the goose she had cooked on the bread she had baked and topped it with a slab of goose liver. To me, that is the most perfect comfort." Very rich, and utterly memorable.

Chef Lidia Bastianich, owner of Felidia and featured cook on the Food Network, opts for pasta, "creamy, preferably homemade ribbon kind. Nothing complicated. . . . It has to glide down. It fills your whole mouth and has a nice warm sensation that reminds me of when I was held by my mother." Another chef, Julie Sahni, says, "Nothing is more comforting than rice pudding." Psychologist Dr. Joyce Brothers stays with dessert, but chooses something creamier: "Floating islands are my favorite comfort food." Straight out of the nursery— albeit a sophisticated one—meringues sailing on a sea of custard. "I love," says Dr. Brothers, "how those cute little meringues float."

Food writers have approached rhapsody in prose when writing about their personal comfort foods: "Every eater, no matter how dedicated, intrepid or sophisticated, now and then feels the need to gain comfort from one of perhaps several security-blanket foods, soothing and satisfying palliatives to frazzled nerves and frayed tempers, or to over-stimulated psyches and palates in need of gentle surcease." So wrote Mimi Sheraton, purplely, in *The New York Times*.

Her personal "security-blanket food": a chicken sandwich. She described several of the greatest, most soul-satisfying chicken sandwiches she could remember having eaten but "If a chicken sandwich was made to be eaten immediately and at home, and if some fresh cole slaw was on hand, I had one of the most lusciously dripping of all chicken sandwiches, made with cole slaw and Russian dressing on dark pumpernickel."

M.F.K. Fisher wrote about the comfort foods of her friends. There was one who depended upon a perfectly baked potato with plenty of butter, and another who preferred the simple luxury of a bowl of milk toast ("Warm two cups of creamy milk....").

Undoubtedly surprising, but Mrs. Fisher herself owned up to *canned* tomato soup. It was her "cure-all, surefire palliative...." Only one brand would do the trick in the middle of the night: "The Secret Ingredient in the ubiquitous can gives my comforter exactly what it needs." The soup was heated with "an equal amount of the best possible plain milk I can buy," and poured into a "little fat pitcher" specially reserved for this purpose—after its bottom had been generously dusted with cinnamon. She then retired to bed, to read, sip, and recover. (The secret ingredient was probably sugar.)

Former *New York Times* food editor Craig Claiborne wrote often about the nursery food which was his comfort food—noodles, creamed vegetables, cream soups, eggs, custards, purees, and puddings. He often said that he wasn't a dessert man as so many amateur eaters are, but whatever else he could manage to push away after dinner, he couldn't resist nursery-food desserts—bread pudding, Bavarian cream, chocolate mousse....

There are national comfort foods. In consecutive polls of its readers, *Bon Appétit* magazine asked for the most comforting comfort food of them all. In 2001, the top food was pasta. In 2002, ice cream was first, cookies second, and pasta had moved to third. The following year, pasta was on top again, followed by pizza, ice cream, and mashed potatoes. Macaroni and cheese, surprisingly, was the comfort food most readers said they could just as happily live without.

Comfort food stays fairly firmly on the feminine side of food—eggs, soups, puddings, chicken, potatoes, ice cream, sweets: all female food—but it crosses all the usual class and ethnic lines of the dinner table. Macaroni and cheese was once a middle-class staple, a couple of steps up the status ladder from a diet consisting largely of Kool-Aid. Black beans and rice achieved a certain nobility among those conscious of their protein sources, but it was not always so. But whatever their class or caste, macaroni and cheese, Kool-Aid, black beans and rice, and many other basic dishes, qualify fully as comfort food.

At the top of the status ladder, success can mean, at the table, exotic dishes—part Asian, a bit French, part goodness knows what, or food that an architect could have built, with crossed chives waving at the top like demented antennae. Other times success calls for a bland diet—quiet food soothes jangling nerves. But nothing reveals one's origins as quickly as food. The man who had couscous for dinner may crave Cream of Wheat in the middle of the night. Mineral water or club soda may do the trick in a crowd, but seltzer is more thirst-quenching when you're all alone.

The sophisticated menu changes with the times. We've gone through all sorts of food fashions—remember beef Wellington? Cassoulet? *Coulibiac?* Onion marmalade? Confit *de* everything? Still, even the most sophisticated have their bad days, and when they yearn, they do as the rest of us do: they yearn backward. Oyster ice cream offers little in the way of comfort.

A group of fashion designers was once asked what food they serve in their own homes. A designer for Chanel said, "I like eggs . . . and a dessert of hot baked custard flavored with sugar and vanilla and really good mashed potatoes made with butter, a touch of cream and an egg yolk beaten in." (So many eggs!)

From Yves Saint Laurent: "I like to eat only sandwiches. I like white food.* Vanilla ice cream. . . . I am greedy for dessert and keep sweet things here all the time."

"I do not smoke, drink alcohol or even coffee," said Karl Lagerfeld, "but I would do anything for a good *Bavaroise* chocolate cake and German whipped cream. The French is too sour." (A diet tip from Lagerfeld, who has lost much weight: "At dinner parties, slide the food to the center of the dish and later squeeze it all together on the side of the plate. So as not to offend the host, occasionally put the fork to your mouth and make believe.")

*See Chapter 10.

Before he died, Andy Warhol had made plans with a group of partners for a Manhattan restaurant they were going to call Andy-Mat. The waitresses were to be dressed as nannies; the cocktail menu was to feature two drinks, one made of champagne and fruit juice, and the other featuring milk on the rocks. (A childhood treat—milk over ice cubes with a bit of sugar and a dash of vanilla.) "When I was a child," said one of the partners, "I loved to drink milk on the rocks and suck the ice cubes."

The food, the partners said, "will probably look like a nanny's nursery food." One elaborated: "My nanny was a great maker of shepherd's pie. In fact, when I go to London to visit my sister, I always gain ten pounds because I eat all the children's food in the nursery."

The partners planned a set of Warhol-designed flatware for each place setting, including a pusher. Comfort food carried to its logical extreme: absurdity.

In London, there is a restaurant that does just that. It's called School Dinners Club, and it offers presumably improved versions of much maligned English private-school food. Greasy sausages with lumpy mashed potatoes—known in England as bangers and mash—and suet pudding appear on the menu as "a selection of specially made English sausages, three different varieties of mash," plus homemade pie of the day, traditional spotted dick, and custard. "It's all here," the restaurant says on its Web site. "There's a matron to be sure everybody behaves. . . . our wicked headmaster likes to personally take charge of the night's fun. . . . Arrive promptly for Registration . . . or you may be punished!" Patrons may be spoon-fed, if need be, by "one of our St. Trinian's girls." Spanking presumably comes later.

Even astronauts need comfort food. Probably more than the rest of us. You're never too big or too far away. When the stars are flying past the window or you're floating in a vacuum, it's comfort food, among other things, that lets you hope you'll get back home again. A taste of sponge cake, a bit of lamb stewed with tomatoes and garlic, a spoonful of chicken stuffing brings a rush of memories: We lived once in the garden, where food was given to us whenever we were hungry and someone loved us.

It doesn't always work. No one would eat the strawberry cubes that were featured on early *Apollo* menus. After a while someone thought of dipping them in Lucite and selling them as souvenirs at the Spacecraft Center in

Houston. The Smithsonian also sold NASA's powdered ice cream in little tinfoil packages.

Sometimes coming upon a taste from home that we had forgotten, a memory of childhood leaps out, like a bubble floating forward from the past, encapsulating a moment long gone. It's like hearing a bit of song that was popular years ago and suddenly remembering where we were when we first heard it—on the beach, dancing, at a party, in school, in love for the first time. The same thing happens with smells: a sudden, intense aroma leads us to a memory, hinged to other memories.

It happened to Marcel Proust, who wrote seven volumes about his lost past—*À la Recherche du Temps Perdu*—all inspired by the memories let loose by just a bit of cookie dipped in tea. ("In the light of what Proust wrote," A. J. Liebling said some years later, "with so mild a stimulus, it is the world's loss that he did not have a heartier appetite," because if he had eaten a full meal, "he might have written a masterpiece.")

As Proust's single madeleine so amply bore witness, comfort foods carry us back. What a cookie does for one, cheesecake might do for another, and grilled sausage for a third. Comfort foods are often encoded ethnic foods, because—until this supermarket age of microwavable veggies and frozen piecrust—ethnic foods were the foods of childhood.

Chicken soup is the classic comforter, for the sick at heart as well as for the sick in body. It is love in a bowl, soup therapy, as all those books testify. And it really does have medicinal value. There have been studies (by a scientist who loves his mother?) that show that chicken soup clears mucus from the nasal passages at the rate of 9.2 millimeters a minute. Cold water has a rate of 4.5 millimeters, half as fast. To be medically effective, though, chicken soup must be taken every half hour—beyond the average Jewish mother's wildest dreams—because its physical effects wear off very quickly. Its psychological effects last forever.

Every culture has a chicken soup. There are international variations on every culinary theme. Gefilte fish is only a step removed from quenelles. Pizza is related to meat pies, pilaf to fried rice. Put them all together, in every tongue, they spell *mother*. And whatever you call the dumplings, they sink or swim in Mama's soup.

These are the foods that warm us in the winter of our souls, filling the empty places and healing the cracks and wounds. These are the foods that restored us when we were sick and lay pale and quiet—playing with our favorite toys—under the quilt. These are the foods of home. No wonder raw carrots and celery sticks never made it to the soul-satisfying level of ethnic food. Ethnic food oozes with a rich, fatty kind of love—olive oil and chicken fat, lard and treacle, goose fat and butter. Ethnic food needs a certain weight to carry its load of love. It takes much more than crunch to do the job.

Ethnic foods become their own stereotypes. Some years back, when a conflict erupted between blacks and whites in New York City's Canarsie area—a largely Italian section of Brooklyn—Al Sharpton led a group of protesters in a march there. Local spectators on the sidewalks derisively waved watermelons at the marchers. Undaunted, one of the marchers ducked into a local grocery store, bought a box of Ronzoni spaghetti, and rejoined the march, waving his spaghetti right back at the watermelon wavers.

Margaret Mead once compared German and Italian eating habits. Italians, she said, tend to keep eating Italian food—pasta, cheese, wine—long after they've grown up and left home. Italians eat Italian food longer than Germans eat German food. She suggested that Italian children are raised with less strictness than are German children, and that Italian homes, warm and noisy, are more overtly loving. At dinner, the tomato sauce is warm and spicy. Mama dishes it up at the noisy table with a big spoon and with a big smile. *Mangia!* she says. Eat!—and she means that it'll feel good, and I made it just for you.

Red cabbage and sauerbraten (*sour*-braten!) are sterner stuff. Once on the plate they *must* be finished. For generations, German children have grown up with an established order and decorum that had to be obeyed. Grown up, Italians go on eating pasta not only because it tastes so good but also because it is a comfort, a reward, a reminder of love and happiness and a warm stomach. Germans eat bratwurst and *kartoffel salat* in a way which somehow suggests they have no other choice.

Ethnic food conveys a sense of character in many ways. French food is sensuous. It can be stylish, trivial, and artificial, or profound and natural in the most earthy ways. Chinese food is subtle; Japanese, full of art. English food—think of the beef that built an empire—is well-defined. Italian food is hearty and speaks to the soul. German food is heavy and sticks to the ribs; an army could march on it, and often has. Mediterranean food oozes with sunshine, but its taste is a culinary relief from the sun's glare.

James Jones wrote about the food tastes of the French and Germans in a similar vein. "Every kilometer north and east that you get from Paris," he said, "you find the French more and more like the Germans: melancholy, alcoholic, therefore intensely military, big eaters of pig sausages against the long gloomy dull and chilly winters, big eaters of fats, big eaters, period."

American ethnic food is the food of its immigrants, one at a time, from pasta to colcannon to chicken soup, or, more recently, chicken tandoori and fajitas. The Pilgrims, America's first immigrants, didn't bring much to the ethnic stew—on board the *Mayflower*, they ate preserved beef, dried fish, hardtack, moldy cheese, root vegetables, and dried peas, none of which lasted as comfort food once they had tasted fresh corn. Sex is good, said Garrison Keillor, but not as good as fresh sweet corn.

We can be comforted by the food of another culture, but our own speaks most clearly and sweetly. Sweets, of course, are a universal language, better even than spaghetti or chicken soup. A cookie, a piece of cake with lots of frosting (the corner piece! That's why square cake was invented!), candy, a chocolate bar, pie with whipped cream: It is the rare soul who never has a need to sugarcoat the day.

In Kuwait, weight gain has been a steady problem since the end of the First Persian Gulf War. Restaurants, fast-food places, pastry shops, ice-cream parlors, and candy stores were suddenly packed during a postwar crisis in 1994. A Danish study diagnosed post-traumatic stress disorder: Excessive eating—especially of sweets—was the most common way of coping with the problem.

It happened once at the Waldorf-Astoria. The famous New York City hotel installed a 2 million-dollar computerized telephone system, and at the same time changed room numbers to conform to the new telephone numbers. At some point during the changeover, everything broke down and the computer went berserk.

Nerves were frayed. There were long lines for each of the hotel's restaurants, and the hotel served free coffee and punch in the lobby. The disaster nearly caused a follow-up crisis: a sudden shortage of chocolate mousse.

The kitchen made more. "People just seem to eat more mousse in crisis situations," the Waldorf's director of food and beverage operations said. "The same thing happened [to the Waldorf kitchens] during a blackout. Maybe it's easier to spoon up than pie or cake." Comfort in a spoon, and chocolate to boot.

A full tummy feels good when things are at their worst. A glass of milk before bed—and, by extension, the midnight snack—tucks us in as safely and sweetly as mother might have. We'll make it till morning. At least we won't starve.

We will never stop needing comfort food, and we will never get enough of the foods that comfort us. Comfort food takes over the prime jobs. It does the work Mother was supposed to do, or it takes over where she left off. It makes us feel better when we are lonely, sad, bored, angry, hurt, or anxious. Food rewards us when we are good. Or even just when we wish we had been.

Part Four

EATING IN AND EATING OUT

You eat terrible. You got no manners.
Taking your shoes off—that's another thing—
picking your teeth. You're just not couth.

—Judy Holliday to Broderick Crawford,
in *Born Yesterday*

Chapter 12

....

MINE OWN PETARD

Some Inside Stories

> To eat is human. To digest is divine.
> —Mark Twain

> This month ends with very fair weather for a great while together.
> My health pretty well, but only wind doth now and then torment
> me about the fundament extremely.
> —*The Diary of Samuel Pepys*,
> May 31, 1662

We have bodies full of holes and hollows, dimples and dents, and they operate under definite restrictions.

Most codified of all are the orifices that remind us of the basic holes, the ones we beget by. The primary genital symbols are five: nose, ears, navel, anus, and mouth. Only the mouth is allowed to make a scene in public, and even it had better watch out. Rules for the others are a bit illogical: It's rude to put your finger in your ear to swab it out and cleaning your nose

121

is taboo in public, but it's quite all right to mop your forehead or to rub your eyes—but they're *all* simple cleaning gestures, involving some degree of necessity and hygiene. What it is, is that the ear and nose lead *in*, and we need to be careful about navigating those dangerous inward pathways in public.

Most of all, the mouth leads in. The adult digestive system, if you could uncurl it and measure it as a straight line, is about thirty feet long from top to bottom. It's all coiled up inside us, working away, and most of the time—if all goes well—we don't pay much attention to it. Digestion is like breathing, another kind of heartbeat. It just happens.

Back when dyspepsia, and not obesity—both food-based—was considered our national disease (most crimes, says a pamphlet published by Shredded Wheat in 1910, "may be traced to indigestion"), the Kellogg Institute was founded to work on a cure. Digestive problems were rampant for a variety of reasons: lack of refrigeration; poor hygiene; a heavy, greasy diet with insufficient fiber. Dr. John Harvey Kellogg came to the Western Health Reform Institute in 1866; eventually, he changed its name to the Battle Creek Sanitarium, but it was known as The San, or the Kellogg Institute.

Dr. Kellogg tended to obsess about the digestive process—on what went into bodies and what came out of them. Patients who were underweight were fed twenty-six times a day, and between meals had to lie motionless in bed with sandbags on their stomachs to help their bodies absorb the nutrients they needed. Patients with high blood pressure were given grapes—nothing else—to eat. Like Horace Fletcher before him, Dr. Kellogg believed that because digestion begins in the mouth, food should stay there as long as possible. Patients were advised to chew every mouthful at least one hundred times.*

Once breakfast, lunch, and dinner had made it through to the stomach, Dr. Kellogg worried about its continued progress. In a pamphlet about the

---

*If they weren't on the grape diet, guests at the sanitarium were given hard crackers for breakfast. Chewing them a hundred times proved hard on the teeth, and dental problems began to supercede digestive ones. Dry cereal flakes—cornflakes—replaced the crackers, and eventually the cereal industry replaced the sanitarium.

Kellogg way of living, a color chart of the Battle Creek Diet System shows breakfast (red) as it enters the stomach at 8 A.M. It moves into the small intestine (still a clear red blob) and is followed closely by "dinner"—what we now call lunch—(blue) at 1 P.M. Blue lunch moves along as it's supposed to and is followed by supper (yellow) at 6 P.M. By bedtime, the digestive system is a color riot, all yellow and blue and red. "Supper residue," says the pamphlet, is "beginning to enter the colon," while "breakfast residue" is "discharged before bedtime."

Dr. Kellogg was not only colorful; he was also a little optimistic. It takes just a little less than a day—about twenty hours—for food to travel the length of the digestive system, inch by inch, from the mouth through the esophagus and stomach to the small and large intestines, through a series of valves, accompanied by secretions from a variety of glands and organs. Breakfast, lunch, and dinner, over and over and over, attacked by hydrochloric acid, pepsin, and bile, but not blue and yellow and red, and not always discharged before bedtime.

Even when everything is working just as it should, not everything we swallow is vegetable, animal, or mineral. Some is just plain air. Technically, the act of swallowing air is called aerophagia. It isn't necessary to go around taking in great mouthfuls of the sky to imbibe air. Our own saliva contains air bubbles, and some things—gum-chewing, candy-sucking, smoking, false teeth that don't fit quite right, or chewing every mouthful a hundred times— cause extra salivation. Eating under stress causes aerophagia, as does gulping one's food. Anxiety, excitement, grief, tension, or even just a bad cold are other causes of excessive air swallowing. For that matter, just plain eating involves a certain amount of air swallowing.

What happens to all that interior atmosphere?

Burping and belching, more formally called eructation, are the first line of defense the body has against too much air. The former—burping—is air released from the esophagus, while the latter—belching—is air released from the stomach. Both come naturally, but we don't consider either to be polite. Hundreds of millions of dollars are spent every year on antacids simply to get it up again, and millions more are spent on carbonated water, from what used to be a two cents plain to imported mineral water, for the same purpose. In Yiddish, *a greps herein iz a gezunt in dein pupik* means, more or less, "a belch is a blessing to your belly." My mother quoted a variation on the same theme: Better to bring it up and bear the shame than keep it down and bear the pain.

If you do keep it down, it gets pushed around in the stomach. *Borborygmus* is the word for a talkative stomach and it means "a noisy, windy abdomen." After the stomach, the stray air that's left, unburped and unbelched, loses any innocence it may have had when it entered. Down at the nitty-gritty, it's still invisible, but when it emerges from the bottom rather than the top, it is quite noticeable. It smells. It has a new name: Air at the bottom is flatus from the Latin for air or gas. (A person who has a great deal of flatus is flatulent.) Flatus rhymes with status, even though it has never acquired much. By other names, still smelling as sweet, it is a toot, a breaking of wind, a cutting of cheese, what Dr. Johnson called "an ill wind behind" and Mark Twain called "the body's sigh," a fart.

In Georgia, what Yankees call a fart is sometimes called a poot, which may derive from the French *pétard*, meaning detonator. That, in turn, traces back to the Latin, *petar*, to break wind, through the Middle French, *péter*, meaning first to break wind and in later usage, to explode. (A *pet de nonne*—nun's fart—is still a French dessert, sweet and puffy, deep-fried and sprinkled with powdered sugar.) In England, a petard (as in hoist with my own) was a small explosive device which sometimes went off unexpectedly.

Fart itself has a long and honorable derivative lineage. According to the Oxford English Dictionary (which describes it as a noun meaning an emission of wind from the anus, and says it can also be used as an example of something worthless—a person could be described as "some old fart," something might be "not worth a fart," fooling around can be "farting around"), the word *fart* comes from the old English *feorting*,* which was from the older German words *verten, ferzan, verzen* or *vurzen*. The later German: *farzen*, or *furzen*. The Old Norse word was *freta;* the Greek is given as both *perdesthai* and *perdo*. Before that, there is the Sanskrit *pardate*. Later, in Lithuanian, *perdzu*, Russian, *perdet*. Albanian has *pjerdh*, which means "to fart loudly," while the mother language, Proto-Indo-European,

---

Feisty comes from a Middle English variation of *feorting, fisten*—to break wind. *Fizzle* comes from the same source—although now, it's what happens when the bomb doesn't go boom.

has *pezd*, "to break wind softly." (There are words that describe sound quality as well as sound level; *crepitus* refers to a crackling sort of noise. A boom is a boom.) The *p* words seem more related to poot and petard; the *f* words more clearly to fart.

The thing about farts, other than their sound, is that they smell, and that is because they are made up not only of leftover air but also of a gas produced in the intestinal tract by anaerobic bacteria, the kind that don't need oxygen to survive. These microorganisms, part of the flora of our internal landscape, do good work, too, producing vitamins, proteins, and antibodies; they are an important part of the digestive process. None of which makes a single fart smell any better, though it has been said that each of us likes the smell of our own.

Children certainly do, boys especially. They have been known, in small groups, to have farting contests to see whose is the loudest and smelliest (just as, at the other end, they spend hours learning how to burp on purpose—while girls are busy training themselves to raise one eyebrow, probably so that they'll know how to look when they hear a burp).

It has not always been considered rude to fart. Not even at the table. In first-century Rome, Claudius was said to be planning a law to "legitimize the breaking of wind at table, either silently or noisily—after hearing about a man who was so modest that he endangered his health by an attempt to restrain himself." The doctors of Salerno, the Mayo Clinic of the Middle Ages, agreed. "Great harms have grown, and maladies exceeding, By keeping in a little blast of wind...." In 1530, Erasmus wrote: "There are those who teach that the boy should retain wind by compressing the belly. Yet it is not pleasing, while striving to appear urbane, to contract an illness. If it is possible to withdraw, it (farting) should be done alone. But if not... let a cough hide the sound. Moreover, why do not the same works teach that boys should not defecate, since it is more dangerous to hold back wind than to constrict the bowel?"

One of the glosses to the Cologne edition of Erasmus's *De Civilitate Morum Puerilium* ("On Civility in Children"), discusses Aethon's epigrams. "Even though he had to be careful not to fart explosively in the holy place, he nevertheless prayed to Zeus, though with compressed buttocks. The sound of farting, especially of those who stand on elevated ground, is horrible. One should make sacrifices with the buttocks firmly pressed together."

Two hundred years later, the winds of time had brought change. Though it was still done, etiquette writers were frowning on farting in public. In 1729, La Salle wrote, "It is very impolite to emit wind from your body when in company, either from above or from below, even if it is done without noise; and it is shameful and indecent to do it in a way that can be heard by others."

Still, even as recently as the nineteenth century, there was farting in the dining room. Frank Harris, in *My Life and Loves,* described a party he attended at which, while his eye was on his hostess, his nose was being attacked by the Lord Mayor of London, Sir Robert Fowler. Harris believed that his countrymen devoted too much energy to food and not enough to sex. "Why shouldn't one speak just as openly and freely of the pleasures and pains of sexual indulgence," he asked, "as of the pleasures and pains of eating and drinking?"

At the party, Harris was seated opposite the Lord Mayor when suddenly he was "assailed by a pungent unmistakable odour." No one seemed bothered or embarrassed. Harris noticed that his hostess, Lady Mariott, looked as unhappy as he felt. "I looked away to spare her when suddenly there came a loud unmistakable noise and then an overpowering odour...." The Lord Mayor asked for more meat. Lady Mariott paled. After another sudden booming noise, the lovely Lady Mariott turned to Harris in despair. "I'm not very well," she said in a low tone, "I don't think I can see it through." Harris was more than sympathetic. "Come upstairs," he said. "We'll never be missed!"

Lord Mayors, these days, are more careful about where they fart. Etiquette writers wouldn't dream of mentioning the subject at all. They don't need to. Farting is a perfectly private business, only a short step removed from defecating and also relegated to the bathroom. Parents instruct their children about both. We all learn to pray, like Aethon, with our buttocks pressed firmly together. The sound of a fart in any public place but an elementary school is totally shocking.

James Jones meant to take advantage of that shock in his final book,

Whistle. He told his friend Willie Morris, who completed the book after Jones's death, about his plans:

> ... he talked one night to me about a scene he was looking forward to writing, and which was all in his head. Sergeant Winch takes his girl Carol to dinner in the staid, family-type restaurant of the Peabody Hotel in Memphis, or, in the book, Luxor. What ensues is a sign both of Winch's suffering from his heart ailment and his increasing craziness. While in conversation at the dinner table with Carol, surrounded by the quiet, respectable citizens of Luxor, Winch lets loose this loud rippling fart which reverberates from the walls of the restaurant. There is a pronounced though short silence all over the place, a discreet turning of heads, and then the people at the other tables go back to their dinners. Winch continues talking as though nothing has happened, and so too does Carol. What else can she do? As Jim [James Jones] described this scene to me in its details, he started laughing. "I know it's supposed to be sad," he said, "but shit, it's funny," and he put his head in his hands and laughed some more. That got me to laughing too, uncontrollable laughter from the belly muscles, and to punctuate all this Jim at that moment farted, and we both dammed near fell out of our chairs.

Farts have been funny for a long time. At the end of the seventeenth century, a pseudonymous fellow who called himself Don Fartando wrote a pamphlet on the subject of "noisy venting" which was widely enjoyed. There were also reports of some rare souls who had perfected the skill of playing tunes by "skillfully regulating and controlling one's windy expressions." Beating trained seals by a long shot, this talent was "regarded as evidence of a most joyous and praiseworthy form of wit."

In *Life on Man,* a marvelous book about the human body, Theodor Rosebury writes about Monsieur Joseph Pujol, "whose virtuosity in this art form was confirmed and explained by physicians who examined him," and who was quite popular fairly recently as an entertainer in France and Belgium. There were those who believed M. Pujol somehow cheated while he farted, but Mr. Rosebury is convinced he was "a man of the greatest integrity." In the final chapter of his book *Learned Pigs and Fireproof Women,* Ricky Jay tells us that M. Pujol—who was also known as *Le Pétomane*—could take air in through his bottom, and control the sounds the air made as it exited, without any accompanying odor. The highlights of his stage performances included his attaching a tube to his body, like a tail, and blowing out gas jets or a candle (which he could also do without the tube). Sometimes, he attached a flute to the tube and played *Au clair de la lune* thereupon. For private performances, he wore a bathing suit with a hole cut out so that members of the audience could see clearly that his art was genuine.

Children worry a lot about how people in stories go to the bathroom. Adults either take these problems for granted or would rather not think about them. Children and adults alike know that some foods cause more gas than others. "Beans, beans, the musical fruit," goes one childhood rhyme, "the more you eat, the more you toot. The more you toot, the better you feel. So eat some beans at every meal."*

Some people are reluctant to eat beans at all because of their inevitable by-product, which strikes about four hours after they've been eaten. Some beans are worse than others, and in 1977, *The Book of Lists* rated them accordingly. Soybeans do the most damage, though if they are cooked with an equal quantity of rice, two thirds of their flatulence is eliminated while their protein value is increased. After soybeans, in decreasing order of fart effect, come pink beans, black beans, pintos, California small whites, great northerns, lima beans (baby), garbanzos, limas (large), and black-eyed peas. It is noted that garbanzos and black-eyed peas are not biologically beans, but are included because they are thought of as beans (as peanuts are thought of as nuts) and because they produce as much gas as a bean by any other name.

Cabbage is not quite so notorious, but almost, and also on the flatus blacklist are broccoli, brussels sprouts, cauliflower, kohlrabi, and sauerkraut,

---

*An old English rhyme speaks of continental rivalry as well as farts:
"There was an old man a hundred and one / Who let out a fart as loud as a gun. / The fart went rolling down the street / And knocked a policeman off his beat. / The policeman pulled out his ruddy pistol / And shot the fart from there to Bristol. / The people of Bristol was doing a dance. / They kicked the fart from there to France. / The King of France was eating a tart. / He opened his mouth and swallowed the fart."

all in the cabbage family. Corn, radishes, tomatoes, and cucumbers are often included as flatus producers because they leave a high residue of carbohydrates, indigestible cellulose, and other unabsorbable material, on all of which intestinal bacteria love to feast. If one wished, one could also avoid nuts, pies, melon, onions, pork, clams, oily fish, hot bread, and all fried food. There is scanty evidence that avoiding all these foods would truly vanquish the farts, though there is one fellow, Vilhjalmur Stefansson, who ate only meat and fish for years and said that as a result, all his intestinal flora died off. Stefansson, who died in his eighties, claimed that his totally carnivorous diet reduced his fecal residue by over 80 percent, all problems with gas ceased, and his feces and farts, what little was left of them, never smelled at all. Stefansson* didn't go on his all-meat diet in order to remove odor from his feces or to eliminate farts. This was simply a by-product, so to speak.

Even with all our farting through the ages, and a natural process it is, we have managed to repress not only the action as we compress our buttocks ever more firmly together, but also the idea. *The Book of Lists* mentions a poll taken of members of the National Association of Teachers of English, on which is based a list of "The 10 Worst-Sounding English Words." *Flatulent* is third. Flatulent as an abstract sound isn't any worse than a lot of others that aren't on the ten worst list at all. It's the thought that counts, the image of that other sound and its cloud of foul air.

Why are farts so much more embarrassing than burps and belches? Well, burps don't smell. And they're closer to the surface. They're upper rather than lower. They're seen—one covers one's mouth (or one doesn't)—rather than invisible. And they are that much further removed, a torso away, from the body's primary holes, the genital shaft and groove, both so surrounded by emotion, myth, and taboo.

It isn't as far away but even the navel—gateway to no place, first innocent notch, proof positive of humanity—has had its problems, though now

---

*Stefansson survived blizzards and severe food shortages on his first trip to northern Alaska in 1908. Later, he lived on floating ice for two months, and existed on bear and seal meat. He wrote three books about his travels, worked on flight plans for Pan American Airlines and on Lindbergh's transatlantic flight route, and also helped map the Alaska Highway.

at last it's having its day in the sun. It was not always so. For years, the Hollywood Hayes Code expressly forbade the exposure of belly buttons* in films. To get around the code, Hollywood directors used belly-button jewels so that all that showed was the bling. In *I Dream of Jeannie*, originally broadcast for five seasons, ABC censors never once permitted genie Barbara Eden's navel to show, even though her costume was otherwise both revealing and suggestive. Times have changed.

Today, the navel, whether or not it has a stud in it, has become a center of attention. Many is the midriff bared even in midwinter, the belly button showcased between a cashmere top and a low-flung pair of jeans. According to *The New York Times*, in a 2003 article called "At Gender's Last Frontier," we're "left wondering whether Dame Judi Dench is the only living celebrity who has not been photographed with her navel proudly on view."

The Times explored explanations for the belly-button mania. As breasts have become more plastic as well as more visible, *The Times* wrote, they've lost some of their power as sex symbols, in a paradox of the way that sex appeal works. (A flash of ankle, normally hidden under a long skirt, was once a sexy turn-on. Now it just connects the leg and the foot.) The contemporary on-display navel is seen as part of the flat stomach syndrome, "a modern-day virginity symbol." If men are hardwired to be attracted to women who have years of healthy childbearing ahead, the flat belly (and the visible waist-to-hip ratio) is a visual cue to what awaits.

There are darker ways of looking at the navel. One suggests that the flat stomach advertises that a woman has triumphed over her appetites; clearly, hunger has won. (Or lost, depending on your point of view.) The naked stomach is sexy, especially when it has a sweet little pad of tummy bulge in the middle of it, but the disciplined body seems to advertise other less sensuous things—a kind of denial and self-involvement which is not really

---

*The word *belly* is considerably more accurate than the more polite *stomach*. Belly drives from the Old English *belig* and the Middle English *bely*, the plural of which was *bellows*. All trace back to the Old Norse word *belgr*, meaning bag or sack. Stomach goes back further, but the original Greek *stomachos* and the Latin *stomachus* simply meant an opening, like the mouth, in Greek, *stoma*.

The navel, our belly button, is more like a buttonhole than a button, but it served once to tie us up and that's what buttons do.

sexy at all. But beyond that thought, *The Times* noted that the stomach is "a body part exclusive to neither sex," and thus, while it may say good things about childbearing possibilities, at the same time it represents "a kind of androgyny among women (acquire rippled tummy, wear low-riding jeans, look like a male underwear model or hip-hop star)...." *The Times* compared the fashionable navel to the fad for leg display that began in the sixties, with that decade's new promise that "women could buoyantly walk away from a conventional life as housewife and mother.... The hip-obscuring miniskirt, paired with tights and flat shoes, turned the leg into the focal point of the female form, making women look like children at a time when sex was equated with play."

Belly buttons were focal points well before Britney Spears and J.Lo were born. Legs, by comparison, are a flash in the pan. Abdomens have been what it's all about for centuries. Belly dancing has been traced to ancient Egypt, where it may have been a fertility and childbirth ritual.

Many Asians consider a deep-set, almond-shaped navel to be a mark of female beauty; Indians find it highly erotic, as does the Bible. "Thy navel is like a round goblet," says the Song of Solomon, "which wanteth not liquor." Middle Eastern dancers decorate their navels with jewels and beads. The Greeks placed an oracle at Delphi because Delphi was the navel (in Greek, *omphalos*) of the earth. Zeus had released two eagles, one to fly west and one to fly east, and they met at Delphi, a cave near the foot of Mt. Parnassus. Delphi was the shrine of Gaea, the earth mother, before it became Apollo's.

In all of this, the innie-outie battle is nothing more than diversionary, if even that, though outies have a phallic symbolism all their own, and that's probably why they seem so wrong. Belly buttons are supposed to be holes, not projections. If the innies and the outies ever got together long enough, they could probably make tiny baby belly buttons all their own.

Belly-button lint is another story, something else to giggle about, a different kind of belly laugh. It is much more innocent than that which collects in noses (and less purely yucky than toe jam). What collects in noses leads in, and belly buttons go nowhere, which is precisely what makes them so silly.

Of all the holes that double as symbols and—unlike the navel—really do lead in, the mouth is the most dangerous. It goes the farthest and it leads down. (Maybe they meet in the middle, those two holes, mouth and genital, and there, where our stomachs should be, is where the babies grow.)

Because the mouth is so threatening in its status as a genital symbol and also as a weapon, it has the most complicated rules. One can eat in public, but anything that hints of digestion—of the inside!—is verboten. The occupational noises of the digestive process are not allowed. Stomach murmurs are very embarrassing and quite uncontrollable; they cannot be stopped, as a burp or a fart can, but despite all this, we still think they ought not to happen. Humphrey Bogart took tea with Katherine Hepburn and Robert Morley in *The African Queen* and writhed as his stomach gurgled, but it simply wouldn't stop. Better-bred stomachs, presumably, speak in more muted tones, if they talk at all.

In the same way—something the body does that can't be stopped—yawning is rude. It seems to show our companions that they are, alas, once again making fools of themselves and boring us beyond endurance. But in fact, yawning isn't a sign of boredom; it's just the body's automatic response to an imbalance of carbon dioxide and oxygen in the blood. The mouth opens wide (unless you grimly try to keep it closed), the chest cavity expands, the shoulders rise, and in rushes oxygen-rich air. Carbon dioxide (the body's waste gas) goes out when you exhale. Yawn-provoking circumstances include being tired or sleepy, sitting still, wearing tight clothes, poor ventilation, shallow breathing—and seeing somebody else yawn. Yawning is contagious from adult to adult—but not from babies, and not from animals. In the face of all this evidence to the contrary, yawning is considered rude in ways that have nothing to do with shallow breathing. It's the *yawner* who's embarrassed. Shouldn't the person who is presumably so boring be embarrassed? The answer is that yawning is rude because of what it reveals: the way in. How unpleasant to see that gaping chasm, full of its works. It is an exposure as well as a threat. Said Archie Bunker, "Stifle yourself!"

Coughing and sneezing are symptoms of disease, but, perfectly irrationally, they're much more acceptable than the burps and belches and yawns which reveal a healthy body at work. Even doctors take extra care when they work on our holes. When they're at our bottoms, they place their hands beneath protective sheets, as if they were working in the dark. (I didn't see anything! Honestly!) They have nurses standing by to reassure us and keep us safe.

The dentist, poor rich man, has made our mouths his lifework, and spends his days with his fingers in our holes. No wonder we are never comfortable in his chair and the toothache always disappears in the waiting room. No wonder that when it is time to spit, he asks us politely to please rinse. If you find a good dentist, hold on to him, because as Bessie Smith said, a good man nowadays is hard to find.

And it's no wonder that most dentists are—still—men. Dental schools (and, in the past, their applicants) seem to have long subscribed, unconsciously at least, to the theory that it is more natural for men to poke fingers in holes than it is for women. Things are changing. In New York State before 1970, about 1 percent of dental students were female: now, the percentage is approaching fifty, according to the state's office of higher education research. Nationally, in 2004, about 40 percent of dental degrees were awarded to women.

Going to the dentist, male or female, inspires fear and trembling in the strongest among us. The dentist means to make us well, we know, but he does it by attacking our primary source of life, our most potent weapon, a wellspring of pleasure from the cradle to the grave, from the first bottle to the last kiss. Teeth are weapons and symbols of power. They grind and tear, bite and gnash. Angry monsters bare their teeth as warnings to us all. Movie aliens are mostly fangs, covered with glittery, slimy drool. Great white sharks are famous for two things: their teeth (some of which are serrated around their edges, the better to bite you with, my dear) and the fact that they will eat almost anything.

Brave dentist, then, who means to drill holes in our teeth. He comes with his little needle and immobilizes us. We're strapped into high chairs like tiny tots, with bibs around our necks as if we were waiting to be fed. We're worse than babies; we can't even scream; he doesn't even let us swallow; and to make it all perfectly insufferable, we're there for our own good. We are defenseless—sedated!—and then he attacks.

Inevitably, given the complex power of the mouth and its varied roles, some dental problems turn out to be psychosomatic. Millions of people grind their teeth when they close their eyes at night, sometimes because their jaws are out of line, and sometimes because of anger and tension. Teeth grinders—bruxists, they are called officially, and bruxism is teeth-grinding while sleeping—can wear down their tooth grooves, enamel, pulp, roots, and all. In the process, teeth loosen, the gums become irritated, and eventually even the bite is affected. TMJ syndrome (painful muscle spasms in the jaw joints) can also be caused by a stress reaction—the tensing of the muscles of the jaw joint until spasm results. Other emotions emerge, like muted words, by way of the teeth. Gums react particularly quickly to upset, becoming as angry and inflamed as any naked emotion might wish.

Despite its close relationship to the power of the mouth, dentistry has never had the status of other kinds of medicine. Dentists have a great deal of hand washing to do, like Barney Cashman, the seafood restaurateur and would-be Romeo in Neil Simon's *Last of the Red Hot Lovers,* who was always washing his hands to get the fishy smell off, or Lady Macbeth, who was worried about the damned spot.

Noses have problems, too. It ought to be a simple matter to clean one's nose, but in fact it's quite difficult—not allowed in any sort of company. We say nose-picking, but why *picking?* Are we picking our eyes in the morning when we wipe away nighttime sand, or are we cleaning them? Why are noses less deserving of being cleaned? Whatever you call it, it is a dirty, childish habit in public, but it's fine in private. People alone in cars pick their noses all the time because they're by themselves and they think no one is watching. When other people are around, we keep our fingers away from our nose holes.

So we believe, at any rate. As part of a study to determine how people catch colds, researchers set up a device on a volunteer's nose that trickled clear fluid at the same rate that a cold would. The fluid contained a dye visible only under ultraviolet light. The volunteer spent a few hours in a room with other people—talking, eating, and playing cards. Then the experimenters turned out the lights and turned on an ultraviolet lamp. The dye had gone *everywhere*—on the volunteer's face and hands, his food, the deck of cards, other people's hands—and *their* noses. In other research, an audience at a medical convention was part of an observational study. The results: One in three adults picked his nose at least once every hour. We think we don't pick our noses in public—but we probably think wrong. We just do it carefully, is all.

With all the decorums and taboos—from navel to dental—it is left to the table to prove that we are living organisms and therefore take in at one end that which we eliminate at the other. We may still eat (even if we can't digest) in the company of our friends. We have codes of behavior to cover the risks and to minimize any animality we might display. With the careful protection of manners, we may still eat in public and open our mouths without cover of hand, words, or linen napkin.

Perhaps that is one reason, of the many, why there are secret eaters. It isn't only the quantity of food to be eaten when no one sees; it is also the sheer pleasure of eating as if your life depended on it.

Manners make it seem as if food isn't necessary; food is just a pleasant and attractive and sometimes expensive diversion. Popular morality does the same thing—certain foods are "bad," as are we for eating them, and dieting and deprival (and broccoli) are "good." Fats were bad last year; carbs are bad this year. Eating becomes a kind of annoyance at worst, and, at best, something to give us pleasure, an amusement. Survival has nothing to do with it.

In the relative scale of time, we are only a tiny distance away from the Victorians, who saw food as the carnal indulgence of bodies, and punished children who ate too well, with too much pleasure, with doses of salts. Adults were punished before they could eat too much with servings of soggy cabbage and sticky pudding and afterward with whalebone girdles and laced corsets. Eating was too closely related to sensuality and to self-indulgence and to the unfortunate tendency of the body to excrete wastes to be really enjoyed or enjoyable. One ate because one was supposed to and one had to, and if it was necessary to think about the table at all or to discuss food and its preparation, then it was as a philosophy, a way of thinking about life and how to manage and control it.

One wonders, with all our refinements today, whether we are the masters of our conventions and manners or if it might not be the other way around. Life was full of lusty pleasures when we ate with abandon, tossing bones and peels over our shoulders, as the Romans did, tearing at the joint with fingers and teeth as the Saxons did (even Robin Hood and Maid Marian didn't mind), sticking both hands into the stew with Queen Anne, and burping and belching as we, the nations, went along.

It was left to our more proper age to invent Alka Seltzer—a medicine for the victims of plenty. It is in our time, in Western society, that hunger has had to become a virtue rather than an inevitable process. "I like a girl with an appetite," the rich hero of a large number of bad post-Victorian novels says as he watches the poor young heroine—on her way up—devour her dinner. "It shows she has spirit!"

Maybe someday, our refinements will reach such a stage that eating will no longer be allowed in public. There is a science-fiction story about a society in which sex is freely available and enjoyed in public, and nutrition has progressed sufficiently so that a pill or two does the trick for breakfast, lunch, and dinner. In that society—how Frank Harris would have loved it!—sex is routine but real food is pornography and eating is obscene. All the flasher would have to do is close up his raincoat and take a sandwich out of his pocket. Open his mouth! Say cheese! Arrest that man.

Chapter 13

. . . .

THE RESTAURANT
DEMOCRACY

Old joke:
Q: What's the best thing to make for dinner?
A: Reservations.

Waiter: Your check, sir.
Driftwood: Nine dollars and forty cents!
This is an outrage! If I were you,
I wouldn't pay it.
    —Groucho Marx, in *A Night at the Opera*

We're all created equal when we're faced with a menu and a fork. Sure, some of us are more equal than others. Those are the ones who pay the check.

Restaurants are democracy in action, and the menu is a restaurant's bill of rights. First amendment: You have the right to eat what you wish. It's as simple as that. You may have your duck sliced rare on a bed of radicchio, or with cherries or oranges, or Peking with pancakes. You may have your steak sirloin, porterhouse, mignon, or rib. Rare or well-done? Baked, mashed, or french fries? At home, someone hands you a dish with potato pancakes on it, and if you don't like potato pancakes, that's your problem. But when you eat out, they ask you questions and you get to answer. You choose your potatoes. Freedom of choice is what menus are all about, and that's the beginning, just the beginning, of why restaurants are—simply—fun.*

In restaurants, all the details are taken care of by other people, and for the most part, they're invisible. The cook stays in the kitchen. The table is set before you arrive. The dishes are removed when they're dirty, and for all you know they're smashed after you've eaten from them.

You can't see the cook or the pastry chef or the dishwasher, but all the people you *can* see love you. Good restaurants are nurturing—uncomplicating, uncomplicated, and, until you have to pay the bill, undemanding. You're going to be pampered and cosseted, well fed and well cared for. They're going to keep you warm. Restaurants are the perfect democracy: Your mother has been voted out of office, and somebody else's is in charge.

Mothers rally, however. Mother's Day is first of the ten busiest days of the year for restaurants, according to the National Restaurant Association. Mother's Day is followed in order by Valentine's Day, Father's Day, Easter, New Year's Eve, Thanksgiving, Saint Patrick's Day, New Years Day, Christmas, and—surprise?—Professional Secretaries Day. But the single day when most people eat out? On a birthday—their own or somebody else's. Most popular day of the week? Saturday. Most popular month? August.

The American Restaurant Association has 60,000 members and lists 300,000 restaurants. Worldwide there are 8 million restaurants, employing 60 million people, and contributing 950 billion dollars annually to the global economy. In America, restaurants are the single largest private sector

---

*Freedom of choice, as luck would have it, depends on your income. The more you have, the more you get. Perhaps freedom of choice is a bit like the idea that if you can afford to live in a gated community, you can choose which house you want to buy. There are also those who can only choose which soup kitchen line to stand on. Fortunately, there's a range between the two, and that's what I'm writing about.

employer, and two out of every five adults has worked in a restaurant at some time in their lives. The restaurant share of the American food dollar is 46.5 percent. That's almost half.

Plainly, we're eating out almost as often as we eat at home. We're also eating take-out food at unprecedented rates. There's even a take-out menu organizer you can buy, if you need one. It offers "the first step toward a cohesive philosophy of menu management." It's a three-ring binder with tabbed dividers and menu sleeves—and thirty-eight cuisine tab labels. For your amusement, it comes with the kind of order pad that waitresses use, pens for writing on plastic, ballpoint pens, a history of takeout, and "essential takeout tips."

There are many reasons for the steep rise in restaurant eating. There are more single-parent families, more two-working-parent families, more singles—male and female—who have no interest in cooking for themselves after a full day of work, or who don't know how to cook. There are more people who look at dinner out as a way to socialize, to connect with the world, to be seen by the world, more people who need a break every day, more people who want a fast-food fix, more people who live in smaller spaces and want a chance to stretch before they turn in for the night, more people with no time; there are simply more people eating out. All this means the kitchen as heart of the home is an empty chamber, sadly in need of medical help.

Adam Gopnik, writing in *The New Yorker*, quotes Robert Frost. "Home," Frost wrote, "is the place where, when you have to go there, they have to take you in." "A restaurant," says Gopnik, "is a place where, when you go there they not only have to take you in but have to act as though they were glad to see you. In cities of strangers, this pretense can be very dear."

That's partly why we're eating out in greater and greater numbers, both in places that need reservations months in advance—if not years (like New York City's tiny Rao's)—as well as in the fast-food restaurants on the edge of town.

Indeed, restaurants, like everything else, come in styles. The main trend in expensive big city restaurants for a while now has been bright, crowded, and noisy, full of short skirts, high heels, and bling. The crowd is spectacle and reassurance at the same time. The subtrend is for innovative food in innovative spaces and places. But if the lights are bright, the angles sharp, and the surfaces hard, it's probably trendy and noisy and a place to be seen—grown-up singles bars, where conversation is hardly the point, and where the music is LOUD and the buzz fills in the blanks. Mimi Sheraton, former restaurant reviewer for *The New York Times*, described the noise level at a restaurant whose food she enjoyed as "like having your head in a pencil sharpener." The noise is the audible signal of trendiness; it just *sounds* as if everybody is having a great time. The noise isn't as isolating as it seems at first—the sound level is an almost physical connection, and everybody bathes in the buzz together. (This is the first generation that seems to believe that adults, like old-fashioned children, are to be seen and not heard.) Or maybe the noisy crowd helps to cure that perennial affliction of the big city: loneliness.

Five of New York's classic French restaurants—the opposite of the crowded, bright, noisy places chronicled in the columns—closed in 2004 and the several months preceding: La Caravelle, Le Cirque, La Côte Basque, Lespinasse, and Lutèce. That makes a trend, too. These were restaurants that pampered their diners. They defined an earlier kind of elegance, more formal, more lavish, and kinder. Pink-rose upholstery flattered ladies who wore Chanel rather than Versace, and there were lavish table linens, enormous painterly bouquets of flowers, and hushed and formal atmospheres.

Trendy restaurants now aren't formal, except in the sense that informality becomes formal when it's the rule—in the same way that nonconformity becomes conformity when it feels as if it's required. Ties are out; sneakers and T-shirts are in.* The floors are often bare, as are the tables. This makes economic sense—the linen and laundry bill at chef-owner Daniel Boulud's Daniel runs to about $150,000 a year. His newer restaurant, DB Bistro Moderne, doesn't use linen tablecloths. Bare tables also contribute to the essential noise level, bouncing the sound off glass and steel and from tile floors to tin ceiling to undraped walls.

*There is no excuse, complained a letter to the editor in *The New York Times*, for the sloppy, bare-midriffed, torn-jeans outfits that we've seen in very good establishments; it's a slap in the face to the venue and to the chef. (Hardly anyone gets dressed up for the opera anymore, either. Sic transit white gloves.)

Many of New York City's newest restaurants, writes Amanda Hesser in *The Times,* are run by young chefs "raised in an era when it was acceptable to serve the family dinner in front of the television, when barbecue became a subject of scholarly debate and when French dining was losing its primacy, suddenly, to that of Spain and California." Not to mention Mexico, Japan, Thailand, Turkey, India, and China, among others. Putting all those tastes together is fusion food, which Felipe Fernández-Armesto, author of *Near a Thousand Tables,* calls "Lego cooking," not so much evidence of a taste for the inventive and the exotic combined with the classic, but rather a meaningless assembly of parts, plugged together this way today and that way tomorrow. As for family dinners, George Carlin says that a family-style restaurant is one where there's an argument going on at every table.

Some restaurants invest in space, and encourage the notion that good food is to be enjoyed in good company. Even the decor lends itself to an outline of the differences between restaurants, a silhouette of style.

It used to be that the more expensive the meal, the fewer windows there would be (unless there was a view). Instead, there were painted landscapes, perhaps a mural, nature as we wistfully imagine it to be or as we remember it as having been—the Italian coast, the French countryside, seascapes. (Peter De Vries said that murals in restaurants are about as good as the food in museums. That was before museums included name restaurants, most recently Danny Meyer's The Modern, in the reconstructed Museum of Modern Art in New York City.)

In that kind of restaurant, the ones with chandeliers and drapery, you're seated by somebody who is probably more dressed up than you are. There are flowers of some sort in a central spot or in a wall niche. The menu may be leather bound, a veritable book, and the wine list is another. You're eating in a room which is very much like a room in a private house—only it's a house owned by someone with a lot more money than you have, and with well-trained servants to boot.

Then there's the dim restaurant—so different from all that downtown flash. If it takes a moment or two to become accustomed to the light (or lack of it) when you first come in, the tablecloths are probably white or peach or a shade of red. If it's high-tech, there's lots of chrome, or sleek gray and black and white. There may be a lot of mirrors. Maybe there's a fireplace oven, or an open grill, or you can see into the kitchen. (Maybe you can even eat in the kitchen.) There's background music—orchestral, chamber, rock, or elevator, but not vocal. The dishes may be square or rectangular—or odd, maybe sort of blobby—instead of round. The tables against the wall fill up first.

In the low to middle price range, there might be candles in pockmarked glasses on the tables, plastic flowers, prints or posters instead of paintings, paper place mats instead of tablecloths, paper napkins instead of linen. The tables are placed between banquettes, making booths, so that *everybody* sits against a wall. The menu is a decorated page or two, or it's chalked on a blackboard, or it's laminated and slightly stained. Maybe the restaurant has lots of plants and nicely grained wood, a message that is supposed to convey good health, or, at least, honesty. Or, failing that, good intentions.

If it's fast food, it's bright and noisy with huge windows all around. There is no menu; the few choices probably hang on posters from the ceiling, illustrated in case you can't read. Tablecloths, no; are you kidding? Plastic trays, yes. Everything is disposable. Everything looks, sounds, smells, and tastes the way it did the last time you were here, and here could be anywhere. The Burger King in Kalamazoo is the Burger King in Boston as far as the food is concerned. You can have it your way as long as your way is their way.

If there aren't as many dimly lit restaurants as there used to be, are we more secure? Lyall Watson, author of *The Omnivorous Ape,* wrote that dark restaurants serve to remind us, on some level, of the caves we used to call home. Once we lived in the forest. We were hunted even as we ourselves hunted. We were most vulnerable when we ate—just like all the other animals. Warning systems shut down during mealtime: Sound gets lost in the uproar of chewing, scent is displaced by the smell of fresh food, and sight becomes peripheral while the eyes are focused on what's being eaten. Animals prefer to eat in selected safe places—the back corner of a cave, for instance, where all they have to worry about is the front door.

There aren't as many cave-restaurants as there used to be, but that doesn't necessarily mean that we've moved away, in such a relatively few years, from an awareness of danger. Perhaps it's that the crowded restaurant, in addition to being a place to see and be seen, feels differently safe in its bright lights and loud noise. It also matches the jittery flash of sex in the big city.

The cave-restaurant, on the other hand, is a refuge, a retreat. It's snug and safe, as warm and dim as a womb. It's a shelter, where women are given the soft seats against the wall while men stand guard in the more exposed chairs opposite. (I always wonder about people who prefer to sit side by side. Thigh to thigh, they meet each other—flesh by flesh, with nothing to meet their eyes but their food and a room full of strange people. Are they groping under the table?)

Womblike restaurants are suffused with a dim red-gold glow. Watson says variations of red light (peach, pink, salmon) is often found in restaurants because red is the color least like daylight. Some scientists believe that red is the color that best aids digestion. Watson writes that blue is the color least often associated with food because food itself is so seldom blue. Most of our food is in the yellow to green to red range, which for a foraging animal would be most vivid, most easily seen. Leafy food is bright green and meat and fish are reddish brown or white. Yes, there *are* blueberries, the only food to fill the red, white, and blank gap on the Fourth of July.

There's another reason for rose-colored tablecloths: They make us look good. Rose-gold light flickers most gently against the skin. Red or pink tablecloths accomplish the same thing; so does candlelight. (It's always such a shock after a drink and a candle to find the ladies' room has fluorescent lights.)

Gourmet magazine has ranked colors to dine by. Yellow, says the magazine, sends fast signals—for motion and action, and in a restaurant, yellow means "eat fast and leave," unless it's slowed down by accents of red, orange, or green. Beige is worse. It's boring and unconnected. "Beige leaves no lasting impression and garners no respect—never interview for a job or ask for a raise wearing beige." It's okay as a background if something else—a colorful painting or some flowers—becomes the focus. Green isn't good—it's forgettable, and it's unflattering. Blue, says *Gourmet*, decreases appetite, and notes that the term blue plate special became popular during the Great Depression because restaurant owners found that diners were satisfied with smaller portions of food if it was served on blue plates. But red—oh, back to red! Red is good. It's powerful; it feels warm and safe, and it goes with any kind of room and any kind of food.

There are other colors that don't do much for the skin and simultaneously take the appetite away. Fuschia. Bright purple. The blue-green shades of aquamarine and turquoise. Howard Johnson's once made orange and turquoise instantly recognizable as the symbol of twenty-seven flavors and too many fried-clam rolls to count, but Howard Johnson's was a slightly gussied up fast-food restaurant, and fast food is different. Its very speed implies a kind of safety, a de-emphasis on eating and an open wariness, a general watchfulness. You can see out of McDonald's as well as anybody else can see in, and the food requires minimal thought.

McDonald's is the same kind of symbol as Coca-Cola: This is corporate America, home of the brave and land of the hamburger and quarter-inch french fries. In France, farmers burned Coke signs in front of one McDonald's and demolished another under construction, and the statement was clear in every language: down with America. When a man who had orchestrated anti-McDonald's violence in France was on trial, banners carried by protesters read, *Non à McMerde* (No to McShit). In Belgium, Coke was dumped by the truckload. In Denmark, a McDonald's was looted and burned to the ground. In Colombia, a McDonald's was bombed. In St. Petersburg ... in Athens ... in South Africa ... in Rio ... in London ... more of the same. "Resist America Beginning with Cola," read a banner at Beijing University in 1999. Across the ocean and a few years earlier, Bill Clinton made McDonald's another kind of symbol in the 1992 race for the presidency: United we eat. E pluribus Big Mac.

It isn't only the openness and speed, the brightness and clamor, and the quality of the food which has made fast food an American institution. (Other countries have more charming (at least to us) equivalents: sausage stands in Austria; crêpe wagons in Brittany; fish and chips in England; small pizzerias in Naples, noodle stands in China; falafel places in the Middle East.) What counts about American fast food as much as the speed is the uniformity and dependability of the food—it's always the same—and the decor is also always the same. The noise, the smells, and the colors all combine to create a nervous, pulsing quality in which nothing is out of place. Certainly not the customers.

The fast-food menu is limited (choosing takes too long; fast-food restaurants work hard at maintaining speed on the lines); there's no inappropriate way to dress; no anything *du jour* to worry about; you can eat with your fingers, you can play with your food—dip it and sauce it and squeeze it. You can even eat it in the car! The food is fun, but it tastes like a kid's idea of grown-up. The sandwiches look sort of homemade (leaf lettuce, marketing tests show, appeals more than shredded lettuce, for exactly that reason); maybe they remind us of Mom in the kitchen and Dad at the barbecue.

That's a vision that has precious little to do with reality, and in exchange we give up the notion of the welcoming home away from home, where the waitress recognizes us and asks if we want "the usual." There's no tipping at fast-food restaurants, and that ends another kind of relationship in which, whether they mean it or not, the serving staff is there to serve. (Would our grandparents have believed that we'd pay more to pump our own gas, that we'd order our food precooked and prewrapped, that we'd pay a fee to get our money from a machine that's bolted to the floor so that it can't be carried away? Who is there left to take care of us?)

Fast food is everywhere. Notes Eric Schlosser in *Fast Food Nation*, fast food is served "at restaurants and drive-throughs, at stadiums, airports, zoos, high schools, elementary schools, and universities, on cruise ships, trains, and airplanes, at Kmarts, Wal-Marts, gas stations, and even at hospital cafeterias." He notes that in 1970, Americans spent about $6 billion on fast food; in 2001, more than $110 billion. "Americans now spend more money on fast food than on higher education, personal computers, computer software, or new cars. They spend more on fast food than on movies, books, magazines, newspapers, videos, and record music—*combined*." (My italics.)

In 1968, there were about a thousand McDonald's. Today, there are 30,000—and 2,000 new ones open each year. One out of every eight workers has worked at a McDonald's; the company hires about a million people every year—"more than any other American organization, public or private." McDonald's is the largest owner of retail property *in the world*, and is America's largest single purchaser of beef, pork, and potatoes, and the second largest of chicken. It spends more money on advertising and marketing than any other brand. It has more playgrounds than any other private company. It has a best-selling line of children's clothing and is one of America's largest distributors of toys. Ninety-six percent of American schoolchildren know who Ronald McDonald is; only Santa Claus is recognized more often. McDonald's golden arches, says Schlosser, are now "more widely recognized than the Christian cross." Farmer Jones has long since been replaced by Old McDonald. With an oink, oink indeed.

How did this happen? Why? The price of the food isn't as crucial as one might think, because fast-food places often edge out competitors who charge less and offer more. (The price of food in a real restaurant is often part of its appeal: Look! I can afford to eat here!) Of course, the price makes a difference for a family—and for the average American, who eats at a restaurant about six times a month. But a survey rating the appeal of fast-food restaurants gave price a low 8 percent of possible reasons for choosing to eat at one. Speed of service was 12 percent. Consistency and accessibility ranked higher and so did taste.

In *Near a Thousand Tables,* Felipe Fernández-Armesto speaks of "the loneliness of the fast food eater." He ranks fast food and microwaves with the dooming of the home kitchen and the family meal. He quotes Thomas Carlyle, who said, "If the soul is a kind of stomach, what is spiritual communion but an eating together?" Fast food *is* lonely, even when we eat it with a friend. And it bears another burden: a kind of morning-after effect. It can taste good while you're eating it, but later your fingers smell greasy, with a lingering, sticky sort of smell. No matter how much you want a Big Mac ahead of time, you don't respect McDonald's in the morning.

Children undoubtedly see it differently—and part of the genius of Ray Kroc, who founded the McDonald's chain, was to see that the children are double customers: Their families come with them, and they grow up to be the customers of the future, eventually with their own families in tow. A Penn State experimenter discovered that children turned loose in a room full of junk food divided into two separate groups. One group didn't eat very much. Those who pigged out were the ones who had been brought up on healthy food—on the theory that if it was bad for them, it had to taste good. Adults work the same way: There's food that we crave not *in spite* of the fact that it's unhealthy, but *because* of it. French fries as the forbidden fruit. Not for nothing did Ray Kroc name his children's bag of unhealthy food the Happy Meal.

Fast food can be called happy, and it can masquerade as comfort food, but by its very definition, it can't be *truly* comforting. Yes, it makes possible a kind of ethnic universality—it's what happened to the melting pot:

Everything turned into a sesame seed bun with special sauce. Real ethnic food eaten in public can carry with it a stigma, an open sense of difference. Immigrants eat ethnic food. Well-to-do people indulge in a kind of table slumming at ethnic spots; they're table tourists. But fast food has no ethnic identity. It has no heredity. Its only genes are plastic and sterile. It's the restaurant on the edge of the universe, and it's open late.

The immaculate conception of American fast food continues to streak toward a homogeneous nation, one out of many, and tomorrow the world. Looking backward rather than forward, there's a line that connects fast food with the world's first official restaurant, which, according to some historians, appeared in Paris in 1765. In this theory of how it happened, the first restaurant had been in business as a tavern. Monsieur Boulanger, the tavern's owner, may have been a genius of sorts, for he had a good idea, obvious and simple, the flash of inspiration which is a mark of genius, however fleeting.

The taverns of M. Boulanger's day were forbidden by law to sell meat. Meat was the prerogative of a privately owned and powerful corporation of meat dealers; only caterers were allowed to sell cooked meat to the public, and even they had to cook whole carcasses. Taverns were licensed to sell drinks and snacks—like the peanuts and pretzels of our day. M. Boulanger's genius was to realize that drinkers get hungry, and that therefore there was a profit to be made in food as well as drink. And his idea was to sell soup. The soup that he made was substantial and thick—lamb in a white sauce base—really only a short step removed from stew. But he called it soup, not meat.

Inevitably, he was sued. The suit was taken all the way to the king for its final appeal. Louis XV tasted the soup, and agreed with parliament that soup is not meat. It's not like a roast, said the king, in fact, it's barely even food. M. Boulanger was in business. The drinkers at his tavern called the soup a restorative, in French a *restorantes**—helpful between drinks.

Before M. Boulanger's stroke of genius, it was possible to buy food away from home, but menus were limited, and so were locations. Country inns

---

*The word had great staying power. In French, English, Dutch, Danish, Norwegian, and Rumanian, a restaurant is a *restaurant*. In Spanish and Portuguese it's a *restaurante*. In Italian, it's a *ristorante*, in Swedish, *restaurang*, in Polish, *restauracja*, in Turkish and Serbo-Croatian, *restoran*, in Russian *restauran*, in Czech *restaurace*, and in Japanese, *resutoran*.

sold meals which were set out on a table at the side of the room (a side-board), the *table d'hote,* table of the host (where *hotel* comes from). There was no choice or selection—what the cook felt like cooking you felt like eating. The great food writer Brillat-Savarin, author of *The Physiology of Taste,* tells us that by and large, the innkeepers didn't cook very well, and he adds that their food was limited to "strict necessities" and was only offered during limited hours.

Brillat-Savarin liked restaurants. They were, he said, "of great scientific importance." He listed their advantages: You can eat at one wherever and whenever you want—not only at a predetermined hour, hungry or not. You can spend as much or as little as you want, and you can eat whatever you choose. A restaurant, he said, is "an extremely useful thing for travelers, for strangers, for those whose families are temporarily in the country, and for all those, in a word, who do not have their own kitchens or are for the time being deprived of them." When there were no restaurants, only the rich could be well fed while they traveled. Onward to the *buffet de la gare!* "A restaurant is Paradise indeed," said the hungry Brillat-Savarin.

Then, as now, there were other reasons for eating out than those on Brillat-Savarin's good list. Some people go to restaurants because they have so much money that it isn't necessary for them to cook, and they'd rather not. Other people eat out for the opposite reason, because they haven't got enough money to have a decent kitchen at home. Some people eat out because they're lonely, or they're homesick—and the neighborhood Korean barbecue place smells and tastes exactly like home. Eating out is fun; eating out is theater; eating out is a respite. Eating out can be a measure of power.

There have been endless articles about which restaurants are "in"—the places where the power deals are made, where the right introductions can happen, where money changes hands without ever touching fingers. *The New York Times* noted a lunch at the Four Seasons ($130 for an appetizer portion of white truffle risotto): Edgar Bronfman Jr. and Roger Ames shared a table "while other captains of industry . . . casually took in the significance of the pairing." A few days later, Warner Music (Roger Ames, chairman) was sold to a group headed by Mr. Bronfman for $2.6 billion, "which sort of puts the price of risotto in perspective."

The old-fashioned expense account two- or three-martini lunch is long gone. ("Business and pleasure don't mix, the old folks used to say," Russell Baker once wrote, "which proves once again that the old folks never did understand the income-tax law.") But the business lunch still matters. Where you eat, who you eat with, and what table you sit at—people watch, and take note.

New York City's '21' Club goes back to speakeasy days, but it's often credited with the invention of the public power lunch. In the crowded downstairs room, toy trucks and airplanes hang from the ceiling—"totems of industrial might," says *The New York Times*. The upstairs room is quieter and more dignified, and it attracts a different kind of power. The sadly defunct Russian Tea Room is supposedly where the concept of restaurant Siberia comes from—upstairs was *not* the place to be seen if you wanted to matter, just like back in the USSR.

Delmonico's was the city's first power restaurant; it opened in 1830. But the concept of power eating is not new by any means. Brillat-Savarin said that savages decided matters of war and peace at their feasts; villagers conducted their affairs at the local inn. "... The table establishes a kind of tie between the two parties to a bargain; after a meal a man is more apt to receive certain impressions, to yield to certain influences; and this is the origin of political gastronomy. Meals have become a means of government, and the fate of nations has been sealed at many a banquet."

Steve Millington, the general manager of Michael's, a favorite media restaurant, put it differently. "It's the high school cafeteria," he said, "and everybody likes to flex their muscles."

The right table matters too, just as it did in high school. The best tables are usually against a wall and they have corners. They're away from the kitchen, away from the bathrooms, away from the serving stations. The bad tables are the opposite, or they're behind a column, too small, or too close to the front door. Restaurant designers try to improve on the worst tables—they're put on platforms, or given a special view—but some tables are always going to be better, and some worse, and there's always going to be a Siberia for tourists. Those who really have power don't need to worry about bad tables; they automatically get the good ones. They worry about who's sitting in which chair.

The power breakfast clocks in before the power lunch. There are breakfast clubs, breakfast meetings, breakfast spots. Breakfast works for everybody: It costs a lot less than lunch would, everybody is relatively alert, the day has been nibbled at, not gobbled up, and the stock market doesn't open until after nine. Restaurants pay rent around the clock, and opening for breakfast helps pay the bills. The good places fill up fast; you need a reservation for breakfast just as you do for lunch and dinner. Florence Fabricant reported in *The Times* last year that every table at Michael's midtown restaurant was filled—at 8:45 A.M. And there was a corporate party in the private garden room. New York City's Regency Hotel, reports *The Times,* has its own power rhythms. The first wave, beginning at 7 A.M., is Wall Street types. At eight, advertising people and media names are breakfasting, as are real estate tycoons, executives with nonprofit groups, lobbyists, and politicans.

Restaurants have always been stars. But today—after breakfast at least—the chef gets top billing, and customers follow him or her from restaurant to restaurant. *The New York Times* has a regular column in the Wednesday "Dining In/Dining Out" section; it's called "Off the Menu," and reports on the comings and goings of chefs as well as the opening, closing, and moving of restaurants. *The Journal News,* a Gannett daily in the northern suburbs of New York City, wrote about Chef Cards, collectible sets of cards featuring the portraits, profiles, and signature dishes of notable chefs in the area. No bubble gum; instead, the cards act as coupons for discounts or complimentary items at each chef's restaurant. The cards are stamped on the back when they're used, and the customer gets to keep them—they're collectible. *Saveur* magazine says that Chef Cards are available in packs of ten, and so far show chefs from Boston, Philadelphia, and Fairfield County in Connecticut. In its October 2004 issue, the magazine notes that cards for New Orleans and Los Angeles are due out soon. In its 2004 restaurant issue, *Gourmet* featured twelve similar cards for chefs in Las Vegas, including Alain Ducasse, Nobu Matsuhisa, Thomas Keller, Bobby Flay, and Andre Rochat. The backs of *Gourmet*'s cards include listings of signature dishes, favorite ingredients, a little known fact, and "I Knew I'd Hit the Culinary Jackpot When...".

Chefs have to work at stardom—programs on the Food Network don't come easily, nor do celebrity-chef cookbooks. In the race for the top, signature dishes sometimes tend to get a little weird or overly complicated. In the Las Vegas cards, Joachim Splichal lists his signature dish as "Foie Gras on a Celery Root Waffle with Strawberries and Balsamic Vinegar." Chef Heston Blumenthal's U.K. restaurant The Fat Duck has three Michelin stars, one of very few British restaurants to have been awarded that honor. He works with specialists—physicists!—to test various factors in the preparation of food. Would you like coffee and garlic crème brûlée? Bacon and egg ice cream? Not terribly far removed from tobacco-infused cake or the foams and splashes that have long since been offered on trendy menus. Cost is part of the attraction. One New York City restaurant offers a six-egg frittata made with lobster, cream, and ten ounces of sevruga caviar for $1,000. It also offers French toast at $28.

Another kind of eating out is the sexy kind. Thirty-five years after M. Boulanger first served his soup, over five hundred restaurants had opened in Paris, and inevitably, they began to specialize. One was famous for cod with garlic, wrote Brillat-Savarin, another for its truffled entrées. Baleine was known for "the great care he took to serve fine fish," and Henneveu for "the mysterious little private rooms on his fourth floor." A restaurant "isn't a whorehouse or anything like it," wrote Adam Gopnik in a *New Yorker* review of two books on alternative histories of restaurants. But often you take someone to a restaurant "because you would like to have sex with that person afterward, and sometimes you do, although, if you get to do it after lunch or dinner, you go and do it somewhere else."

Not always. Henneveu's "mysterious little private rooms" shortened the distance between dinner and other delights. They were a literal memory of the first public eating places, which were indeed brothels, combining two eternal needs, two glorious pleasures.

Some of the old restaurant love nests were semipublic; others were secret. Some separated the bed from the table, putting it in an adjoining room; others offered a comfortable couch to sit on during dinner, and to lie down on afterward. Restaurant boudoirs were meeting places for men and their mistresses, for those who had high hopes, and for discreet lovers. How much more appealing than a motel on the outskirts of town!

There's a Guy de Maupassant story about a restaurant bed used by—of all people—a husband and wife. In "Forbidden Fruit," Henrietta and her husband have lost their first passion, and are beginning to be bored with each other. Henrietta asks her husband to take her to "a gallant inn," and he does, to "a very chic place" where he's—aha!—already well-known. He orders a splendid meal and champagne. The room is candlelit and it has a large mirror; names have been scratched on the mirror with a diamond, and it looks a bit like a huge cobweb. They're served by "two grave waiters, mute, accustomed to seeing everything and forgetting all." Henrietta is enthralled. She drinks a little too much and she begins to ask her husband questions. Has he had many women? (Yes.) How many a year? (Twenty or thirty or sometimes just four or five.) Is it amusing to go from one to another? (Yes, very. Each woman is different—in body as well as in everything else.)

"And are men different, too?" Henrietta asks.

We aren't told how her husband replies. They embrace, the waiter closes the door, and after a discreet interval, comes back with dessert. Henrietta is holding a glass of wine and looking thoughtful. "Oh yes!" she says. "It must be very amusing, all the same!" We know what's going to happen.

Restaurants and restaurateurs whose specialty is a bit of sex with dinner are not always as discreet as de Maupassant paints them. Some, in the pre-AIDS years, were out-and-out flamboyant, like New York City's Plato's Retreat, where couples (singles were not allowed) found snacks, a swimming pool, private rooms, and one grand orgy room with padding on the floor. Today, there's less flamboyance, but the opportunities remain.

In England during the eighteenth century, one could dine naked, from the soup to the nuts, at the exclusive Hell Fire Club. Guests concealed their faces, if nothing else, with polite masks. They "often formed some weird familial entanglements while at table," and they ate voluptuous French dishes, interrupted by refreshing drinks, meant to be restorative, with such naughty names as "Strip Me Naked" and "Lay Me Down Softly." Londoners whispered that venereal disease was so widespread among the club's aristocratic members that they sometimes referred to each other as "Signor Gonorrhea" or "Monsieur de la Croix de Venus."

Another nineteenth-century London restaurant offering was revolving stages hand-cranked over customers' plates, each stage featuring a menu of naked men and women for after-dinner delectation.

Americans also appreciated the tradition of the dinner orgy. Herbert

Barnum Seely (nephew of the circus Barnum) gave a party at Louis Sherry's in 1896, for example. Afterward, it came to be known as "The Awful Seely Dinner," but that may have been the judgment of those who hadn't been invited. The main course at the dinner was a belly dancer who began her performance by gyrating naked—well, she was almost naked; she wore a pair of black stockings and high-heeled shoes—in the middle of the table.

Stanford White, who later figured in one of the most scandalous murders of his day, once gave a dinner after which the guests were told to pull on a long ribbon. The ribbon was attached to a pie, out of which popped not four and twenty blackbirds but a single lady wearing only a red satin armband. She was followed, in short order, by a number of other young women, similarly dressed but lacking the armband. Each sat down on a guest's lap and proceeded to hand-feed him his dessert. An early lap dance.

We're not any different today. *The New York Daily News* lists restaurants that offer "cocoon dining," places, says the newspaper, "where you can enjoy a night out and still be a shut-in." One restaurant surrounds each table—for two or for twenty—with chiffon tents, leaving room for a belly dancer if requested. Another has one table inside a tall tubular enclosure. "We call it the love shack. You feel like you're in your own private room." At a new Japanese restaurant, there are four curtained spaces, each with its own fireplace. At least five restaurants in New York City, including one with a branch in Miami, feature beds in their dining rooms or even separate bedrooms. (Sheets are changed after each set of diners leaves.) Guests use pillows and bolsters to help them manage their meals, and they tend not to order soup.

Some of Manhattan's strip clubs—like those in Dallas and Las Vegas, among other cities—come with doormen, valet parking, and well-known chefs. They have chairs in plush velvet or leather and there are private nooks with candlelit tables. There's onstage dancing as well as women who strip for individual customers. The executive chef at one club formerly worked at Le Cirque and Daniel. About the club where she works, one dancer says, "It's not a brothel. It's a fantasy we're selling."

The acting out of sexual fantasies is nothing new; only the degree of the fantasy changes as does the line between what can be done in public and what can't. Eating is the body's second most sensuous act. Two people in love, desiring each other, have to eat, and restaurants are busier than ever.

In his *New York Times* column on restaurants where you can eat for $25 and under, Eric Asimov described one place as "a great first-date restaurant." He goes on to describe what that means: "... the primary task of a first-date restaurant is to enhance feelings of well-being. Such a restaurant needs to make daters feel at ease, confident that they are good looking, important and desirable, while offering food that accents the evening without overpowering it or getting caught in one's teeth."

Love affects the appetite. Some people eat more when they are in love and others eat a lot less. In the wonderful movie *Charade*, Audrey Hepburn alternated between ravenous hunger and no appetite at all, depending on the state of her romance with Cary Grant. Love makes changes. It also puts attention in new places. Lovers watch each other's eyes as they eat (each of them is filled with a particular beauty, enhanced by the knowledge that the other sees it), but they have to eat carefully. There is a constant awareness of the body and of its processes.

Lovers need to order their food thoughtfully. It isn't wise to order soup. Soup requires a steady hand and regular breathing. Chicken is messy. Cutting it takes too much attention and it's too much work. It distracts. Sandwiches are a problem—too many fingers. Too much biting. Teeth. Corn on the cob drips. No one wants to hold hands across the table with someone who has butter on his chin. Or, worse yet, greasy fingers. Coffee is sobering; it puts a damper on the emotions. (The Turks called it "the black enemy of sleep and copulation.") On the other hand, the memorable dinner scene in *Tom Jones* demonstrated very clearly that if you eat with the right attitude—happy lust—greasy fingers don't matter at all; they're not a hindrance, they're a help.

The very public act of eating together—making love with the mouth in a roomful of people—makes eating out together exciting. Of all the body functions, eating is the only one that consenting adults may perform together in public without apologizing or blushing or dissembling or being arrested.

And restaurants thrive on love, as they do on power. Everything about them is conducive to lovemaking. The separateness of the lovers is emphasized, which simultaneously emphasizes their desire to be together. They are alone in a crowd, and their togetherness, their simple need to belong to each other, is thus heightened. "The presence of the other near-invisible diners," writes M.F.K. Fisher, "makes the promised isolation seem even more desirable."

As they eat, lovers share the consciousness of what may come later, even if they already have fond memories to sustain them. Eating is so private, so personal, so devoutly of the body. The covert knowledge of lovers is a nervous, exhilarating secret, a swelling excitement and warmth.

Good waiters, at the restaurants that lovers love, baby their romancers, offering a sweet paternity like that of the very rich. Lovers, when they eat out, are almost like siblings, children of the indulgent parent who is their waiter. They are brother and sister alone at the table, twins at the nipple, in their shared pleasure. Lovers entrust themselves to waiters; waiters wait and watch their lovers laugh, and they keep the wineglasses filled. They make discreet suggestions—"The lamb is very good tonight"—and they approve of everything. A good waiter is, like a good restaurant, almost an adjunct to a love affair. While it eats, he is responsible for its sustenance.

There is a kind of safety for lovers who eat in public: They are in neutral territory. They are at a certain distance from the bed. Neither of them has cooked. Nobody has to carve the roast. True, a suitor must know how to order, how to tip, how to taste the wine. These were once the manly arts of the table, offerings to a fair lady, request for her favors. Today, men suffer less. Male or female, once sophistication has been proved, innocence can be indulged in.

There is something else about a restaurant: Sooner or later, the check will arrive. There's always a price. Somebody has to pay for the food. And there are all sorts of ways to pay.

Tipping is one. There's no free lunch, and there's no free service either. Everybody expects a tip—the upscale wine steward, and the kids at Starbucks. According to the Internal Revenue Service, Americans paid over $14 billion in tips in 2002. Another (nondeductible) estimate is considerably higher: over $25 billion each year to waiters alone. According to one international survey, countries with the most extroverted and neurotic citizens (top line: the United States) tip the most. Extroverts are social, and tipping guarantees good kinds of attention. Neurotics tend to feel guilty and anxious, and tip more to feel better about the difference between their status and that of the server, or they just want to be liked.

Americans once thought tipping was undemocratic, and thus the Anti-Tipping Society of America, an alliance of one hundred thousand traveling salesmen, successfully had the custom outlawed in seven states from 1905 to 1919. Today, tipping is more popular than ever in America as it is around the world, from baksheesh to the bill that already includes a charge for service. (In China, tipping a waiter is considered rude, though that will probably change as more and more tourists leave more and more money behind.)

A Cornell University study says that waiters and waitresses who introduce themselves by name—"Hello, I'm Gladys, and I'll be your server tonight"—receive much greater tips than those who don't—53 percent more, even though so many diners are irritated by what they call an unrequested intimacy. Who cares what your name is? Maybe they feel guilty about feeling that way, and they leave more money. (Or maybe things are different in Ithaca, where Cornell is.) However it works, Gladys makes more money when she says who she is. Servers who bend their knees and squat at the tableside (it would never have happened at Le Cirque), thus making better eye contact, also make better tips, as do those who write "Thank you!" on the back of the check. Women who draw smiley faces on the bill up their tips, but males who do that decrease them. Other good things for servers to do if they want larger tips: smile, smile, smile; and touch gently (as on the shoulder, or on the hand) when giving change. Using a tray to hold the check increases tips by as much as 25 percent. *The Atlantic Monthly* reports that servers who leave a piece of candy with the check average 18 percent more in tips than those who don't.

That still leaves the rest of the bill to be paid.

Daphne Du Maurier, in *Kiss Me Again, Stranger*, explored the debts eating out can incur. "You start off with a long evening ahead of you, and by the time you've been to a picture or a concert, and then had something to eat and to drink, well, you've got yourselves acquainted, and it's the usual thing to end up with a bit of kissing and a cuddle, the girls expect it."

So do we all. In a Norman Rockwell sort of picture of adolescence, an ardent youth once paid for a hamburger and french fries, hoping to drive away afterward and spread a blanket over the ground in the tall grass at the side of the road. A loaf of bread, a jug of wine and thou may be paradise enow, but a milk shake and the backseat of a car could have taken their place for a few heated moments along the time line of love.

Hungry prefeminist girls faced two important questions about adolescent dating. How can I *not* kiss him good night after he's spent all that money on me? Or the reverse: Should I let him take me to the movies and buy me something to eat afterward, spending all that money, if I know I don't want to kiss him good night? (Today, the venue is different—oral sex is the expectation—but the choice is the same.)

In a way, back then, a girl might have learned to trade her body for a piece of goods, be it dinner or a diamond, a bit of cash or a marriage license. Some women knew enough to pay their own way; others chose what they wanted because they wanted it. There were always some who ordered the most expensive items on the menu, on the theory that you should take what you can get while you can get it. In that case, the trade was implicit. He paid for supper; the bill included a few after-dinner treats. They just didn't call it what it was.

Prostitution is a seesaw of supply and demand: The customer pays for what he wants and hasn't already got (no matter why) and the prostitute supplies it. An indirect food-sex equation of sorts emerges. The working girl wants money; the customer wants sex. Money buys food; a hunger for sex works out to be the equivalent of a hunger for food. Oversimplified, yes (and leaving drugs out of the equation), but prostitution, as women who work at it will tell you, is work like any other, and the reason we all work—whether or not we like what we do—is to put dinner on the table and to pay the rent.

The pseudonymous author of *My Secret Life*, Victorian pornography first published in 1888, once asked a young prostitute, aptly named Kitty, what she did with the money she earned on the street. "I buy food," Kitty said. "I can't eat what mother gives us. She is poor and works very hard; she'd give us more, but she can't.... Sometimes we have only gruel and salt; if we have a fire we toast the bread, but I can't eat it if I'm not dreadful hungry." Asked what she likes best to eat, Kitty replies "Pies and sausage rolls." "[Is that] what you let men fuck you for?" the writer asks. "Yes," Kitty answers, sausage rolls and meat-pies and pastry, too.

Pornography spread like hotcakes in the 1970s and the 1980s, an age of decadence which was juxtaposed, in retrospect, with innocence, as if everyone believed there would never be a price to be paid. At the same time, and equally quickly, fast-food restaurants bloomed from coast to coast. There was a clear danger of having lovemaking become as personal as eating a hamburger at McDonald's—all wrapped up before it was even ordered. Both pornography and fast food de-emphasize the personal and the intimate. Both are mass order; they're tailored for people in a hurry, people avoiding intimacy, people seeking easy satisfaction, people who wish to make no commitment or take any undue effort, who at heart would prefer to eat and to love alone.

A long time ago, America was obsessed with purity and its young people were advised about how to keep their innocence by taking cold showers and going for long walks (alone). In those days, eating made you healthy. Zaftig was not a bad thing to be. It was good to be chubby, and good to be pure. Atkins hadn't happened yet; neither had AIDS.

Now, the pendulum has swung again. We aren't as careful about sex as we used to be just a few short years ago, but we still worry about food, more and more as we try to eat less and less. How many carbs? is the question of the day; not how good does it taste, or how will I feel after I've eaten it. Whether or not anatomy is destiny, we want lines of muscles where we once had curves, and our lore is the virtue of being thin.

But we seem not to be totally convinced—or, at best, we're a little confused (just as we are about sex, making out while we talk about safety). Still, somehow, despite everything we've read and done and not eaten, we weigh more than ever. We talk a good game, but no matter what we say about carbs and fat, premium ice cream sells. When we eat out, we carefully have our salad dressing on the side, and then we order white chocolate mousse with raspberry sauce and whipped cream for dessert. Restaurants are busier than ever—at home, there's no time to cook and no energy for fussing; eating out is fun, you never know whom you might see, food is trendy, and I know a place that makes the greatest french fries . . . with mayonnaise sauce instead of ketchup. Yum. I'll worry tomorrow—I'll diet tomorrow; I'll pay the charge card tomorrow; let's eat out tonight!

Chapter 14

CHEWING THE SOUND BITE

Political Gastronomy

Seeing is deceiving.
It's eating that's believing.
—James Thurber

I t's all part of election season: promises, negative ads that pretend they're
not, and eating ethnic and local food, from knishes in New York to tacos
in New Mexico.

"Good political food," said an article in *The New York Times Magazine*
just before the 2004 presidential election, "... must be democratic. The
barbecue, the clambake, the chili contest, the fish fry, the hamburger cook-
out, the pancake social, the fried-chicken potluck, the spaghetti dinner—
these are the great entrees of American politics...."

Election eating is done in the hope of tilting a few undecided voters,
and indeed, from the voter's point of view, the food bite can mean more
than the sound bite. After all, eating shows that the candidates are human.

And because eating is so revealing, what they choose to eat tells us more than they might have meant for us to know. When we open our mouths to eat, our souls fly out. Tell me what you eat, and I'll tell you whether or not you'll win.

The food bite has always mattered. During his 1840 campaign, Martin Van Buren was attacked on the grounds that he had used public money to raise strawberries for his dining pleasure. "How delightful it must be to eat his *pâté de foie gras, dinde désossée,* and *salade à la volaille* from a silver plate with a golden knife, to sip with a golden spoon his *soupe à la Reine,* to wash his pretty tapering soft white lily fingers after dining on *fricandeau de veau* and *omelette soufflée,*" said Charles Ogle in a speech in Congress that became known as the "Gold Spoon" speech. Ogle said *his* candidate, William Henry Harrison, was happy with "hog and hominy and hard cider." Harrison won.

If hog and hominy then and Philly cheesesteaks now are campaign eating, first lady recipes are campaign cooking. They began appearing in 1920—not coincidentally, surely, the year that women won the vote. It was Florence Harding's waffles that year—even though she admitted to not liking to cook, she was reported to be a whiz at the waffle iron. Her waffle recipe became a symbol of her husband's "Back to Normalcy" campaign, just after World War I. Hillary Rodham Clinton's infamous comment about not staying home and baking cookies echoed Mrs. Harding's reluctance to cook, but in a similar spirit to Mrs. Harding's waffle recipe, Mrs. Clinton presented a recipe for the voters—the cookies she didn't usually stay home to bake.

Mrs. Coolidge was another who didn't take honors as a cook—"Don't you think the road commissioner would be willing to pay my wife something for her recipe for pie crust?" Calvin is supposed to have asked after eating a slice of her apple pie—but her blueberry muffins were cited as an example of Coolidge wholesomeness, and thus another first lady recipe was made public.

In 1928, Herbert Hoover partly echoed France's King Henry IV when his campaign called for "a chicken in every pot and a car in every garage." Hoover won, but four years later, after the Great Depression had begun, the slogan came back to haunt him. He denied ever having said it. (It had originally appeared as the headline of an ad in *The New York World,* paid for by a group of "Republican Business Men.") The denial didn't take; the promise hadn't been kept; pots were empty, and Roosevelt won.

A later food link for Richard Nixon began even before he became president. In the summer of 1959, as vice president, Nixon was traveling in Russia. He visited a model American home, part of a U.S. exposition in a Moscow park, and had a series of exchanges with Russian Premier Nikita Krushchev, most famously a verbal dueling match in the model home's kitchen that became known as the Kitchen Debate.

During a Smithsonian twenty-fifth-anniversary celebration of the Kitchen Debate, Nixon recalled that American experts had had doubts about Krushchev's Kremlin leadership. "The verdict in the United States intelligence community," Nixon said, "was that Krushchev wouldn't last because he wore ill-fitting suits and he liked to drink too much...." Even so, Nixon later ranked Krushchev at the top of the world leaders he had met. "He had a fast mind, a marvelous sense of humor, and he was highly combative," Nixon said. "He was a man of great warmth...." Indeed, Khrushchev was as round and cuddly-looking as a teddy bear. Obviously, he liked to eat. He was also known for his public tantrums. They had more than a bit of calculation in them, but they were breathtaking even so.

"Khrushchev," wrote A. J. Liebling, the great writer on food, sports, and politics, "looks like the kind of man his physicians must continually try to diet, and historians will someday correlate these sporadic deprivations, to which he submits 'for his own good,' with his public tantrums. If there is to be a world cataclysm, it will probably be set off by skim milk, Melba toast, and mineral oil in the salad."

According to Liebling's theory, if Khrushchev had to forego his kasha and kissel, somewhere deep in his Russian soul it would surely have made him angry. So he came to America and went to the UN and took his shoe off and banged it on a desk, and made page one of every newspaper in the world.

If only one of those UN interpreters had understood. "I'm hungry," someone in the glass booth would have said to the world at large, as Nikita pounded his desk and his bare toes wiggled with rage. "Give me my dinner," the blank voice of the simultaneous translator would have intoned, allowing us to understand this strange, angry Russian. "And I want two desserts." The cold war would have been over in as long as it takes to heat up a stove.

As open and sunny as Khrushchev seemed when he had his shoes on—the wily peasant, eating boiled potatoes with sour cream and coveting caviar—Nixon seemed to be the reverse, dark and hidden, perpetually hungry, as if he scorned eating what he might be served, just like Groucho Marx not wanting to belong to any club that would have him as a member, or like a king who no longer trusts his tasters. It's easy to forget—Nixon seems so much wiser now that he's safely dead—how menacing he seemed in his public years, first the old Nixon, then the new Nixon, and tricky Dick throughout.

His mother loved him.

As a boy, according to Dr. David Abrahamsen, who wrote one of the most popular contemporary psycho-biographies of the former president, Nixon loved to help his mother mash potatoes. Abrahamsen went on—and on—about Nixon and the spuds: "The extent and intensity of this activity might suggest that this potato mashing was a form of aggression against an inanimate object which was a substitute for people. Potato mashing allowed this apparently tense and moody child to express his unconscious anger." His mother saw it differently: "He never left any lumps. . . . He was the best potato masher one could wish for."

What came later in Nixon's kitchen psyche was his fondness for cottage cheese and ketchup, a snack that threw our nation's food editors into a frenzy of nothing. What could they say about cottage cheese and ketchup? Nixon apparently retained a fondness for mounds of mushy white stuff on his plate.

We're back to Leland Hayward's white food (see chapter 10)—still innocent and pure, while red food is violent and erotic. The two sides of Nixon; the new and the old. White food speaks of childhood, purity, and safety. It's mighty clean; any dirt would show. Cottage cheese even tastes clean and innocent. It's mild, reassuring food—milk just one step removed. Covering it with ketchup is a violent act. It is a defilement. The image is one of blood on snow. Or blood on a mother's breast. It is a corruption of mother's milk, a cutting of the flesh of the breast, so that the red, red blood spills over the sweet milk, and the anger of the child is gratified at the same time as his hunger. It is the violating—and the violence—of an innocent.

It all goes together: cottage cheese, ketchup... Cambodia... Watergate... "skim milk, Melba toast, and mineral oil," just as Liebling said. (Adolf Hitler was a vegetarian; he never ate meat; he preferred lime blossom tea and vegetable-nut soup.)

Nixon named Gerald Ford as his vice president after Spiro Agnew was forced to resign in a bribery scandal. When Nixon resigned, Ford followed him into the White House.

The Ford presidency was heralded with newspaper stories about how he toasted his own English muffins, a warm, buttery picture of a small, homey chore that seemed to thaw the cold darkness of the Nixon years. The muffins, hand-toasted by the man who was suddenly president, led Americans to anticipate a cozy, family sort of presidency, and that is almost what we got. The Fords had a well-publicized double bed—Gerald Ford was the first president to admit that he slept with the first lady (the existence of presidential children somehow never feels like adequate proof). After the nihilistic Nixon years, America so desperately yearned for a sense of reality about its president and his family that we had to invent warmth and personality and love. We did. And we called it Betty Ford. And she drank too much and took too many pills in order to invent exactly the same thing.

Jimmy Carter was more of a true reaction to Nixon than Ford had been; eventually that seemed part of what, at the time, was misunderstood and was therefore sad about his presidency. Carter's ultimate image in the White House years was bland. So was his taste in food. More than any other food that he ate, he was inevitably associated with peanuts—because he was a peanut farmer—and with grits because he was from Georgia. And both are funny.* (Both are also like Carter's toothy smile: innocent, gawky, country.)

Willie Clark, the old vaudeville comic in Neil Simon's *The Sunshine Boys,* says that words with a *k* in them are funny. "I'll tell you which words

---

*Peanuts grow funny, too, bending over, blooming underground. They have a long history—they were brought to America by slave ships from Africa. The word *goober*—funny—comes from the African word *nguba*, peanut.

always get a laugh," he says. "'Chicken' is funny.... 'Pickle' is funny.... 'Cupcake' is funny.... 'Tomato' is not funny.... 'Roast beef' is not funny.... But 'Cookies' is funny.... 'Cucumber' is funny...."

Peanut is funny, whether or not it has a *k* in it. Ask Charles Schulz; he knew what to call Charlie Brown and the gang. Not Cookies. "Peanuts."

Peanuts are funny because they're little and curved; they have sexual connotations, but they're safe because they're so small. Bananas are bawdy; peanuts are funny.

Grits have less of a history, but they, too, sound funny and earthy, determined and plain, even though in the years since Jimmy Carter ate in the White House dining room grits have come to find their fifteen minutes of fashion and fame.

We learned only a little about the rest of Jimmy Carter's diet. He was a private president, the toothy grin hiding as much as it revealed. His press aides said he liked steak, rare. Good. Steak is a power food, masculine, aggressive. A male president does well to eat his beef rare. (Ronald Reagan avoided beef; he preferred veal, which is not politically correct and is a little neutral, not to mention effete.) Carter also liked ham with red-eye gravy and corn bread. He feels good, then, about his heritage. He didn't drink much, but when he did—at least in the White House years—he sipped wine or scotch. Good again. Wine is intelligent. Scotch is masculine, unlike vodka,* which is neuter. Both wine and scotch are drinks of maturity.

All that was made public about Ronald Reagan's drinking habits is that he preferred California wines. That was good politics for the former governor of the state. As for food, he was all-American, except for the veal which he explained on the basis of health but which smacked of his wife's White House clothes and china; stylish and expensive. Nancy Reagan frequently chose menus that included both veal and raspberries—again, both stylish, both expensive, both for what George W. Bush later called "the haves and

---

*"The standard of perfection for vodka," A. J. Liebling wrote in *Between Meals*, "[is] no color, no taste, no smell.... it accounts perfectly for the drink's rising popularity with those who like their alcohol in conjunction with the reassuring tastes of infancy—tomato juice, orange juice, chicken broth. It is the ideal intoxicant for the drinker who wants no reminder of how hurt mother would be if she knew what he was doing."

the have-mores." During the Reagan years, when a mother wrote the White House that she couldn't feed her family of four on what the reduced food stamp program covered, the first lady's staff inadvertently sent back Mrs. Reagan's crabmeat and artichoke recipe. The woman took the recipe to her local newspaper, and it soon became a national press item: crabmeat and artichokes, when the Reagan administration had just declared ketchup to be a vegetable for federal school lunch purposes.

Aside from veal, crabmeat, and raspberries, according to a White House list of trivial facts (hat size: 7; pajamas: yes; lucky number: 33), Reagan's favorite food was macaroni and cheese. He also loved vanilla ice cream. And all the world knew about the jelly beans. What an image! Bland, bland, bland! And nursery food to boot! (He called his wife Mommy.)

Reagan spiffed up his jelly bean image a little bit. He didn't eat just any jelly bean: the candy of choice was Jelly Bellies, "the original gourmet jelly bean," colored and flavored throughout and made with natural ingredients "whenever possible." Reagan said that "you can tell a lot about a fellow's character by his way of eating jelly beans." Well, yes. Does he eat only one color? If so, which? Or does he just grab a handful in a careless and uncaring way? Does he eat one at a time? Reagan didn't say how he himself ate jelly beans.

Did he realize that way down deep, jelly beans are kid stuff? They're what the Easter Bunny brings if you've been a good little boy or girl. They're sweet and pretty—fairly innocuous, like his macaroni and cheese. They're sticky, not just sweet, and they can require a certain amount of sucking. (As do cigarettes. He took up jelly beans when he stopped smoking.) Mainly, they are nursery candy. Pralines, for instance, are more sophisticated. Chocolates are sexy. And bittersweet. Even M&M's are more grown-up than jelly beans.

No matter; a great many voters loved Ronald Reagan and his jelly beans. At least he *had* a food image. George Bush the Elder was said to love pork rinds and barbecue but the image of sauce dripping down his chin simply jarred with the prudent man he claimed to be and the elite easterner (Yale grad, Skull and Bones member, son of an old-line old-money Connecticut senator) that he really was.

It was Lee Atwater, Bush's 1988 political deputy, and master of the sound bite, who told him he had to do something about his preppy image—it wouldn't sell in the voting booth. Pork rinds replaced popcorn as Bush's favorite snack, and with the Oak Ridge Boys and the American flag became the official new image of George Herbert Walker Bush.

Bush Père doesn't look like a man who enjoys food. His popcorn was probably air-popped. He's thin—scrawny, in fact—and he has the kind of legs that Brillat-Savarin said trousers were invented to hide. As president, his food was particularly notable for not being broccoli. On March 22, 1990, the president declared that he never, ever, wanted to see another piece of broccoli on his plate. "I do not like broccoli," Bush said, "and I haven't liked it since I was a little kid and my mother made me eat it. And I'm President of the United States, and I'm not going to eat any more broccoli!" So there! Broccoli was banned from meals on Air Force One as well as the White House.

Covering the broccoli story, *The New York Times* reported that Bush really was a fast-food addict. "Junk food is his lifestyle," said an aide, and *The Times* listed some of his favorites: beef jerky, nachos, tacos, guacamole, chili, refried beans, hamburgers, hot dogs, barbecued ribs, candy, popcorn, ice cream, and cake. That's a list that covers both parts of his heritage, Texas and Connecticut, and it does give credence to the pork ribs and barbecue image. It certainly is the food of the common man, not the Republican Right. Is it picky to say that it isn't heavy on the vision thing? It doesn't have a lot of real substance; it's fast and easy eating, and not what the president himself would have called prudent. Candy, popcorn, ice cream, and cake, occurring as they do together at the end of the list, seem like a kid's birthday-party food, and apparently that's how Bush ate, like a kid at a party when the grown-ups aren't looking. The same *New York Times* article described the way he eats: ". . . with a shoveling motion, bent over his plate, sometimes sticking his napkin into his shirt like a bib so he won't soil his shirt and tie." That shoveling motion surely didn't make his mother happy.

"I'll do whatever it takes to get elected," Bush said before his second go-round with the electorate The first time, he was running against Michael Dukakis, relatively unknown, consistently misunderstood, and battered by Lee Atwater's smarts. The second time, though, was different. Bush was up against Bill Clinton, a hungry man, a *real* eater.

The fire in Bill Clinton's belly was not just to win the election. As a candidate, his relationship with food bordered on national mythology. (Bush, by comparison, wasn't really hungry. He had already eaten.) On his hungry path to victory during the campaign of 1992, Clinton ate *everything*. He extended the multicultural food line for the first time (from pizza and knishes) with chicken enchiladas, and he added the all-American Big Mac and coffee. Perfect political eating: common denominator all the way. And a weight problem to boot. We can relate to that. Much better than Reagan's jelly beans (how cute!) or Bush's upper-class Texas barbecue, preppy picnic version.

Among the foods listed then as Clinton's favorites (and there are many) are doughnuts, lemon chess pie, chips and salsa, Coke with ice, chicken enchiladas, hamburgers, biscuits, mango chutney ice cream, cinnamon rolls, and peanut butter and banana sandwiches. Wow! This man likes to eat! This was a man with a real appetite, and his favorites are as American as apple pie. There's plenty of real food here, and heritage food, sweet and spicy and meaty and sophisticated (mango chutney ice cream!). This, it seemed, was a man really—really—happy being who he is. There's even a bit of Elvis tucked in—Elvis's favorite was *fried* peanut butter and banana sandwiches.

On the one hand, it seemed a relief to have a candidate who could eat for pleasure—and that's what we saw on his face, not slickness, not a problem making a choice and sticking to it, but the ability to indulge, to overeat, to satisfy a sensual appetite. And on the other hand, that made some of us uncomfortable. And, as it turned out, maybe it was right to be uncomfortable about Bill Clinton's appetite. What was true about food was true about interns, too. He ate so much because he could.

Bush never seemed to realize what he was up against—he seemed stunned and tired during most of the second campaign. At one point, he made a visit to a Texas bar in a town where he was staying with a friend. He signed napkins and menus. He ordered a mug of beer. *Lite.* (He was with Wyoming Senator Alan Simpson, who was not campaigning and who ordered Chablis.) He stayed about fifteen minutes and then left, because, he said, he had told Barbara he'd go to bed early. Sounds like a guest at a dude ranch; certainly not one of the cowboys.

When Clinton ran for *his* second term, his opponent was Bob Dole. For a public figure, Dole was a remarkably private man—at least before his Viagra commercials. His food choices were muted, as was his campaign generally.

A spokesman, late in the campaign, listed some of Dole's favorite foods: hamburgers, fried chicken, chocolate milk shakes, and cherry pie. Can't go wrong there; nothing controversial. A very American menu, middle-American right down the line. But in terms of image, it's bland, careful, traditional, and safe.

When he ate in the Senate dining room, Dole's choice was usually a bowl of Senate bean soup—smooth, sophisticated, yet homey and by definition Yankee—and a slice of that favorite cherry pie—sweet/tart, innocent with a touch of complexity, and as American as George Washington and his ax.

During the campaign, Dole asked voters, "Who would you trust your children with? Bob Dole or Bill Clinton?" and the president took him up on the idea, though his question to the guests at a White House correspondents dinner was different. If you go home tonight and order pizza, he asked, who would you trust to select the toppings, Bob Dole or Bill Clinton? *Time* magazine and CNN repeated the questions in a poll of over a thousand Americans. The results were a clear indication of what was to come in November: 54 percent chose Clinton as the man to select what goes on top of their pizza, 26 percent picked Dole, and 20 percent were undecided. The election was just a formality.

Clinton's legendary appetite changed even before his open-heart surgery in 2004. While working on his autobiography, he lost a great deal of weight on a low-carb diet. But back in 1999, this is what the Clintons had for Christmas dinner: relishes; crudités; winter vegetable soup; turkey with herbed bread stuffing; peppered ham; winter greens; sweet potato casserole; mashed potatoes; peas and carrots; sauté of root vegetables; rolls; salad with asparagus, artichokes, and roasted tomatoes; and, for dessert, chocolate cake with white icing; pumpkin pie with glazed ginger; lemon meringue pie; and cherry pie. Those days are gone, and the appetite, in all its glory, seems to be under control. The thought of Bill on a diet (or seeking forgiveness) has become every bit as real as Bill eating banana and peanut butter sandwiches; it's just the other side, the penalty we all have to pay for pleasure. Both food images, equally convincing and equally sympathetic, are also equally appealing as far as the hungry voter is concerned. And it is the hungry voter who decides.

During the Gore–Bush campaign of 2000, *Family Circle* magazine's annual presidential cookie contest was between Tipper Gore's gingersnaps and Laura Bush's "Texas governor's mansion cowboy cookies," a cookie that seemed by its name alone to cover all the bases. Ditto for the ingredients: butter, chocolate chips, coconut, and chopped pecans. The gingersnaps were flavored with molasses, and sounded nicely spicy-sweet, but, said *Family Circle* food director Peggy Katalinich, "If you have chocolate chips in your cookies, you're ahead of the game." Did the Supreme Court get to taste the cookies before they voted on the outcome of the election?

Laura Bush made many changes in the White House she inherited from the Clintons. One of the biggest from the food point of view: The Bush White House kitchen closes after dinner; during the Clinton administration, it was open until midnight. (Doesn't anybody in the Bush family ever get hungry in the middle of the night?) And everything runs on time. *The New York Times* reported that if Bush "is not on time, he is a half-hour early; his aides say he does everything fast, including eating meals."

Food doesn't seem to be of great importance to George W. According to *The New York Times*, Bush wakes every morning at 5 A.M., has coffee, and reads the newspapers (despite his statement that he leaves reading to others). By seven, he's in the Oval Office; his national security briefing is at eight. Lunch is often a salad, eaten alone, watching TV in a small dining room off the Oval Office. He's back in the residence by six, and dinner is usually at seven. Back to bed at nine, even when there are guests. He takes a giant briefing book to bed with him; lights out at ten. Bush ran, and now bikes, daily, no matter where he is.

Laura Bush says that she's the gourmet in the Bush family. She has a large collection of cookbooks, mostly for the pleasure of reading them. Her Texas governor's mansion cowboy cookies faced a second campaign in 2004, against Teresa Heinz Kerry's pumpkin spice cookies—not unlike Tipper Gore's gingersnaps. (Someday, will *Family Circle* publish the candidate's *husband's* cookie recipe?)

Both President Bush and John Kerry are peanut butter and jelly sandwich men. A PB&J on white bread is about as all-American as you can get. It couldn't possibly offend anybody who is eligible to vote. (There are plenty of people from other countries who think peanut butter is ridiculous, but they're not eligible to vote in American elections.) A peanut butter sandwich is plain-speaking food, honest, unpretentious, upright. It's what we ate when we were kids; it's comforting. It's what we revert to when we're home alone and there's not much in the fridge. It's almost snack food. True, it doesn't do much in the field of international diplomacy. It's not adventurous. It's hardly distinguished. And it's not the least bit presidential. But both candidates loved it, so the field seemed even. For a while.

Vice President Cheney, who has had four heart attacks, undoubtedly eats a careful and stringent diet——fruits and vegetables and not much in the way of butter and cream. During the 2004 Democratic primaries, vice presidential candidate John Edwards appeared on *The Tonight Show.* Jay Leno asked him if he'd been eating well on the campaign trail. "No," said the man who became Kerry's vice presidential candidate. "I had two double cheeseburgers for lunch today." Edwards and his wife traditionally celebrate their wedding anniversary at Wendy's, and in 2004, the Kerry-Edwards campaign bus stopped at a Wendy's in Newburgh, New York, for their twenty-seventh anniversary meal. Mr. and Mrs. Edwards each had a cheeseburger, fries, and a Diet Coke, and they shared a Frosty for dessert. The Kerrys had a bowl of chili each. "It's good chili," Mrs. Heinz Kerry said. "It could even be made by Heinz." There's a rumor that after they all got back on the campaign bus, they found a meal that had been smuggled in from the Newburgh Yacht Club (Newburgh is on the Hudson River): shrimp vindaloo, grilled scallops, prosciutto-wrapped stuffed chicken.

John Reynolds, in his *New York Times Magazine* food page, discussed American attitudes about money, politics, and food. "Americans long for money——but vote for those who don't look as if they've got any: LBJ, Nixon, Carter, Reagan, Clinton." Both George W. Bush and John Kerry are rich men by any standards: Both inherited money; Kerry also married money. Both are American aristocrats (Bush is a Bush and a Walker; Kerry is a Kerry and a Forbes); both went to elite prep schools; both went to Yale, where both were members of Skull and Bones, the top-drawer secret society. (The similarities end there.)

Many American presidents—beginning with George Washington—have been men of wealth, either inherited, married, or earned. It's the others—poor or middle class—who are the exceptions. Certainly, three of the five on the Reynolds list—LBJ, Carter, and Reagan—had money before they arrived in Washington or earned it, one way or another, shortly thereafter. John Fitzgerald Kennedy came from money—and, like Kerry, from Catholic Boston. Franklin Roosevelt, arguably the twentieth century's greatest president, was born to wealth, as was Teddy Roosevelt. Harry Truman was a haberdasher—a plain Missouri man who made an excellent president. Abraham Lincoln was famously poor. Does money matter? It all depends.

During his primary campaign in 1972, advisors to Sargent Shriver (Maria Shriver's father, JFK's brother-in-law) suggested he visit a working-class tavern because his image was too patrician. At one point in the New Hampshire race, he sidled up to a small town bar, reporters, photographers, and TV cameras close behind. He announced that the next round was on him.

"Beer for the boys," he said, "and I'll have a Courvoisier."

He lost.

In 1976, Gerald Ford campaigned in the Republican primary against Ronald Reagan. In a Mexican-American community in Texas, Ford was offered some tamales, traditionally served wrapped in corn husks. He made the mistake of eating one with the husk still on. The cultural gaffe made the newspapers. After Ford lost the general election to Jimmy Carter, he was asked what lessons he had learned from his defeat.

"Always shuck your tamales," Ford said.

Politicians have always used food, be it pork rinds or Big Macs, Courvoisier or lite beer, strawberries or smoked ham, on their way to the top and to wheel and deal over dinner so they can stay there once they've gotten there. We—the hungry voters—can also use food when it comes time to take their weight at the polls. And then, sooner or later, we'll find out what they *really* ate for dinner—who they really are—when the photographers are gone and the hot dogs and knishes and pizza have been sampled and put away. Did they shuck their tamales? There are good reasons for wanting to know.

Part Five

SOME EATING HISTORY

The belly is the reason
why man does not mistake himself for a god.

—Friedrich Nietzsche

Chapter 15

THE CIVILIZING PROCESS
Manners at the Table

Civilization has taught us to eat with a fork,
but even now, if nobody is around,
we use our fingers.
—Will Rogers

There is a history of humanity in our hungry search for food. It may begin with the Garden of Eden's bright red apple shining through the leaves or with the man-ape who first learned how to hold a stone and a stick to hunt with. It expands with the search for trade routes to reach the spices of the East. It becomes modern with the kitchen revolution that accompanied the industrial revolution: the beginnings of processed food—baking powder and packaged yeast, Gail Borden's canned milk and Alexander Knox's powdered gelatin—and the gas and electric kitchens that liberated generations of women and turned the serving class into the labor force and the middle class into consumers.

There's another history that follows the first, step-by-step, and that is the history of our table manners. Hunger led first to the search for food for right now, and then, once we had eaten, to thoughts about food for tomorrow. When we stopped traveling with the herds and stayed in one place long enough to see the cycle of food from seed to table, foragers became farmers, and civilization began. Manners began to count, from the earliest fertility rites in the fields where we spilled semen among the seeds of next year's harvest, to the extended pinkies of the lower classes on the way up over cups of tea.

At first we were surely more concerned with efficiency than with style. Our early meals must have been like a baby's, frantic and greedy. Manners are a kind of altruism—a bartered self-concern—and hungry people are selfish eaters. Children have to be taught their manners, from fingers to forks, before they are ready to take their places at the table, and in the same way man, as he grew, learned his.

Learning how to behave is first a practical lesson and then a moral one. Caring about other people is on a higher level than worrying about one's self. Our first reason for eating politely is that we would be terribly embarrassed, ashamed, and uncomfortable if we didn't. And what's just as bad or worse, if we didn't eat politely, no one would like us very much or ever invite us back. But if we do manage to eat as we ought to, with awareness of the nuances of forks and wineglasses, if we learn, once we're out of the high chair, to chew with our mouths closed and not to talk with food in our mouths, no one will know whether we, like Professor Higgins's Eliza Doolittle, are princesses or flower girls.

Manners have always been visible proof of position in a way which money cannot be. Manners are the way we turn class into a code. Manners begin with the elite, the upper crust, and the higher up you go, the more complicated they are, so that the code is harder and harder to break. But it isn't unbreakable. Manners are imitated step-by-step down the social ladder. As this happens, the quick, visible differentiation between the classes disappears and new refinements have to begin at the top.

The same thing happens with clothes, only faster and more obviously. If everyone is wearing bustiers or cashmere sweaters, then no one can be special by wearing them. On to the next trend! Sometimes, the top runs out of ideas and borrows the best from the bottom, like Marie Antoinette playing farmer. A look that used to cost $9.98 can be priced at hundreds, or even thousands, of dollars when it reaches the right designer or a good shop. Jeans, which used to be work clothes for laborers and farmers, get carefully torn and shredded—or embroidered. Baseball caps come in colors and boast slogans and designs instead of team logos. Sneakers cost more and more the higher up they climb on the social ladder.

The same thing happens to food. White bread used to be a mark of privilege, because producing it takes longer, requires more intensive labor, involves more waste, sometimes is based on a more expensive grain, and in the end has a more subtle flavor. After the industrial revolution, white bread could be cheap, packaged, and sliced. The lower classes wanted white bread because it had status—it was what you ate when you could afford to eat it. What was left for the top? Peasant bread.

Chicken, too, used to be status food. Henry IV, King of France, aimed for a chicken in every peasant's pot (echoed in the Herbert Hoover campaign of 1928). Now there is, finally, a chicken in the pot of almost everyone who wants one. At the top? Free-range chicken, the kind that used to peck in lower-class backyards, and now costs much more than mass-produced chicken. According to Felipe Fernández-Armesto, in *Near a Thousand Tables*, pasta didn't become a universal food in Italy until the invention of the kneading machine and pasta press in the mid-eighteenth century. Before that, pasta was a luxury. Caviar used to be commonplace until it became rare and thus expensive. When the rivers of western America were so filled with salmon that the fish had to be pushed away from canoes with paddles, apprentices in 1787 refused to have salmon more than twice a week. When cod was plentiful, it was poor man's meat, salted and dried for the lean days. Now that there's less of it, cod has swum to the top. It happens over and over again, from oysters to white wine. "It is hard," writes Fernández-Armesto, "for elites to monopolize select foods. It is almost equally hard for the underprivileged to claim their stake to their own dishes without exciting elite envy . . . Goldilocks is always transgressing class boundaries and stealing other people's porridge."

From Escoffier to fusion food, from Spanish rice to quiche lorraine, from nesselrode pie to melted-center chocolate cake, from crudités to crudo, food travels up and down and all around the town, time and time again. The same thing happens with *how* we eat, whether the kitchen is a room for servants or the heart of the home.

At the table, there aren't many ways for the rich to differentiate them-selves from the rest of us. Obviously, they can eat more. And they often did. (Think of the kings of France—there was even one so named, Charles the Fat, who was really Charles III, and reigned from 884 to 887.) When there's plenty of food for everybody, they separate themselves by eating less. ("You can't be too rich or too thin.") They can eat food that's hard to get—Japanese kobe beef—or hard to find—truffles—or slightly bizarre—tomato foam—or brand-new to the table—fennel powder. They can make what they eat look elaborate—the wildly garnished food of yesterday, and today's architec-tural food, islands in the middle of a plate, with dots of sauce and flecks of something green afloat in the sea of china. And finally, they can develop com-plicated codes of etiquette, a language that makes them instantly identifi-able, and makes it possible to identify social status just by the proper use of a fish fork. Manners are a secret handshake, the Skull and Bones of the table; initiates know who they are and who everybody else is as well.

What matters, then, as much as *what* we eat is *how* we eat it. Through our history, the trend in manners—how we eat—has been constant, always mov-ing toward control of the easy instinct, restraint of the impulse, the repres-sion of anything which links us with animals, or which hints at our inner workings. Manners are the table's civilizing process. Fernández-Armesto writes that manners are "...signs of our renunciation of the savage within..." He compares table manners to sauces. In a way, sauces make food less natu-ral, less like *food*; sauces "remove food from the state of nature and smother it in art." Manners, he says, are the sauces of gesture.

We didn't arrive at a state of table grace all at once. We had a long way to travel—we may even still be on the road. An example: For hundreds of years it was perfectly all right to pick your nose at the dinner table. It took generation after generation of etiquette writers, saying the same thing ("Don't!") with variations before people stopped poking their fingers first in their noses and then in the communal sauce. For ages, nobody objected; everybody did it. The feeling of revulsion we have now about nose-picking and the resultant offending finger is relatively modern, and it has to do with the way we feel about what goes into and out of our bodies, and how we feel about the exchange in question. Cleanliness, for a long time, simply had nothing to do with it. Cleanliness is just an excuse.

Even blowing one's nose *without a handkerchief* and at the dinner table was not much of a problem in the long while before handkerchiefs existed. People blew their noses when they needed to, wherever they happened to be at the time. In the thirteenth century, gentlemen were told: "When you blow your nose . . . turn round so that nothing falls on the table." It took two hundred years longer before the next step was reached: "It is unseemly to blow your nose into the tablecloth." In the sixteenth century, Erasmus advised that "if anything falls to the ground when blowing the nose with two fingers it should immediately be trodden away."

In 1594, Henry IV owned five handkerchiefs. If the king had only five, the peasants had none. Before handkerchiefs, a distinction had evolved: One was expected to blow one's nose into the left hand if the right was used for eating. When those who set the fashion began to use handkerchiefs, they still had to be careful *how* they used them. "Nor is it seemly, after wiping your nose, to spread out your handkerchief and peer into it as if pearls and rubies might have fallen out of your head."

In 1672, Antoine de Courtin wrote that to blow your nose at the table "into your handkerchief . . . and to wipe away your sweat with it . . . are filthy habits fit to make everyone's gorge rise." Obviously there were people who had filthy habits, or de Courtin would not have felt obliged to write about them.

By 1774, nasal refinement had set in, and polite people didn't wish to discuss the subject *at all.* "You should observe, in blowing your nose, all the rules of propriety and cleanliness," La Salle wrote. And that was it. It was assumed that children would be taught when, where, and how to blow their noses. Adults did not need to be told, just as today, no etiquette book would bother warning its readers not to eat with their fingers when they dine out. The lesson instead is which fork to use.

It has taken a long time, but to date, we have learned our manners quite well—so well that it sometimes seems as if they are part of our basic nature. Children displease us when they have to be told to chew with their mouths closed. But we are not born believing that forks are good and greasy hands bad. It takes learning before we are ready to enter kindergarten and drink our juice and munch our cookies in the presence of our peers.

We teach our children to eat politely. They grow up to believe, as we do, somewhat vaguely, that forks and knives must have been part of every caveman's basic equipment, or a dowry, perhaps, that his wife clutched as he dragged her by the hair to the cave.

Cavemen did have cutlery of a sort. When men and women were ready to use them, there were sticks and stones, shells and branches to make life easier.

The first knives were made from sharp stones and were used to tear at meat when fingers wouldn't do. Later, pieces of flint were ground and chipped at until they were sharp. Sometimes, the flint was mounted on an antler or a piece of bone, because it was easier to use that way and more effective. Bronze knives came later and were sharper and sturdier, and iron, when it had been tempered, was hardier still.

By the Middle Ages, men were carrying clasp knives with them to use during the hunt and later at dinner. Clean the knives first! courtesy experts had to write. Only the noblest men had knives kept just for eating, and they brought their knives with them when they ate out, because they didn't expect to find any put out for them.

Hosts provided food and placed it in large bowls and on trays where it was speared and then placed on individual trenchers—flat, thick pieces of bread, slightly hollowed in the center (thus the term *trenchermen*—hearty eaters). Trenchers were sometimes shared by two people—companions, which comes from the Latin *panis* (bread), and *com* (with). After they had chosen their food, knights selected pieces of meat from their trenchers and placed them in their ladies' mouths with their fingers, or, if they were just that much more refined, carried the meat to her lips on the tips of their knives.

Bones, fat, and gristle were thrown on the floor, which was thickly covered with rushes. (The floor rushes were changed every so often; to do so daily was considered overly fastidious.) Dogs scavenged for the morsels of food. When dinner was over, some of the leftovers were saved for the poor*—who waited outside for their food—and the rest was thrown to the dogs.

Since no one used forks at the table, knives had to be sharp and pointed to spear food. Some had very broad blades, almost like a spatula, in order to carry slabs of food from the serving dish to the trencher. And since everybody of any importance carried his or her own knife, inevitably knives became more and more elaborately personal. Some had blades etched with flowers and words. Handles were made of ivory and silver and gold and sometimes they were studded with jewels. Some knives were made in different colors, to match church holidays: There were black knives for Lent and white knives for Easter and, in England, checkered knives for Whitsun, made of black horn and mother-of-pearl. Some of the most elaborate knives boasted biblical scenes. The Victoria and Albert Museum in London has a set of fourteen knives, handles carved to be the kings of England from Edward V to James I, each wearing a crown and carrying his orb and scepter. Most valued of all the knives, at the time, were those made of unicorn horns, because unicorn horns were magical and could cure anything and everything. Even then, unicorn knives came supplied with written guarantees of their authenticity, but since nobody has ever seen a unicorn (maybe they were all turned into knives), some poor rhinoceros probably gave up his own authentic horn instead.

Until the end of the seventeenth century, brides were dowered with a pair of "wedding knives." The handles were usually of silver and sometimes made in the form of clasped hands and engraved with a quotation from the Bible. Young brides often wore their wedding knives in satin sheaths at their waists like phallic trophies, public proof of their new marital status.

It is partly the knife's power as a phallic symbol—as well as its overt potency as a weapon—that has made it, at the table, the subject of all sorts of taboos and careful definitions in books of courtesy. It has almost always

---

*It has ever been thus. The hungry have always waited for the spill from the rich man's table. When Consuelo Vanderbilt became mistress of England's Blenheim Palace in 1895, she changed the method of distribution of leftovers to the poor. Food was still dumped into large jerricans to be wheeled out to the needy, but for the first time in the history of the palace, she separated the cans by course—meats, fish, vegetables, and sweets—instead of mushing them all together.

been bad manners to clean one's teeth with one's knife. In the Middle Ages, it began to be considered rude just to point a knife—even at one's own face. "Bere not your knyf to warde your visage," Caxton wrote in his *Book of Curtesye*, "for therein is parelle and mykyl drede." This was so even though for hundreds of years before Caxton, men had been eating with knives, using the knife to put food in their mouths at no peril or dread at all. Soon it was rude not only to point a knife at one's own face, but also to point it at anyone else's face while passing it.

There have been other restrictions about eating with knives, many of which have to do with round or egg-shaped—female—food. The union of phallic knife and female food is not a comfortable one, though it seems as though it ought to be. For a long time, fish was eaten with a special knife all its own; in many of the best homes, it still is. Potatoes, dumplings, and eggs were not supposed to be cut with knives. The most sensitive courtesy writers even thought that apples and oranges were too ladylike for the use of a knife. "I may hint that no epicure ever yet put knife to apple, and that an orange should be peeled with a spoon," said *The Habits of Good Society* in 1859, and again in 1889.

As we have become more and more civilized, we have used knives less and less: "... everything that can be cut without a knife, should be cut with fork alone," says *The Habits of Good Society*. Lettuce and tomatoes thus should be cut with the side of the fork, though it seems as if hardly anybody remembers that.

The Chinese—civilized long before Westerners were—don't use knives at all. Food in China is cut in small pieces *before* it's cooked. It cooks faster this way, and food writers usually explain precutting by saying that both food and fuel for cooking have always been scarce in China. Chinese food uses a variety of ingredients in small amounts, all cut into pieces that cook very quickly. But that was just as true for the emperor as it was for the peasant.

On the other hand, the Chinese say that Europeans are barbarians, because they use knives. "They eat with swords." It is more civilized not to have to cut food while it is being eaten; if food is more refined, manners are more refined; if manners are more refined, society is more refined. The Chinese need no knives at their tables; even in the kitchen, cutting is done with a cleaver. "One may surmise," writes Norbert Elias in *The Civilizing Process*, that this custom is connected with the fact that for a long time in China the model-making upper class has not been a warrior class but a class pacified to a particularly high degree, a society of scholarly officials." Warriors would eat with swords; knights ate with daggers; gentlemen used chopsticks.

Slicing food before it's cooked is the ultimate refinement, a very civilized way of eating meat. There was a time, not so long ago, when animals were brought to the table whole, to be carved and served. Birds (sometimes still wearing their feathers), fish (with eyes and tail intact, and, when cold, with scales carefully imitated with slices of cucumber), rabbits, and lamb appeared whole on platters; pigs, oxen, and venison were roasted whole on a spit, the pig with an apple in its mouth as if it were still having lunch. The man who carved the meat was a very important person; carving was an honor and an art.

Gradually, households grew smaller and thus needed less meat. Simultaneously, the means of producing food—slaughtering animals, for example—moved out of the house and into the hands of specialists. People developed a different kind of sensitivity—the sight of a whole animal at the table became slightly repulsive, gradually more so, and then disgusting. It's nicer not to be reminded that dinner was once an animal, lately on the hoof or the wing. We don't want to know that hamburger once mooed. We worry about our children—whether they'll make the connection between the illustrations in their picture books and the food on their plates—because the thought bothers us when we ourselves suddenly face it.

As we grew more human, we became less animal. Now, we prefer it if our meals do not remind us of their former state, or, indeed, of any relationship to the animal kingdom at all. Even in England, where the Sunday "joint" lasted longer than it has in other countries, the meat brought to the table is just a small part of the total animal, hardly recognizable at all. Leg of lamb never walked, it just grew.

Spoons are much less threatening than knives. They have no status as weapons, and they are much less obviously phallic. In *Femininity*, Susan Brownmiller wrote about her first awareness of gender differences as a child. She and her mother played a game called "setting the table," in which her responsibility was to put out the cutlery. If she dropped a knife or a fork, "that meant a man was unexpectedly coming to dinner. A falling spoon announced the surprise arrival of a female guest." Whether or not the man or woman actually arrived wasn't as important as knowing that the knife was what announced the male and the spoon the female.

Spoons were probably foretold by scooping fingers. They were leaky, to be sure, but they did their work as best they could until someone thought of folding a leaf or using a shell instead.

The French word for spoon, *cuiller*, comes from the Latin *cochlear*, which in its turn derives from a Greek word meaning cockleshell. The first spoons were shallow. They were used first more as shovels, to scoop up food, than as little ladles to convey liquids to the mouth.

Eventually, spoons were carved out of wood or horn or, much later, formed out of metal, though the wooden spoon for the table (as opposed to the cooking spoon) lasted long enough for it to be used in Wales as a love gift from a man to the woman he wished to marry. A love spoon was a hand-carved proposal, and it meant love; thus, our old word *spooning*.

Knives were appropriately phallic wedding gifts, and about nine months after the ceremony, spoons were the resultant presents at English christenings. The rich gave what were called "apostle spoons," sets of thirteen, one each decorated with the twelve apostles and one master spoon, usually bearing an image of Christ raising his hand in blessing. In Shakespeare's *Henry VIII*, when Cramer says he is unworthy of being sponsor to the infant Princess Elizabeth, the king replies, "Come, come, my Lord! You'd spare your spoons."

There were those who *had* to spare their spoons. Thriftily, they chose for christening gifts only four spoons, one for each of the evangelists. The poor did what they could, as usual, and if they gave anything, it was a single spoon made in the form of a saint.

Guests at dinner parties soon brought their own spoons as well as knives when they were invited out to dinner. Sometimes the knife and spoon were one piece, with the blade at one end and the spoon at the other, hinged so they could be carried more easily. Knives speared the food and spoons carried it; for the rest, everyone ate with their fingers. Forks had been around for a long time—since the first branch was sharpened to hold food over the fire—but they were used as cooking tools and never saw the table at all.

Most people, if they didn't have a knife or weren't good at using the one they had, simply used their fingers to take food from the communal plate to their trenchers, and then picked it up by hand and dipped it into the common sauce bowls. For centuries, etiquette concerned itself with the use of fingers and hands at the table, because that was what mattered.

"... It is a great breach of etiquette," wrote Erasmus, "when your fingers are dirty and greasy, to bring them to your mouth in order to lick them, or to clean them on your jacket. It would be more decent to use the tablecloth." The Talmud also says that the fingers ought not to be licked during a meal. (The Talmud also discusses burping, yawning, and bad breath.) The admonition not to lick had to be repeated again and again over the years. In the fourteenth century, it was necessary to warn diners not to butter bread with their fingers. In early English courtesy books, picking one's nose, ears, or teeth was forbidden at the table. Italians were reminded not to scratch themselves at the table; neither were they to spit. Erasmus spoke again on this subject: "... sit not down until thou have washed, but let thy nails be prepared before, and no filth stick in them, lest thou be called sloven."

Chaucer's prioress had obviously studied the etiquette books of her day and learned her lessons all too well. She ate with enormous daintiness, barely allowing the food to touch her body at all, except in so far was absolutely necessary, since it had, after all, to be swallowed. It was reasonable, then, for Chaucer to make fun of someone who was so careful when she ate that nothing fell out of her mouth, whose fingers never touched the sauce, whose food didn't spill on her clothes, and who wiped her lips before she drank. For those who ate less neatly than the prioress, napkins and cloths were supplied.

Eventually, finger bowls solved even more of the problem, though they created a few in their own time. Some less-sophisticated diners were known to use their finger bowls to swish out their mouths. There is also the story of the man who was misled by the slice of lemon garnishing his finger bowl; he picked up the bowl, drank its contents, and then complained to his neighbor about the weakness of the lemonade.

Forks were to be the answer to the problem of greasy fingers and slippery food, but they were a long time coming and they were much resisted along the way. They were considered kitchen implements; they did not belong in the dining room. Small table forks appeared at some Mediterranean tables by the tenth century, after having been used in the dining rooms of Byzantium. From there, they traveled to Greece, and from Greece to Italy. And there they stayed. Italians were noted for elegance at the table (they even had "grace knives," with broad blades on which were etched the words and music of various graces to be sung before and after dinner). Italians were envied for their manners, but the table fork just didn't catch on in other countries. A French silk merchant wrote home about forks as early as 1518; Catherine de Medici took the whole kitchen with her to France, it seemed, when she married the dauphin in 1533, but still no one used forks. They belonged in the kitchen.

In 1608, an Englishman wrote home at considerable length and some precision about the forks he had seen in Italy, but when he got home, people thought he was trying to be affected and even his friends made fun of him and called him "Furcifer," or silly fork carrier. Forks were denounced from the pulpit, where they were called impious. They were laughed at on the stage, where Beaumont and Fletcher joked about "fork-carrying foreigners." In the kitchen, cooks thought of table forks as an invasion from the south, and announced firmly that foreign forks were poisoners of good food. In short, forks were for fops and fools. As late as 1897, British sailors were not allowed to eat with forks because forks were unmanly and "prejudicial to discipline." Fingers, everyone agreed, were made before forks.

Gradually, by the seventeenth century, more and more people, from a sprinkling of avant-garde eccentrics to, finally, those who set the fashion, began to use forks. Queen Anne was supposed to eat not only with her fingers but with both hands, and Louis XIV absolutely refused to eat with a fork, but Louis's grandchildren were taught that good manners meant using forks at the table. By the time of Thomas Jefferson, Philadelphia could claim the distinction of having the first public eating house in America to offer its customers forks.

Now we take forks for granted—but still, not everybody uses them. Consider chopsticks, for instance. And fingers. In Muslim countries and in India, food is eaten with the fingers of the right hand. Eating with the left hand is unthinkable; the left hand is used for cleaning oneself in the bathroom and can *not* be used at the table. For Muslims, eating with the left hand is incredibly dirty, and anyone who eats with it is either a devil or is imitating a devil.* In India, food is scooped in the three fingers of the right hand (minus the thumb and pinkie) and is pushed into the mouth— without the fingers touching the lips—by the thumb.

Plainly, what works in one society is shocking in another, what your mother approves of would make somebody else's mama blush. The classic example: It isn't rude in Japan to smack your lips, slurp your food, or belch during the meal.

If you're invited to dinner in a country not your own, you need to know many things. In some places, it's polite to take your shoes off at the door, because outside is where the dirt is. Be careful what kind of gift you bring: In eastern Germany, roses mean romance; in Bulgaria, yellow flowers mean hatred. Funeral flowers—like American gladioli—vary from country to country, but on the list are carnations, chrysanthemums, and any kind of white flower. Don't bring wine in Spain, Portugal, or Italy—there, it would mean you didn't trust your hosts to choose correctly, or that you felt they couldn't afford to choose well.

In American restaurants, the host tastes the wine in order to approve it before the guests get to drink it. In some countries, the host tastes the *food* before it's served to the guests—to show that they needn't worry about poison. Some cultures have clothes specifically designed for eating, as we have clothes—pajamas and nightgowns—reserved for sleeping. The Japanese tea ceremony sometimes includes an interval during which the guest is left alone in order to admire the room and its appointments, while the host changes into a special tea-drinking robe.

Western dinner parties mean careful seating plans, so that honored guests sit next to the host and hostess. In many Arab countries, guests and host sit in a circle around a tray of food, indicating that all are of equal importance to the host.

Even in those countries that routinely use forks at the table, they aren't used in the same way. In America, the fork is held in the right hand and

---

*Devils are often associated with the left hand—maybe because most people are right handed. Spilled salt is supposed to be thrown—with the right hand—over the left shoulder—to throw salt into the devil's face; he lurks behind the left side of your body.

switched to the left in order to cut; it goes back and forth. In Europe, the fork is held in the left hand throughout the meal. In America, food is speared or carried by the fork with tines curved up; in Europe, food is carried on what Americans would call the back of the fork, tines down, and the knife is used to help put food there, because otherwise it wouldn't carry as well. One story has it that the barbarians—the Goths, Franks, Visigoths, and all the others—held on to their daggers with their right hands while they ate, just in case. (The right hand was the dagger hand because most people are right handed, so that was the more powerful hand.) The left hand thus held the fork. And still does. Sometimes things work the other way around—customs change in order to show that the initial worry is no longer a concern; in the old West, hands stayed on the table, evidence that there was no weapon hidden in either hand beneath the table. Now, it's better not to have your hands on the table while you eat.

With the advent of complete sets of cutlery in the West, eating became a little less messy. Napkins began to be more decorative and less essential. Table settings became more elaborate. Guests, when they began their meal, were supplied with knives and spoons and forks; they didn't need to bring their own. Not only that, but before dessert, each guest was given a *new* knife and fork. Finger bowls were placed upon small fringed napkins, and they, too, were a nicety rather than a necessity.

The finger-bowl napkin, in England, was often supplied by a linen draper named Thomas D'Oyly. Its purpose was to prevent the table from being soiled. It was called a *D'Oyly*, or, soon, a doily. Doilies seem the ultimate refinement, after hundreds of years of dripping and dousing, nose blowing and head scratching. When we finally learned to eat neatly, as if by nature, doilies began to seem silly and finger bowls became, with the servants they required, passé.

Tables and chairs also evolved over the years. Getting the food off the ground, away from bugs and small animals and bits of sand and grit, must have been the first impulse, and a flat rock or a tree stump the first table. (The words *tray* and *tree* come from the same root.) A plank or a board—in Latin, a *tabula*—would have been the next development. A board balanced on two rocks would have held a reasonable amount of food—and a particularly nice board could even have been moved from place to place, if necessary.

Eventually, the *tabula* was placed on trestles, with separate adjoining benches. There was no special room set aside for eating—no dining room—so the tables had to be movable. The trestles could be folded up and put away; the top could lean against a wall. They could be taken from room to room, even from house to house. The French word for furniture, *muebles,* literally means movable.

In the best homes, the host and hostess and their favored guests ate at a table that was often fastened on a platform. The silver saltcellar was kept on that table; everybody else ate "below the salt." When woodworkers learned how to join separate pieces to make a whole, they began fashioning tables that could be made larger with extra leaves, and drop-leaf and gateleg tables with sides that folded down when they weren't needed.

Eventually, houses were built with separate rooms, one each for sleeping and cooking and eating. Anyone who could afford to live in that kind of house could now keep eating tables out all the time, in the center of a room to be called "the dining room." (And some houses had breakfast rooms, and even tea rooms and coffee rooms. It took apartments to make the eat-in kitchen something special.)

Dining rooms were usually rectangular, so tables followed suit in order to be placed in the center of the room. The rectangular table inherently means a hierarchy: It most often has two ends at which only one person can sit, and those two people are automatically of a higher rank than the people on the long sides. Round tables avoid that problem; so does sitting on a carpet on the floor in a circle around the food, as is the custom in many countries.

The rectangular table, with its important people at the short ends, is echoed at banquets, or in some college dining halls, and sometimes the table is on a raised platform, and sometimes people sit on only one side of the table. If the table is long enough, (or often on a regular basis in France and some Latin American countries), the host and hostess sit in the middle of the long side, across from each other, with honored guests on their sides. The short ends of the table then become the least-favored places to sit— hardly in the center of whatever is going on. The table as stage was once common at great feasts, where guests were seated at one side only, and crowds of standing spectators watched parades of servants carrying trays of lavishly garnished food, course after course after course.

Today, our tables can be cluttered with cutlery, a far cry from the common sauce bowl and separate trenchers of yore. There may be fish knives, meat knives, butter knives, and fruit knives; soupspoons, dessert spoons, sugar spoons, teaspoons, and demitasse spoons; and hors d'oeuvre forks, fish forks, shellfish forks, meat forks, salad forks, and cake forks. Each has a certain place on the table; each is used in a certain sequence.

In 1994, Sotheby's auctioned a table setting for eighteen people. Each place setting had eighteen pieces—forks, knives, and spoons, from an oyster fork to an ice-cream fork and an ice-cream spoon. Six pieces in each setting were made of solid gold. The service had been created by Tiffany in 1910. It sold at auction for over 2 million dollars. Today, it would probably sell for more. Having all this on the table at the turn of the last century also meant having a large enough staff to polish, wash, and tend to all the pieces, as well as everything else in the house. The grandest households had dozens of servants, and the ratio of waiters to guests at a formal dinner was often at least one to four. There had to be a butler, just to supervise the staff and to keep everything straight and moving forward, the house in order, the table correctly set, and the silver clean and polished.

In the Middle Ages, you could tell a man's class by whether he brought his own plate with him to dinner or used a trencher. Since then, things have had to get more complicated. For thousands of years (the first behavior book appeared in 2000 B.C.), manners have had to do with the same sorts of things. The first rules of good conduct were set down on papyrus sheets by an Egyptian priest, who said that he had copied much of his work from the teachings of the fifth dynasty, five hundred years earlier. And still today the marvelous Miss Manners must tell us what to do and why.

America's founding fathers had a problem with manners. Oh, they all knew exactly how to behave—they were aristocrats, and men of wealth—but they believed in the equality of all men (at least of all white males) and they did not like false civility and fussy manners. As president, Thomas Jefferson tried to ease the rigid rules of diplomatic ranking, which he saw as making distinctions among men who had been created equal. Or mostly equal.

The American battle has been between the artificiality of a certain kind of fussy manners and the simple straightforward behavior of the frontiersman, even between the use of the spittoon versus the use of the floor by the middle (spitting) class. Americans admire the same manners that they like to ridicule; insecurity is a disease of the middle class.

Manners have evolved over the years, and they've also deteriorated. Families don't eat together as much as they used to—everybody has something to do, and a different time to do it in; women are tired after a day at work or driving from soccer practice to piano lessons. It's not pleasant to tell your children how to eat, especially if you yourself aren't sure. Everybody knows how to eat pizza, but how to eat soup is almost in the realm of folklore.

We've also come to value individual freedom—or just plain individuality—more than we do decorum. At Yale University in the 1950s, there were no codes about dressing for dinner for the simple reason that none were needed. No young man would dream of going to dinner without a jacket and tie. In the 1960s, the university had to develop a rule about the necessity of wearing shoes in the dining room.

Things have not improved (in the sense of old-fashioned good manners) since then, and many graduates of many colleges—not just Yale—know that yes, they ought to wear shoes at dinner, but they don't know what to do with their napkins, or how to eat their bread and butter, or even just when to begin eating. To fill the need, we have a host of etiquette books, many of which (like *Miss Manners' Guide to Excruciatingly Correct Behavior,* first published in 1981) have gone on to be best sellers. Universities sponsor research, symposia, and studies on manners and civility—or on incivility. Some offer courses on table manners so that their graduates will be ready for what happens when they trade their diplomas for a job. *The New York Times* headlined a story about private etiquette courses, "A Lost Generation of Executives Needs Help at the Business Table." ("Keep your shoes on and turn off your beeper," said a subhead.) First of all is the need to impress interviewers when they test you by taking you out to lunch; then impressing your boss; then your clients; and last of all, your colleagues. All of these people, presumably, have either learned their manners at home, or have taken the same course you did.

Miss Manners is definitely the best of the manners mavens, past or present. She is a paragon of common sense, and a good writer. She knows that good manners are not simply a matter of knowing which fork to use—though she certainly knows and is happy to tell you in her crisp third-person voice. She knows all the rules of etiquette backward and forward, and she knows something more important, that courtesy and manners are based on the need to respect other people as well as oneself. Manners are a matter of morality and generosity.

There are many ways of thinking about manners, not as a question of how to comport ourselves at the table, but above that, as an indication of who we are and what we believe in. Without any question, manners are an indication of social rank, even a way of maintaining the class system as a check against "too much" democracy. When men and women needed a wardrobe of kid gloves, when tableware was made of solid gold and each person needed eighteen spoons, knives, and forks to get through dinner, the upper classes could rest secure. The working class had no chance; the middle class could only gaze upward in awe and dream of better days. This kind of etiquette is a way of maintaining power and distance; it is for the privileged, and the rest can eat with their fingers if they want. Etiquette has much to say about a society—the long table on a platform with a saltcellar on it, against the circle of equals sitting on a carpet around a tray of food. One group is a hierarchy; the other may have rankings, but it also has genuine courtesy. The best kind of manners are not a structure of domination, but an awareness of other people, and a wish to put them at their ease, to help them feel good about themselves.

Manners are a cultural history and a signpost; they tell you what's important in a society and they tell you what the society is worried about. Manners are a way to change class: Learn what they do one level up, and you can do it, too. And manners are an index of shame on the one hand, and of civilization on the other.

In an early issue of the newsletter *Simple Cooking*, food writer John Thorne wrote similarly about cookbooks and manners. "The cookbook is more than an organized repository of recipes; it is a bible of refinement and economy, the worst two bugbears to find on any pathway to a good time. Its historical place has been to preach (under the guise of nutrition and tastefulness) submission of the body pleasurable to the socially accept-able, to a nation composed of immigrants, most initially innocent of Protestant-ethic prudery. Almost always, therefore, the cookbook belongs on the shelf, not next to the *Kama Sutra,* but beside Emily Post."

The word *snob* offers an interesting perspective on manners. The snob may not always have been someone who looked down on his or her inferi-ors; it may just have been the other way around—the betters looked down upon the snob. One theory of the word's origin has it that it was taken from an abbreviation from the Latin phrase *sine nobilitate*—without nobility. Thus, *S. Nob.* would have been used, in the eighteenth and early nine-teenth centuries, on ships' manifests, to indicate the passengers who should *not* sit at the captain's table on the basis of insufficient nobility. The same abbreviation would have been on the footman's list at grand gatherings to indicate that there was no title that needed to be announced, or on the list of students at Oxford and Cambridge, to show quickly and clearly who were the commoners (the snobs) and who were not.

More likely—but keeping the same idea of the snob as a person of lesser rank—the word probably comes from a dialect word meaning a cob-bler, indicating someone of humble status. The Oxford English Dictionary defines a snob as "one who meanly or vulgarly admires and seeks to imi-tate, or associate with, those of superior rank or wealth; one who wishes to be regarded as a person of social importance." Thus, the first use of snob was as someone below, looking up. The Victorian author William Make-peace Thackery wrote a series of articles in *Punch* in the 1840s, republished as *The Book of Snobs.* He dissected various kinds of English snobs—the mili-tary snob, and the country snob, for example. George Bernard Shaw first used the word to define someone who despised those of lower rank—the first recorded use of snob in that sense. But how transient the snob's glory is!

The civilizing of the table (to date) has taken nearly four thousand years and a series of small steps, each more refined—in the civilized sense—than the one before. Because we can look back on the process, it seems logical. But as it happened, slowly and tediously, with each change as laborious and lengthy as the one from fingers to forks, there was only the doubtful logic of expedience and the uncertain rationale of snobbish fashion to point the way. There was no way of predicting what it was that would come next. Forks did not follow certainly and logically from fingers except with hindsight. When you are traveling in a strange country, there is no way of determining your route, even when you know your destination, unless you have a map.

Chapter 16

IMMORTAL MEAL

Cannibalism

Two cannibalism jokes:
First cannibal: I can't stand my mother-in-law.
Second cannibal: Just eat the noodles.

Is it true that cannibals don't eat clowns
because they taste funny?
— George Carlin

Foreigners cannot enjoy our food, I suppose, any more than we can enjoy theirs. It is not strange, for tastes are made, not born. I might glorify my bill of fare until I was tired; but after all, the Scotchman would shake his head and say "Where's your haggis?" and the Fijian would sigh and say, "Where's your missionary?"

— *A Tramp Abroad,*
by Mark Twain

Incest and cannibalism were once civilization's last taboos. The idea of either gave you that horrible cold, sinking feeling; both were shocking, sickening, barely thinkable. But today, in the immortal words of Cole Porter, anything goes. Survivors of incest have support groups. That leaves cannibalism. Nobody survives cannibalism.

Even so, cannibalism may be losing its position as a savage and utterly inhuman act.* These days, it has begun to be humanized in a way, its horror diminished as we become familiar with its details. We've read about the contents of Jeffrey Dahmer's freezer and admired the cool self-possession and intense intellect of Hannibal Lecter. Now, cannibalism just barely holds its rank as the ultimate horror. Cannibalism is almost a bad joke.

History's most famous cannibals, though hardly its first, were the Carib Indians, who lived in the islands of the sea named after them, to the east of Central America. They were brave, ferocious, and frightful warriors, who covered themselves with red war paint before they went to battle. In their own language, *Carib* meant valiant man.

Tales of the Caribs circulated among the early explorers of the Central and South American seas. They were supposed to have an insatiable appetite for human flesh—they even castrated their victims and kept them in special pens, like capons, to be fattened before being roasted.

The Caribs were said to be gourmets of humanity; it was rumored that they preferred some nationalities of man to others. According to a seventeenth-century writer, the Caribs found the Dutch to be tasteless and dull, the English not terribly tasty, the Spanish so stringy they were almost inedible even after they'd been boiled, and the French—*voilà! c'est la gastronomique*—simply delicious. The writer was French.

The Caribs were indeed fussy eaters, as the Frenchman wrote, but their taste for their own species had nothing to do with its point of national origin. Some historians say that they never ate women or children, wherever they came from. Of men, they chose to eat only those who were their enemies, again no matter where they came from. Their masculine meal was a

---

*In German, the word for eat is *essen*. But *essen* is a word describing what people do. Animals feed, they devour—they *fressen*. The German word for cannibal is *menschenfresser*—literally, an animal devouring people; by implication, cannibals are like animals.

token of victory, and they kept the skulls of their victims as trophies, visual notches in the gun belt, game balls of a fatal encounter.

In the end, they and their trophies turned to dust. They were defeated by the inedible Spanish. Valiant they may have been, but they were no match for better weapons and imported germs. Before too long, there were only a few hundred of them left in all of the Americas. Their name became best known as a derivative. The Spanish changed Carib into Canib, and human flesh eaters became known as cannibals.*

Cannibalism preceded as well as survived the Caribs; cannibalism goes back to our earliest beginnings, our first hungers. It was part of the rites of our first religions, the dark gropings with which we tried to make sense out of the chaos of rain and wind, starlight and sunshine in which we lived. People have been eating one another for thousands of years—just as long, it turns out, as there have been other people around to eat. The taste of human flesh is a mortal memory.

There is evidence. Peking man, who was just barely out of the trees, left a few remarkably well-preserved garbage heaps pressed in the memory book of time. From that dry rubble, archaeologists have sorted into piles the leftovers from Peking man's dinner. In among the bare bones of deer and otter and all the other animals he was able to catch are the humerus and femur of his fellowman, split, as a soup bone might be, to reach the marrow.†

Among the litter of Stone Age households, piles of human skulls speak of practicality after meals—the skull, after the brain had been eaten, made a nice cup. Later, skull cups were decorated with pretty stones and lined with leather. The first cannibalism was probably functional, a matter of hunger. But decorated skulls indicate more complication than just a need for protein.

---

*The Caribs gave us words in addition to *cannibal* and *Caribbean*. They preserved their meat by smoke-drying it on a wood lattice over a slow fire. The French called the lattice *boucan*, and from *boucan* came *buccaneer*. The Spanish word for the lattice was *barbacòa*, and meat cooked over an open fire, thus, is *barbecue*. According to one theory, at least. Another, that barbecue derives from the French *barbe à queue*, from beard to tail, seems to have been discredited.

†Telltale signs of cannibalism include cut marks on human bones that are like the ones on animal bones in the same pile; abrasions made by stones hitting larger stones placed on the tops of heads; burn marks—charring, scorching, and cracking; bone breaks meant to make marrow accessible; no signs of animal gnawing; and the polished edges caused by boiling.

Human beings were small things in a world where the sun rose without reason. Today, we dwarf ourselves on purpose, to prove our own power. We identify with our machines, our cars, our buildings. Their erection is ours. But once we were terrified by sunset and we knew no more about winter than we did about ourselves. If we survived despite nature, through a near infinity of small adaptations and good fortunes, we have grown to master nature, like former slaves, triumphantly and a bit vindictively. At our most rational, we perceive the world as indifferent to us, but we saw it first as personal, hostile, and terrifying. We begged it to allow us to live. Creation, we believed, must have been agony and we were its bloody afterbirth.

Many creation myths are filled with rivers of blood overflowing to create mortal life. The Babylonians believed that the earth and its heaven began as the aftermath of a violent battle of the gods. Marduk rode against his grandmother, Tiamat, and killed her. Then he sliced her down the middle and used half her body to make the sky and the other half to make the earth. Her breasts were the hills and the rivers flowed from her eyes. Later, Marduk's father, Ea, made man. The gods took Tiamat's captain, Kingu, and Ea used the blood that spurted from his veins to make man, "to be his servant and to worship him."

Many other myths, just as bloody, are part of the ancient belief that blood waters the soil and gives it life; blood, the ancients knew as clearly as they could see, was life itself. Without blood, flesh cannot live. More: Blood is the *visible* proof of the spirit which animates the flesh. Flesh is strength and blood is life. Each has its own magic.

The first fertility rites, orgies of blood and semen to please and propitiate the bloody gods of creation, needed sacrificial victims, one to represent all, to be offered to the gods in reverence and hope. The victim was a simple gift of food—as we give a box of chocolates to a lover, a loaf of bread to a new neighbor, an apple to the teacher—but here, instead, the gift was a human being to be eaten by a hungry god. Food soothes the emotions; we are kinder after dinner than we were before. The gods, it was to be hoped, might be no different.

The victim, the symbol, having been eaten would become a part of the god. But at the same time, the gods themselves were everything and part of everything. Everything that grew was the gods incarnate, and therefore food was a holy meal—when we eat, man reasoned, we take in the divine being itself.

This kind of cannibalism was mystical. Flesh contained the strength, the energy, the nature—the force and the attributes—of the body from which it came, and when one man ate another he absorbed all of that as he ate the flesh itself.

In some places, parents, after their death, were shared by their children as a legacy. Pieces of the wise man might be distributed among the tribe so that his knowledge and wisdom would not be lost. The warrior's strength remained in his heart and his muscles, and by being eaten, could be passed on to his brothers. The viscera contained courage; the tongue eloquence; the hands, dexterity; the feet, agility. It all seems quite logical, in its way, and even comforting in a world where we are all born to die. Our own choices for the disposal of our bodies may be ecologically sound—"dust to dust"—but they are hardly heartwarming. "When you die," a nineteenth-century Mayoruna cannibal asked a dismayed European visitor, "would you rather not be eaten by your own kinsmen than by maggots?"

All of this is a particular kind of cannibalism, *endophagy*, the eating only of one's friends. *Exophagy*—eating one's enemies—is animated by a similar spirit. If you feast on those you conquer, their power is incorporated into your own. Their strength is yours; their courage is yours; their heart is yours. And if you don't eat the enemy, his powers remain *outside* of you. They could come back, and, next time, eat *you*.

And there's more: Eating the enemy is total victory. The appetite is whetted by contempt. This is an enemy that could not be more helpless, could not have fallen lower from a pinnacle of potency. Dead dinners were taunted at victory feasts, with toasts full of sneers of triumph. How stupid this piece of meat must have been. First it was killed and now it's going to be eaten!

There might be sacrifices to the god of war. Special morsels—the heart, perhaps, or the brain—might be reserved for the high priest or the village chief. The whole village might share in the victory feast as it had shared in the killing. Sometimes only young boys swallowed the required pieces of humanity, like a dose of medicine, to give them courage and make them men.

Egyptians, Scythians, Chinese, Maoris, Hurons, Iroquois, Ashanti, Aztec, Europeans—French, English, yes, Americans, all and more, at one time or another, fed, in Blake's words, on the "delightful food of the warrior, the well fed Warrior's flesh of him who is slain in war." * Enemy eating has no particular date or location. It is as old as time, as ancient as hatred and as current as today's news.

When David Berkowitz, the "Son of Sam" murderer, was finally captured after a rampage of shootings of young women parked in cars with their boyfriends, one survivor showed a passion for the most primitive kind of revenge. His girlfriend had died in his arms after having been hit in the back of the head by two bullets. "I wanna feel the guy's blood," he told a reporter from *The New York Post.* "I wanna put my hands around his throat and I want him to know he would be dying by my hands ... I want to eat ... yeah, eat the guy with my mouth."

In 1997, a Long Island man banged on his neighbor's door at 3:30 in the morning, furious because he said the neighbor had damaged some bushes on his property. They got into a fight, and he bit off a considerable piece of his neighbor's nose. The bitten-off piece was later found by police and brought to the hospital to be reattached

Another man bit to the bone the index finger of his estranged wife's new boyfriend, causing extensive nerve damage, but the New York State Court of Appeals ruled that teeth could not be classified as a "dangerous instrument." Why? Because they aren't something picked up ahead of time to inflict harm. The court noted that the biter's teeth "came with him." There was a passionate dissent in the five-to-one decision, invoking the infamous Evander Holyfield–Mike Tyson fight, in which Tyson bit off a sizable portion of Holyfield's ear.

All of this is a cannibalism of rage, of passionate anger. More people are bitten by people every year in New York City than by rats. Rats are hungry; people are furious. Babies have to learn that teeth are for chewing and not for biting. Grown up, full of words, most of us forget that the mouth itself is a weapon, the first weapon, the most primitive one.

---

*We still use food names for our enemies. The French call the English *les bifteks*—beefsteaks—while English call the French *frogs*, for frog legs, and Germans are called *krauts*—cabbages, probably short for *sauerkraut*. As for Yankee Doodle, the old song tells us he stuck a feather in his hat and called it macaroni.

We all nibble at ourselves in various ways—out of anger, or like explorers or lovers, making as perfect a circle as an animal that swallows its own tail. This is another kind of cannibalism, the eating of the self, *autophagy*.

Children joke and feign disgust over others who pick their noses and pop the offending finger in their mouths, but they have almost all—at one time or another—done the same thing. They taste various parts of their bodies: scabs, the sand around their eyes, bitter earwax, the tops of pimples.

Adults nibble away at their fingers—the nails, the skin at the corners of their fingers, the cuticle around the nails. They chew surreptitiously on the inside of their cheeks or the tender skin of their lips. The hero of Joseph Heller's *Something Happened* describes his own eating habits—perpetually "nibbling and gnawing away aggressively, swinishly and vengefully at my own fingertips."

During a prolonged fast, the body automatically eats itself. It draws nourishment from its own parts as long as it can, finding protein and energy in the meat of its muscles. In the same kind of way, people have sometimes eaten each other simply because they had to do so in order to survive.

There are barren bits of this green earth where the ground is dry, where livestock cannot graze, and where farmers scratch at hard soil to grow a meager supply of vegetables. In such places, cannibalism flourishes. It may be cloaked in the mysticism of religious rites, but it still remains what it is: the eating of the people by the people for the people.

The Aztecs* had such a society, in a country where regular sources of protein were scarce. Their religion was founded in catastrophe: They believed that the world had been born and annihilated four times, in great cataclysms of destruction, and that they lived in the fifth world. It, too, would end in chaos, in a moment when earth and sky would be torn apart and men and women and everything they knew would be devoured by the monsters of twilight.

They believed that a god had sacrificed himself to give birth to the sun,

---

*Some anthropologists believe that cannibalism flourished in different places and times, for different reasons. Others deny that it existed at all, except in rare cases, and there is a range of opinion in between. The Aztec cannibalism was documented by contemporary Spanish writers. Some accept that as valid proof, and others do not.

that the sun rose from the red-gold flames that encompassed his body. But once risen, the sun could not move until it had been given life and strength in the form of heart's blood. Only after the remaining gods and goddesses had offered their own lives did the sun begin its climb to the top of heaven.

Such a sun, born of blood, needed fresh blood every day in order to rise again. Every day, victims had to be supplied and offerings made. Blood had to pour from heart after heart to provide the red glow of sunrise, the pink promise of a new day.

The gods were insatiable, but men were hungry and they shared the meals they offered to their bloody heaven in the daily sacrifices. Children were drowned as gifts to the rain god. Men and women were pierced with arrows so their blood would flow over the earth in honor of spring. Women died for the goddesses of the salt waters and of young maize. There were tokens for the god of fire. And there were still the hungry agricultural gods, and the god of hunting, the war god, and the mother of the gods.

As sacrificial victims, the Aztecs used prisoners of war, when they had them (it was largely in order to take captives that war was waged) and slaves when they did not. All—victims and victors alike—had believed from birth that this kind of death was an absolute necessity if the sun were to continue its passage across the sky, if the world were to continue to exist. Dying for the sun was honorable, even holy.

For the Aztecs, there was no possibility of making the transition from human sacrifice to animal, another step in the civilizing process. There was simply nothing suitable available. The native horse was already extinct. Sheep and cattle were unknown until they arrived with the Spanish. Buffalo, bison, and caribou didn't graze so far south. Wild deer, ducks, geese, and other game were seasonal and they couldn't begin to fill the everyday demands of the sunstruck rituals. The only livestock successfully domesticated were dogs and turkeys, and neither was considered to be worthy of the gods.

Eventually, the Spanish came to Mexico, bringing with them crucifixes and contempt. The Aztecs were impressed by the Spanish, but not, apparently, by their God. Moctezuma listened when Cortes explained about Adam and Eve and false idols and eternal damnation, but he didn't convert. The Aztecs may have thought that the Spanish, too, ate human flesh, not only because it's natural to expect others to be like ourselves, but also because at first they believed the Spanish to be gods, and all the other gods they knew, their own gods, ate human flesh. The same process happened in other places: Native Hawaiians worried about Captain Cook and his men. In Africa, there were tribesmen who thought white men captured their people in order to provide fresh meat for feasts. The white men, needing slaves for other purposes, were offended that these savages thought them guilty of the horror of cannibalism. So they confronted each other, again and again, the civilized man believing the native man to be less than human, and the native believing the civilized man to be more, "... thus posing the question," anthropologist Marshall Sahlins writes, paraphrasing Claude Lévi-Strauss, "of who did more credit to the human race."

In Mexico, when he discussed religion with Moctezuma, Cortes probably didn't mention such refinements as the Inquisition, the stake, the rack, or the Iron Maiden. His soldiers brought other kinds of weapons: disease, injustice, and exploitation. Millions died from smallpox and measles, even from the common cold, as well as from work in the mines, hunger, and imprisonment. The Aztecs must have thought that the fifth world was finally approaching its end, as the sun continued its bloody trek through the sky, shining as dispassionately on death as on life.

The Spanish saw that the natives were starving. They were, one wrote, "so thin, sallow, dirty, and stinking that it was pitiful to see them." They also noted that even so, the Indians were not eating Aztec flesh, only that of the few Spanish they had been able to capture and then to sacrifice, according to ritual, in a last desperate attempt to hold their world and their bloody sun-filled heaven and earth, together. Why didn't they abandon their pagan beliefs and convert, allowing themselves to be baptized as their conquerors wished them to be? Perhaps it occurred to them that if they died and went to heaven, they would only find, once they got there, more Christians.

The cannibalism of survival is not always as enmeshed in religion and its mysteries as it was with the Aztecs. Even the most civilized man is liable to eat his brothers (though less often his sisters) when starvation threatens.

One of the most famous instances of survival cannibalism occurred in 1972, when a plane carrying members of a Uruguayan rugby team, the Old Christians, and some of their relatives and supporters, crashed in the Andes Mountains. Piers Paul Read's book *Alive*, on which the movie of the same title (with Ethan Hawke and John Malkovich) was based, tells their story.

In the frozen, barren mountains, the survivors of the crash found toothpaste and chocolates in some of the suitcases they were able to salvage. They spent hours melting snow in containers they made from pieces of the wrecked plane. They did their best, but it was obvious that they couldn't survive on a diet of toothpaste and snow. The dead bodies of the other passengers, well preserved by the cold, were their only real source of food.

The idea of cannibalism was horrible, but the drive to live persuaded most of the survivors. The final argument was a religious one. "It's like Holy Communion," one of the group told the others after he swallowed his first slice of flesh, hacked with a piece of broken glass from a body whose face was carefully covered. (All the bodies were placed facedown in the snow.) "When Christ died he gave his body to us so that we could have spiritual life. My friend has given us his body so that we can have physical life." Others began to agree. "This is food that God has given us," one said, "because he wants us to live."

At first, the rugby players ate their meat raw. Gradually, they developed refinements. Slices of fat were placed on the top of the airplane to dry in the sun; when a crust formed, the meat was ready to eat. Once or twice a week, they lit a small fire (they had, for fuel, a few empty Coca-Cola crates and one book) and cooked bits of meat with snow, though some argued that there was a protein loss at high temperatures and that the quantity of meat shrank during cooking. Each corpse was completely eaten, except for the head, skin, lungs, and genitals, before the next was started. The liver, heart, kidney, and intestines were thought to be particularly high in vitamins and were reserved for the men who, if no rescuers found the crash site, were to attempt an expedition to search for help. After a while, they began to eat the brains and lungs they had discarded at the beginning. That meat had now begun to rot and it had a higher flavor; they believed it contained the salt they desperately craved. The bodies of the few women were saved for last, partly because the husband of one and the brother and son of another were among the survivors.

Finally, after seventy days, they had no hope left that they were going to be rescued, and two of the group left on a life or death mission for help.

They finally reached a small valley where a Chilean peasant was shepherding his cattle for the summer. They were saved.

The Uruguayan crash is unique among many incidents of survival cannibalism because it happened relatively recently and it is thoroughly documented. But there have been many other stories—shipwrecked sailors and Arctic explorers and unfortunate travelers like America's Donner Party.

The Donner Party was a large group of pioneers who, in 1846, took a wrong turn (they thought it was a shortcut) on their way West. As a result, it was late in the season by the time they reached the Sierra Nevada Mountains, and they were the last of that year's wagon groups. The snows began early. The first storm dumped five feet of snow on the summit of the mountain they were trying to cross. (It turned out to be the worst winter ever recorded in the Sierras.) They made a winter camp, but their supplies were already low. They tried again to cross the pass—but snowdrifts were now twenty feet high.

Finally, a group of the most able-bodied men and women, calling themselves "The Forlorn Hope," set out for help. They were blinded by snow; and they were soon lost. They had nothing left to eat. Inevitably, the only available food was from the bodies of those who had died. The corpses were butchered, and the meat carefully divided into bundles so that no one would have to eat kin. A month later, the few who remained reached a settlement, and relief parties began getting ready to rescue those who were still on the other side of the Sierras.

There, the cabins of the winter camp were now buried in snow. The last of the food was gruel made from cow hides. As people died, their bodies were dragged to the top of the snow. When the first rescue party arrived, one woman asked, "Are you from California? Or do you come from heaven?"

The rescuers had been able to bring only a limited amount of supplies, and could take only some people from the camp back across the pass with them. Thirty-one remained behind, and as they died and joined the heap on the top of the snow, they were eaten by those who were still alive. Jacob Donner's children survived because they ate their father's corpse. "Mrs. Murphy said here yesterday," read one diary, "that she thought she would commence on Milt and eat him."

Another rescue group arrived, and more people were able to leave. In mid-April, the last of the rescuers reached the camp. Only one person was still alive. Lewis Keseberg became the only survivor to talk publicly about the cannibalism. (He eventually opened a restaurant in Sacramento.)

Alfred (or Alferd—he spelled it both ways) Packer is rumored to be the only American ever tried for cannibalism, but the truth is that he was tried—and convicted—of murder. (Cannibalism isn't illegal. Murder is.) Packer and a group of men eager to find gold left Provo, Utah, in the winter of 1873, bound for Colorado's San Juan Mountains. They were already hungry when they arrived at a Cheyenne camp in northwestern Colorado. Most of the group stayed there, at the chief's urging, but Packer and four others couldn't wait for the weather to improve. They left to continue over the mountains, aiming for Los Piños Indian Agency. They believed they were on a forty-mile trip and took a ten-day supply of food. In fact, it was seventy-five miles to Los Piños. The first snowstorm hit on their second day out. By the fourth day, they had only a pint of flour left to eat; soon, they were surviving on rosebuds and pine gum. They came to a lake and cut holes through the ice to fish, but caught nothing. Two months after they had left the Cheyenne camp, Packer arrived in Los Piños. He had plenty of money in his pockets, but he said he wasn't hungry—he just wanted a drink.

Nearly six months later, bodies were discovered at Slumgullion Pass—later to be called Dead Man's Gulch. Packer was arrested, but he escaped from jail. He lived free for nearly ten years under the name John Schwartze, but in March 1883, a member of the original Provo Party recognized his laugh in a saloon in Fort Fetterman, Wyoming. Packer was captured, rearrested, and tried for the murders of the other prospectors.

Over the years, he told different stories, but basically his tale was that one of the group had killed the others and begun to eat them while he himself was away from the camp looking for game. When he returned, he said, he killed in self-defense. He had no food, so was forced to eat the other men. When the snow began to thaw, he packed a few pieces of flesh, a gun, and money that he'd found in the other men's pockets, and continued toward Los Piños, eating the last pieces of meat just before he arrived.

He was found guilty, and sentenced to hanging. (More Packer legend has it that the judge, calling Packer a "Republican cannibal," complained that when Packer arrived in Hinsdale County there were seven Democrats, but that he had eaten five of them. The death sentence was to warn any-body else against reducing the number of local Democrats.)

Later, he won the right to a new trial, and this time he was sentenced to forty years. Eventually, in a letter to the Denver *Rocky Mountain News,* he wrote of being "surrounded by the midnight horrors of starvation as well as those of utter isolation.... No man can be more heartily sorry for the acts of twenty-four years ago than I." He was finally paroled and ended his days—a vegetarian—in Littleton, Colorado, where he died in 1907. Some years later, the citizens of Lake City, Colorado, erected a monument to his victims, and celebrated with a community fish fry.

The site of the massacre, a remote wilderness in 1874, is now about five minutes south of the Lake City miniature golf course. In downtown Lake City, the Hinsdale County Museum, a stop on Colorado's Cannibal Trail, displays a collection of Packer memorabilia—some buttons from the clothes of the men he ate, a skull fragment from one of them, and the shackles used on Alfred in the Lake City jail. The museum sells an Alfred Packer cannibal collectible doll.

A popular spot at the University of Colorado at Boulder is the Alfred Packer Memorial Grill. Serving, among other things, Packerburgers, Pack-ersnackers, and a burrito called *El Canibal,* the grill was dedicated by then Agriculture Secretary Robert Bergland, who noted in his dedication speech that the grill "exemplifies the spirit and fare that this agriculture depart-ment cafeteria will provide." (He was joking; the name was meant to be a student comment on the quality of the food.)

Rather than abetting survival, cannibalism has also sometimes served as an early form of population control, keeping the birthrate at an even level with the food supply. (Some science fiction has speculated that it might do so again in the future. In the movie *Soylent Green,* the population has in-creased to such a point that the land—what little of it can be saved for farming—cannot support the people, and the citizens of the future fight for the right to eat each other.)

Mythology provides a pedigree for cannibalism. The Greek god Cronus killed his children—to prevent their dethroning him—by swallowing them. When his wife could stand it no longer, she saved their child Zeus, and he grew up to save his siblings by feeding his father a poison which made him regurgitate the babies—Hestia, Demeter, Hera, Hades, Poseidon—one by one. Then Zeus struck his father down with a thunderbolt and banished him forever.

Infanticide (usually of females) is common in history. It makes sure there are enough warriors for defense, and just enough women for food gathering and reproduction. Infanticide is not always linked with cannibalism, but it isn't at all unusual that it should be.

A tribe in Australia ate every tenth baby, in order to be sure that they wouldn't outnumber the production possibilities of their land. Another, the Kaura aborigines, ate all their newborn children during times of famine; at other times, when the food supply was more normal, the tribe replenished its population.

Children, as dinners, were often thought to hold special medicinal qualities. In China, during the Manchu dynasty, boys and girls were roasted and then prepared as prescriptions for the ill. The medical theory of the time was that eating roast children would restore lost vitality. The livers of young boys, the Chaldeans believed, were a sexual restorative for old men. Children were also often prized simply as delicacies, just as we value suckling pig, spring lamb, or milk-fed veal.

In France, Baron Gilles de Rais was born in 1404. He is also known as Bluebeard, *Barbe-Bleue*. A man of enormous wealth, he fought against the English at the side of Joan of Arc, and was her good friend. He retired from the army with the reputation of being one of the finest minds of his time, and began a study of alchemy and magic. And he began killing children—in total numbers that vary from 150 to 800, depending on who is telling the story. The baron liked to eat the entrails of infants. He preferred them raw. He drank their blood. He is supposed to have done other things, even more unpleasant, with their bodies. Eventually, he was arrested, tried, and found guilty—not of cannibalism or murder, but of witchcraft—and simultaneously hanged and burned at the stake, nine years and five months after Joan, the Maid of Orleans, and far less nobly.

If there is a line that separates the "normal" cannibal from the psychotic, Baron de Rais crossed it. But many "normal" cannibals also developed particular tastes in food. Their preferences vary, in so far as they are recorded, from place to place, but there is general agreement that the meat of dark-skinned people is better than that of whites. Among the cannibals of the South Seas, the Polynesians, Maori, and Fijis (who gave the name "long pig" to human flesh) believed that the white man's poor taste, when he was served up, was due in part to his habit of smoking tobacco. A traveler in 1651 quoted a Fiji Islander as saying that European sailors—white—were so tough, they weren't worth the trouble it took to cut them up.

Most cannibals, or at least the ones who eat and tell, have said that human flesh tastes like pork. Sometimes, less often, they say veal. Cooked person, then, is apparently quite palatable. In 1931, adventurer William Seabrook wrote that he had eaten human rump steak and wine-braised loin of man. He said that the meat was less red than beef, firm, coarse in texture, and "good to eat...." The crusaders were supposed to believe that infidels tasted better than spiced peacock. Idi Amin, former Ugandan dictator, said that human flesh is saltier than leopard meat. There were Nigerian tribes who believed man to be "the most succulent of meats, though monkey was almost as good."

Favorite cuts of person vary, too, from place to place and time to time. Some bits of meat—the sole of the foot or the palm of the hand, for instance—are sometimes considered delicacies. Some prefer knuckles, either finger or toe. A tribe in southern Nigeria once specialized in young boys who had been fattened on bananas. Another did almost exactly what we do with turkeys: They pumped palm oil into the body so that it would marinate from the inside out. Easter Islanders told a priest, who was hoping to convert them, that fingers and toes were particularly good. Cannibals in New Guinea ate everything, even the testicles and vulva, and swore by the penis, split and roasted over hot ashes, as a particularly tasty dish.

A description of a Fijian feast tells of a hungry king, waiting impatiently for his dinner. Finally, he orders the butcher "just to slice off the ends of the noses." The king plans to roast them as an hors d'ouevre while the cook works on the rest of the meal, and he puts them on hot stones; but he's too hungry to wait very long and soon he begins chewing on one nose, barely cooked, as he waits for the others to finish. Another gentleman explorer, lucky to return home, reported seeing a native pop a human eye in his mouth.

Many tribes tabooed the eating of women, but among those who did not, female flesh was preferred over a masculine meal. Breasts were supposed to be particularly tasty, followed by arms and legs.

There are various styles of cooking human flesh as well. Some cannibals liked their meat best raw. Others roasted or boiled it. Some, like the Caribs, preferred barbecue. Some smoke-dried their dinner; others burnt it to a crisp and ground the ashes into a powder which was used to flavor soups and drinks. In the South Seas, meat was often wrapped in leaves and baked over hot stones in holes dug in the sand, just as we do a clam bake. From the point of view of a lobster, clam bakes are horrible, too.

It's possible that some of the most sophisticated cooking techniques were for human meals cooked in Europe. Cannibalism is not limited to ignorant savages, head-hunting primitives, a few stray psychotics, or rugby players whose plane has crashed in the Andes. In medieval Europe, children were sold in butcher shops and innkeepers sometimes found some guests to be tempting victims who could be cooked up to supply meals for the other travelers.

In times of famine—Italy in 450 A.D., England and Ireland in 695, Bulgaria and Germany in 845 and 851, Scotland in 936—people turned to their own kind for physical sustenance. In the eleventh century, Europe was again plagued by hunger and people ate horses, dogs, cats, rats, and—finally—each other. A monk in France wrote, "On the highroads, the strong seize the weak; they tear them apart, roast them and eat them. . . . They even attack whole families of mountebanks and strolling minstrels, with their children, killing them and selling their flesh in the nearest market." Children were tempted with pieces of fruit and bits of sweets. Once lured, they were killed, butchered, and eaten. It went so far, the monk added, that "animals were safer than people" when you met them in the forest.

There were even cannibals in the British Isles.* Remnants of the Atta-

---

*Is this cannibalism? In 1998, the BBC featured a program in which a mother, Rosie Clear, celebrating the birth of her daughter, Indi-Mo Krebbs, made placenta pâté and offered tastes to relatives and friends. Only nine viewers complained, but one was a Labour Party MP, who found the program "offensive." The BBC said "the programme was not a conventional cookery show," but that it was designed to challenge conventional wisdom. An English Web site (www.mothers35plus.co.uk) reports the carryings-on, and offers two placenta recipes of its own, one for roast placenta in tomato sauce, and the other for dehydrated placenta, to be shredded and sprinkled on other foods.

cotti, a cannibal tribe from Argyllshire, clung to their hungry ways for a thousand years after the Roman Army had left English shores. But probably the two best-known English cannibals are Sweeney Todd, a legend, and Sawney Beane, possibly quite real.

Reputedly born in the sixteenth century, Sawney Beane eventually fathered eight sons and six daughters who went on to produce, through incest, eighteen grandsons and fourteen granddaughters, and all three generations lived in a cave and survived by robbing, killing, and eating as many people as they could. They hunted together by the Galloway shore for twenty-five years, and went uncaught because the entrance to their cave flooded twice a day with the tide. They killed and ate over a thousand men, women, and children (even salting or pickling some of their victims to last through the lean times) before they were captured by an expedition that was personally led by King James. The whole bunch of Beanes was finally executed.

Sweeney Todd had been immortalized by the English as their favorite cannibal well before Stephen Sondheim set him to music with lyrics discussing the relative merits of meat from a lawyer versus that from a doctor. Todd first turned up in a London newspaper serial in 1846, under the title *The String of Pearls: or The Sailor's Gift, A Romance of Peculiar Interest*. The next year, Sweeney's story was made into a play by George Dibdin Pitt, who called his work *The String of Pearls, or the Fiend of Fleet Street*. Christopher Bond was next, nearly three-quarters of a century later, in 1973, with *Sweeney Todd, the Demon Barber of Fleet Street*. Sondheim saw the Bond play in London and decided to turn it into a musical. It was Sweeney—perhaps originally based, before even the newspaper serial, on a murderous barber hanged in London in 1802—who deposited his customers from their barber chair through a trapdoor to the basement, where their corpses, with throats already cut by the barber, were neatly carved and made into meat pies by the lady next door.

Like Sweeney Todd, werewolves and vampires lived in stories. The tales of bats and beasts were certainly easier to swallow than the thought of fellow villagers who were strangely thirsty in the middle of the night. There were many such neighbors. In Hungary, for instance, there was a countess who supervised the killing of thousands of girls, peasants all (she thought nobody would bother to look very long for peasant girls), because she wished to bathe in their blood. She believed it to be good for her skin.

Among his delights, the Marquis de Sade recommended human flesh as an aphrodisiac. In a way, the marquis was right. The tales of Dracula have amused and titillated thousands since Bram Stoker's Victorian classic first appeared in 1897. Stoker capitalized on the always ready connection between food and sex, between love and the love bite, in his story of the bloodsucking vampire who found his way to the staid, repressed side of a pale English lady. At the beginning of his story, an innocent Englishman spending the night in the count's Transylvanian castle, awakes to find three ethereal ladies bending over him. He watches them "in an agony of delightful anticipation" as one of them "went down on her knees and bent over me. . . . There was a deliberate voluptuousness which was both thrilling and repulsive. . . ." The story is essentially a bedroom drama, as the Broadway and Hollywood versions of our time have emphasized.

Stoker's original Dracula wasn't really an appealing fellow. He had pointy bat ears, hair on his palms, and bad breath. Never mind, the hint of forbidden sex had enormous appeal for Victorian readers. Bela Lugosi substituted a weird accent for the pointy ears, and brought a certain aristocratic charm to his vampire in the movie *Dracula* in 1931. And Mel Brooks summed it all up in his vampire movie of 1995, *Dracula: Dead and Loving It*.

There were vampire stories before Bram Stoker and Mel Brooks, and there have been vampire stories since, from Anne Rice's *Vampire Chronicles* to *Buffy the Vampire Slayer*—and what seems like a new vampire musical every other year. Vampire myths cross cultures and times (the Chinese vampire is called Kiang-si, and he's covered with green hair), shaped by the eroticism of the bite, the ways that vampires control human beings, and their state of being alive after death—undead and loving it.

But mythological blood-drinking vampires were the least of it; there was ritual cannibalism in Europe, too. Devil-worshipping witches were supposed to murder newborn babies and save their fat to use as an ingredient in an evil salve, eating the remainder of their bodies at Sabbath feasts. The Franks found it necessary to have a law against cannibalism—but the only penalty for conviction was a fine. By the time of Charlemagne, the punishment had become more appropriate for the crime. Those who were found guilty of eating human flesh—or of feeding it to others—were condemned to death.

Cannibalism—and the appeal of cannibal stories—is universal, difficult as that may be to accept. Whether it is the eating of a departed family member, the devouring of a defeated enemy, or just adding whoever signs in for the night to the menu, cannibalism is part of our history as human beings, even aside from the textbooks of psychosis or the novels about Hannibal Lecter.

The myth of cannibalism is not that it exists; rather, the myth is our belief that cannibalism is one of man's oldest, most universal taboos. When cannibalism occurs in public, we are shocked and repelled by it, though not so much so that we don't want to read about it. How many newspapers were sold with stories of Jeffrey Dahmer's grisly meals on the front page?* Cannibalism fascinates us even as it sickens us, and we devour words, in our horror, instead of people.

Alive, the book about the Andes crash, was a best seller for months, before it was a movie. The world was hungry for the story of the rugby team and their seventy days in the mountains, but the most amazing thing about their story was not their cannibalism, which was inevitable. It was that even when the evidence stands right in front of us—the surviving "Old Christians" held a press conference after they returned to Montevideo—it is difficult to think of young white men as cannibals. Two of the boys were nephews of the president of Uruguay; one was the son of a well-known heart specialist; another the son of a famous painter. How could attractive, affluent, intelligent young men like these be cannibals?

Apparently, they couldn't. In the flurry of newspaper stories that followed their rescue, only two Chilean newspapers used the word *cannibal* in their headline stories about the crash. All of the others referred to *antropofagia*, a word from the Greek *phagein*, to eat, and *anthropos*, man. In English, the word is *anthropophagy*. It is surely easier to think of those elite young sportsmen, trained in a Jesuit school, as having survived through anthropophagy. Their story became one of "human courage." If they had been a black basketball team from Harlem on tour, would we speak of courage? They would have been cannibals for sure, and anthropophagy would have stayed in the

---

*Dahmer confessed to seventeen killings, from 1978 to 1991. He lured victims to his apartment with promises of beer or money in exchange for posing for nude photographs, then drugged their drinks, and killed them. He told investigators he killed them because he was lonely—he didn't want them to leave. He stored his dismembered victims in his freezer. He was sentenced to serve fifteen consecutive life terms and was killed in prison.

anthropologist's textbook glossary. Worst of all, if they had been black and their dinners white, they would undoubtedly have been greeted by outrage and scandal instead of the world's fascination and sympathy.

It is not only to Western (white) eyes that cannibalism seems horrible. When the Chinese deputy prime minister made an historic visit to America in the winter of 1979, after lines of communication between America and China had been reopened, *The New York Times* reported on his invitation to a family dinner of roast beef at the home of President Carter's national security advisor. The Chinese, *The Times* noted, like beef cooked in small pieces, and are somewhat horrified by bloody slabs of meat like American steaks and roasts. "... the sight of red, rare beef conjures up visions of a live animal. Only barbarians like the Mongols of old times would fancy such a dish, in Chinese eyes."

Perhaps the Mongols were cannibals. The Chinese certainly were. As early as 334 A.D., there were reports of a ruler, Shih Hu, in northern China, who, when guests dropped in, would behead for them one of the girls in his harem. While the company dined on her body, her head—uncooked—was exhibited on a platter as proof that he had given them a particularly beautiful dinner. In the ninth and tenth centuries, Arabs wrote that the Chinese sold human flesh in their markets. In Hangchow, there were restaurants that featured human specialties based on the flesh of old men, women, girls, or small children.

In a country where the devotion of children to parents is a matter of religious virtue, sons and daughters often gave their own flesh to ailing parents. At least two such cases were reported in Chinese newspapers as late as the 1870s. In one, a son cut a piece of flesh from his arm and used it to make soup for his sick mother. In the other, a daughter steeped a slice of herself in her dying father's medicine. According to the newspapers, both parents recovered.

In the 1890s, Chinese warriors sometimes ate their fallen French enemies (*exophagy* again, this time in the belief that the flesh of foreign warriors stimulates domestic courage). In 1901, a Chinese officer was sent to Kwang-si to pacify the residents. He failed. They ate him.

It didn't stop after the turn of the century. Documents disclosed by Chinese government sources in 1993 revealed a record of cannibalism by Red Guards and provincial communist officials about twenty-five years earlier.

"At some high schools," reported *The New York Times*, "students killed their principals in the school courtyard and then cooked and ate the bodies to celebrate a triumph over 'counterrevolutionaries'." One report noted the varieties of cannibalism: "killing someone and making a late dinner of it, slicing off the meat and having a big party, dividing up the flesh so each person takes a large chunk home to boil, roasting the liver and eating it for its medicinal properties, and so on."

According to the documents, at least 137 people were eaten, and probably many hundreds more. In most cases, notes *The Times*, "many people ate the flesh of one corpse, so the number of cannibals may have numbered in the thousands." The paper adds that this cannibalism, the most extensive in the world during the last century, differs from most in that it seems to have been motivated by ideology: People apparently took part to prove their revolutionary ardor. Some of those who were involved received minor punishments when the Cultural Revolution ended after Mao's death in 1976; ninety-one people were expelled from the Communist Party, and thirty-nine others (nonmembers of the party) had their wages cut or were demoted at work. No one faced criminal prosecution.

"Almost everywhere," writes Reay Tannahill in *Flesh and Blood*, "human attitudes and divine commands alike forbid murder for whatever purpose ... [but] the tabu on eating human flesh is by no means the oldest tabu in the world—just one of those most deeply ingrained in the religions which have shaped the societies and the attitudes of the richer nations of the western hemisphere today."

This was not always so. In the Judeo-Christian rites as we celebrate them today, there is a hint of what once was. The words of Mark describe Christ at the Last Supper: "As they were eating he took bread, and blessed, and broke it, and gave it to them, and said, 'Take; this is my body.' And he took a cup, and when he had given thanks, he gave it to them, and they all drank of it. And he said to them, 'This is my blood of the covenant, Which is poured out for many.'" From John, there is this: "My flesh is meat indeed, and my blood is wine indeed."

These religious reverberations of cannibalism were echoed in the Andes, in the words of the Old Christian rugby team. "When the moment came," one of them said at the press conference after their return, "... we thought to ourselves that if Jesus at His last supper had shared His flesh and blood with His apostles, then it was a sign to us that we should do the same—take the flesh and blood as an intimate communion between us all."

Some members of the church agreed. A Vatican priest, writing about the boys in a letter published in Rome, said their "cannibalism is theologically and morally justifiable." The archbishop of Montevideo added, "I see no moral objection to this self-survival...." Even so, the church balked at making cannibalism an overt act of Holy Communion. The term *communion* in this instance, the auxiliary bishop of Montevideo said, "is not correct...."

But there was a time when the church was more literal. In a singular leap of faith, Catholics under Pope Innocent III in 1215 began to believe that they were not eating a symbol of the body and blood of Christ during the Mass, but an actuality.

Less than forty years after the Definition ("The body and blood of Jesus Christ are contained under the appearance of bread and wine in the sacrament of altar, the bread being transubstantiated into the body and the wine into the blood"), a wave of anti-Semitism swept through Europe because Christians had begun to believe Jews guilty of torturing the wafers which were the transubstantiated body of Christ. The wafers had been seen to bleed, and there was no other possible explanation. A Jewish community near Berlin was wiped out in revenge; there was a massacre in Paris; another in Vienna. Jews were burned in Ratisbon, Cracow, Gustrow, Deggendorf, Poznan, Prague, Breslau, Segovia, and Brussels. Centuries passed before scientists discovered a red bacillus that grew on wafers kept in a warm place. Its colonies, nourished on the innocent food of the wafers, grow until they look like spots of blood.

In 1247, Pope Innocent IV condemned the idea of the blood libel, that Jews murdered gentile children in order to use their blood to make matzo, the unleavened bread of Passover. The pope, in his condemnation, noted that the fate of Jews in his own time was "perhaps worse than that of their fathers in Egypt." The Holocaust was yet to come.

It was blood that formed the Jewish covenant with God, made first between Abraham and the Lord. "This is my covenant, which ye shall keep," God told Abraham, "between me and you and thy seed after thee; every man child among you shall be circumcised." The blood promise—made by the reproductive organs of each generation—is contracted over and over again.

When an adult male converts to Judaism, a few drops of blood are shed, even if he is already circumcised, as a symbol of the ancient ritual and promise.

There are many stories of animal sacrifice in the Bible and there are tales, too, of human sacrifice. Abraham was one hundred years old when his son Isaac was born, but when God tells him to bring the boy, "thine only son Isaac, whom thou lovest," as a burnt offering, Abraham is ready. Isaac himself carries the wood for the fire, and Abraham the knife. At the place God has chosen, Abraham builds an altar, and binds Isaac and lays him on the wood. "And Abraham stretched forth his hand, and took the knife to slay his son," ready for the sacrifice to God.

God allowed Isaac to live, and some say that this moment of *non-*sacrifice is the turning point in the history of religion, from the sacrificing of life for an all-powerful God to a new religion of love. In his story, "The Scrolls," Woody Allen envisioned it this way: "At the last minute the Lord stayed Abraham's hand and said, 'How could thou doest such a thing?' And Abraham said 'But thou said—' 'Never mind what I said,' the Lord spake. 'Doth thou listen to every crazy idea that comes thy way? . . . I jokingly suggest thou sacrifice Isaac and thou immediately runs out to do it.'" Abraham falls to his knees. ". . . I never know when you're kidding," he says.

From Adam and Eve and the apple, through the manna of Exodus, to the time of Jesus and the Last Supper, the link between religion and food is strong. It takes us through the calendar year, from Easter and Passover in springtime to Christmas in the winter, through feast and famine, in celebration and in fasting.

The story of Passover is a powerful example of religious feasting, and of sacrifice and ritual slaying. After Pharoah had refused again and again to let the Israelite slaves go free, each of the families in bondage in Egypt sacrificed a lamb and smeared its blood in a mark on their doorposts. That night, in their darkened rooms, they ate roast lamb. Afterward, as they lay, waiting, in their beds, "the Lord smote all the first-born in the land of Egypt," except for the children in the houses with blood on the doors, who were safe. The blood was the sign of the covenant with God.

Religious fasting, the deprivations of Lent and Yom Kippur and Ramadan, is not only a sign of remorse, a penance and purification, but also a memory of devotion and sacrifice. One rabbi put it this way in a prayer:

"Lord of the world, when the Temple was standing, one who sinned offered a sacrifice, of which only the fat and blood was taken, and thereby his sins were forgiven. I have fasted today, and through this fasting my blood and my fat have been decreased. Deign to look upon the part of my blood and my fat which I have lost through my fasting as if I had offered it to Thee, and forgive my sins in return."

Some fasts are meant to benefit others. The prophet Isaiah fasted to loose the bonds of wickedness and undo the yoke of the oppressed. Charity is an important part of Ramadan. The forty-day fast of Jesus announced good news for the poor, sight to the blind, and health to the sick. Gandhi fasted to focus attention on British colonialism and harsh treatment of the Indian people. Cesar Chavez fasted to bring public attention to the miserable treatment of migrant workers in America. Several hunger strikers in Northern Ireland died during their prolonged fasts, again to focus attention on political injustice.

A complete fast—no food and no water—brings death in just a few days; most fasts are either for a limited time, or they allow varying amounts of water. A fast which allows no food but does permit water can last for weeks without threat of death.

Starve originally meant to die—in any way at all: To starve meant to die. Later it came to mean to go without food—and later still, just to be very hungry, or to be deprived of something. Anorexia is self-starvation, a fast which is the extreme of cultural narcissism—going without food in order to look better. There are many kinds of starvation. Kafka's Hunger Artist fasted in the service of his art, though as he fasted longer and longer—the more successful he was as an artist—fewer and fewer people were interested in coming to watch him.

The Hunger Artist's fast was neither moral nor religious, though it may have been spiritual. Among the best gifts we bring to God are gifts of sacrifice, the giving of ourselves. Denying ourselves a pleasure, establishing a discipline over our lives—these are religious sacrifices more sophisticated but only steps away from the religious fast, which is another difference in degree from the offering of the whole self.

"The true sacrifice," writes Norman O. Brown in *Love's Body*, "is human sacrifice. Animal sacrifice is a false substitute, a pale imitation, a shadow. Abraham departs from human sacrifice, and Christ returns to it." The substitution of the animal—the lamb, the oxen—for human beings as gifts of the altar was a mark of the civilizing process. The substitution of Christ for all other men is a symbol of all kinds of sacrifice as well as a reminder of our bloody heritage. The crucifixion, writes Brown, is the last of the old sacrifices, with Christ as the lamb. The Last Supper is the blood of the New Testament. "The supper is the last thing, not the cross; eschatology is eating. . . ." Eschatology is the doctrine of last or final things: death, judgment, immortality. It is also resurrection. "Eschatology is eating."

"The oldest and truest language," Brown goes on, "is that of the mouth; the oral basis of the ego." Life begins outside the womb with the mouth, with hunger, with a voracious appetite, a gluttonous giving up of the self into a repetitious cycle of hunger and fulfillment out of which the self will emerge, whole and with a smile.

The baby is born savage, as purple as a primitive king, glowing with rage at his own impotence. He screams for food, not knowing and caring less, that it is food which will civilize him.

He will learn his potency, that his cries bring help, that his pleasure is returned by someone else's. Eventually, he will learn who he is, that his body stops at his mouth and that the rest of the world begins there. Discovering that the mother's breast is not part of the baby's body is the first step the infant takes toward identity, the knowledge of a separate self.

Before that knowledge is gained, the hungry baby is filled by simple things: hunger and satisfaction, greedy love and its pleasures. Babies would, if they could, devour their mothers, and thus banish hunger forever. They would start with the breast, sucking and sucking till their mouths, their cheeks, their stomachs were filled with milk, till all their world was the creamy bluish/white of mother's milk, sweet, warm, spilling everywhere in the first, warm fantasy of sensuous abandon.

"The great sorrow in human life, which begins in childhood and continues until death," wrote Simone Weil, "is that seeing and eating are two different operations. Eternal beatitude . . . is a state where to see is to eat." "The original aim," says Brown, "is to eat, and to eat all."

Babies see with their mouths as well as their eyes. As soon as their fingers can make the journey, everything they touch is explored in the mouth. It is licked, gummed, sucked, tasted: known.

Rage is also an emotion of the mouth—for the screaming baby no less than the shrieking adult. Babies would, if they could, bite in anger, using their most powerful—their only—weapon, to obliterate the enemy, transient as he or she may be, using the mouth to consume them, and then banishing them to the darkest world, where everything whirls into nothing. Hatred and rage are, like so many emotions, intestinal.

Babies, in their turn, must logically worry about being eaten. Universally, the stories of childhood are filled with horrible people who eat little children. There are hungry ogres, mean and wicked stepmothers who ask for hearts to be ripped out of innocent bodies, giants who devour babies for breakfast, and witches who fatten poor lost toddlers in order to make better meals out of them. The language of fairy tales is based on the fears of children: good, loving, naughty, frightened, angry, hate-filled children. They are all afraid they will be eaten and they cannot say so. They don't have words; even if they did, the words could not be uttered—to say them, even to themselves, would seem too dangerous.

Babies would be cannibals, if they could. They would eat their mothers out of love, or the need to know, or in a rage. To a mind system based on the mouth, the idea of being eaten is very real. The possibility of being devoured by a hungry, angry parent—father or mother—is one of the very first fears, along with the fear of abandonment. No matter how ruffled and pink the nursery, the dark imaginings of childhood exist and are real in the middle of a long, lonely night, a night perpetually filled with obscure shadows beneath the bed and dark waitings at the window.

Historically, as we have seen, children had every right to worry. Their parents ate them or sold them to butchers for others to eat. They were looked upon as particularly juicy morsels, with their tender, milk-fed bodies as sweet as young veal in springtime.

Babies grow older. They lose their first wildness. The mouth no longer holds its place as the source of all pleasure, all knowledge, all power. The rest of the body grows and we are overcome with a succession of new worlds, inner and outer. The memory of that first glorious, awful primacy is lost. But we were all cannibals once, even if we have forgotten. We were all born hungry.

Chapter 17

....

ADOLF HITLER,
VEGETARYAN

... Wagner celebrated ... Aryans as the globe's noblest race. ... But, he lamented, the Aryans' age of gold had passed, their godly purity ... vitiated ... by the supplanting of their natural vegetable food by flesh-eating (an evil brought about by Jews, "former cannibals," educated to be the business leaders of our society). ...
— *Richard Wagner: The Man, His Mind, and His Music,*
by Robert W. Gutman

In the beginning was vegetarianism. What Adam and Eve yearned for was fruit, not meat.

Even after they ate the apple, their diet was low protein. "Thou shalt eat the herb of the field," an angry God said to Adam. "In the sweat of thy face shalt thou eat bread, till thou return unto the ground." Herbs and fruits, cereals and bread: the food of God's first children. And grandchildren, too. Abel was a keeper of sheep; Cain was a tiller of the ground, and it was Cain who lived. Through all the begats, there were no meat eaters until Noah; God cleansed the earth with the flood but then gave up on both human goodness and vegetarianism.

There have been many other vegetarians since Adam—more every year, from Paul McCartney to Madonna. George Bernard Shaw was a vegetarian for aesthetic and hygienic reasons, avoiding meat, tea, and alcohol. Mahatma Gandhi at one point eliminated meat and milk products from his diet as a way to remove what he felt were animal passions, in order to keep his spirit calm. Leo Tolstoy and Albert Schweitzer were vegetarians. So was Adolf Hitler.

"No sane man," wrote A. J. Liebling, "can afford to dispense with debilitating pleasures; no ascetic can be considered reliably sane. Hitler was the archetype of the abstemious man. When the other krauts saw him drink water in the Beer Hall, they should have known he was not to be trusted."

Hitler's empire was built on broken glass, blood, and flames, but his eating habits were nothing short of dainty. His daily menu, pieced together from various sources, verged on what used to be called "invalid food." Vegetarian soup and herbal tea. Bowls of oatmeal soup. Eggs and lime blossom tea. Meat for dinner, he was sure, would destroy modern man. He cited elephants as his proof. Elephants are the strongest animal we know of, he said, and elephants don't eat meat.

He began each day, according to his valet, with eight biscuits, two glasses of warm milk, and a bar of bitter chocolate, carefully broken into small pieces. Lunch was his favorite meal and always began with vegetable soup. In *The Woman Who Lived in Hitler's House*, Pauline Kohler, one of his servants, listed the ingredients for Berchtesgaden Soup: onion, celery, parsley, potatoes, turnips, carrots, nut compound, apple, water, flour, and salt. Soup was followed by fish with butter sauce (despite the fact that elephants don't eat fish—or biscuits, chocolate, or butter sauce, for that matter); sautéed potatoes, and a bowl of nuts. Dinner was a simple meal, perhaps just mashed potatoes, or a tomato salad.

Like many vegetarians, Hitler was also a teetotaler. He drank herbal teas and infusions made of blossoms and peels. He also drank coffee—enormous amounts of coffee, sixteen or more cups every day, and then fretted because he couldn't sleep. He loved sweets, and often finished off two pounds of chocolates—more caffeine—in a single day. He ate huge amounts of butter—half a pound a day—and eggs.

These are all strange eating habits. They speak of a man obsessed with food, as he was with so much else. Physically revolted by meat (though he did allow it to be served to guests at his table), he believed that what he saw as the decay of modern civilization was directly linked to the way meat decays in the intestines. He believed that what he called "the specific decadence of Jews" had its origin "in the abdomen—chronic constipation, poisoning of the juices, and the result of drinking to excess." His vegetarianism, like his anti-Semitism, was modeled after that of Richard Wagner.

Wagner's daughter-in-law Winifred (married to Wagner's son Siegfried) called Hitler "the saviour of Germany" and *"unser seliger Adolf,"* our blessed Adolf. Hitler considered Bayreuth, the Wagnerian shrine, to be the musical capital of Nazism, and used many of the devices of Wagner's operas—torchlight parades, mob choruses, ever-building climaxes, the grand gestures of Nordic heroes—to mesmerize his audiences.

He took on many of the Bayreuth trappings—vegetarianism and anti-vivesectionism, and bits of Buddhism and Indian lore. Buddha's footprints were said to be swastikas. (The Sanskrit word *svastika* means well-being and good fortune.) The earliest examples of the swastika, symbol of the Nazi Party, date from around 2500 to 3000 B.C., in India and Central Asia. Before Hitler turned its ends around and it became a symbol of hate and terror, the swastika was a universal symbol of good luck. Swastikas are woven into Navajo blankets; Jewish synagogues in North Africa were built with swastika mosaics. Rudyard Kipling incorporated a swastika into his signature; they were part of the Bauhaus logo under Paul Klee; Coca-Cola issued a swastika pendant; during World War I, the American Forty-fifth Infantry Division had an orange swastika shoulder patch; until 1940, the Boy Scouts of America had a swastika badge.

It flourished in Germany, too. An anti-Semitic group called the *Germanen* order used a curved swastika on a cross as its emblem. In 1914, the *Wandervogel*, a militarist German youth movement, made it their emblem. The Nazi Party claimed it in 1920. Hitler reversed the direction of the right angle tips of the cross, making it appear to spin clockwise.

Before the world knew the worst about Hitler, Janet Flanner, *The New*

Yorker writer known as Gênét, wrote about him in 1936. "Dictator of a nation devoted to splendid sausages, cigars, beer, and babies, Adolf Hitler is a vegetarian, teetotaler, nonsmoker, and celibate. Emotionally, Hitler belongs to the dangerous small class of sublimators from which fanatics are frequently drawn."

Food, sex, and sleep are the keystones of our personalities, according to psychiatry. Anything too far off base in any one of these three categories means a personality equally out of kilter. Hitler managed to have problems in all three: He had trouble sleeping, was obsessive about food, and had a very strange sex life.

The Book of Lists includes him as one of ten "Famous Men Who Were Full-Time or Part-Time Virgins." The evidence is scanty, but he was most likely part-time, verging on full-time. He liked to talk about beautiful women and be seen with them, but his close relationships with women were few and far between. Each of the three or four women with whom he was truly emotionally involved attempted suicide. That's an amazing statistic. Two succeeded—without even counting Eva Braun, his deathbed bride. "Rather an unusual record for a man who has had so few affairs with women," Dr. Walter Langer wrote in his remarkable wartime study of Hitler for the Office of Strategic Services, forerunner of the CIA.

Rene Mueller, an actress, was one of the successful suicides. She had told a friend what it was like to have sex with Hitler. He "fell on the floor and begged her to kick him. She demurred, but he pleaded with her and condemned himself as unworthy, heaped all kinds of accusations on his own head, and just groveled in an agonizing manner. The scene became intolerable to her, and she finally acceded to his wishes and kicked him. This excited him greatly, and he begged for more and more, always saying that it was even better than he deserved and that he was not worthy to be in the same room with her. As she continued to kick him, he became more and more excited."

But being kicked was the least part of his sexual pleasure. What he liked best, according to several psychiatrists, and "the only way in which he could get full sexual satisfaction was to watch a young woman as she squatted over his head and urinated or defecated in his face."

And if it's true, that's the link: his fascination with feces and urine connected to his obsessions about food. He wrote about "the specific de-cadence of Jews [having] its origin in the abdomen" because of the eating of meat, and the way meat decays in the intestines. The unconscious mean-ing of meat, said the Jewish Dr. Freud, is that it is a symbol of feces. Beer is clearly related to urine. Hitler made a fetish out of swallowing neither meat nor beer. Langer's theory was that Hitler's vegetarianism was an emotional compromise which allowed him to function. It was a way of dealing with an unacceptable obsession, "a compromise between psychotic tendencies to eat feces and drink urine on the one hand, and [the wish] to live a normal, socially adjusted life on the other."

Hitler spent an amazing amount of time underground. As the war wore on, the only time he spent aboveground was to travel from one bunker to another. He began to live beneath the ground—and chose to die there—in the bowels, as it were, of the earth. Here, in the earth's abdomen, among the decayed leaves and the rotting grasses, he felt safe. It was a decadent womb, dark and colonic. It begs the eternal question about the Nazis: What could have produced such madness? There have been—and still are—other horrors in our world, to be sure, but none has ever been so care-fully organized, so calmly efficient, so coldly documented by records and photographs, measurements, and memoranda. Hitler and the Nazis man-aged to schedule genocide and then organize it.

Can Hitler be explained? *Should* he be? There are those who say no, he should not be; that explanations risk sympathy, that sympathy is unthink-able, and that evil simply exists, without being understandable, without needing to be understood. The gap between Hitler as a child and the adult Hitler who was responsible for the icy murder of 6 million Jews—and mil-lions of other people as well—is a chasm that cannot be leapt over, nor should it be. There is no "why"; there cannot be. Others say that his evil must be understood, that sympathy is not empathy, and that if we can un-derstand Hitler, we can begin to understand human wickedness, and dream about preventing its return.

We don't know much about Hitler's childhood. Other World War II leaders, Churchill, DeGaulle, and Roosevelt (though not Stalin, another tyrant and murderer), came from the upper classes; Hitler emerged from the anonymity of the lower-middle class. His childhood was obviously not happy—that can surely be inferred by what it produced, but aside from that, Hitler went to great lengths to obliterate any record of his past. What there is left begins with his own self-revealing passage in *Mein Kampf*, describing the life of an anonymous boy in a lower-class family:

"... There is a boy, let us say, of three. When the parents fight almost daily, their brutality leaves nothing to the imagination... mutual differences express themselves in the form of brutal attacks on the part of the father toward the mother or to assaults due to drunkenness. The poor little boy, at the age of six, senses things which would make even a grown-up shudder.... When [the husband] finally comes home... drunk and brutal, but always without a last cent or penny, then God have mercy on the scenes which follow. I witnessed all of this personally in hundreds of scenes."

Hitler's father, Alois, was the illegitimate son of Maria Anna Schicklgruber. According to one story, Fraulein Schicklgruber was employed as a servant in the Viennese home of Baron Rothschild when she became pregnant. When her condition was discovered, she was returned to her family home. Her son, Alois, Hitler's father, was born in 1837. If the Baron was his father, Alois was half Jewish, and Adolf was one-quarter Jewish—Jewish enough to be sent to the camps. (This theory is credited to Chancellor Dollfuss of Austria, who had his police force investigate Hitler's lineage in a search for a weapon to be used against him. Dolfuss was later assassinated at Hitler's instigation.)

When Alois was five, his mother married Johann Georg Hiedler, a wandering miller whose name was sometimes spelled Hiedler, Huetler, Hüttler, or Hitler.* Hiedler did not legitimize the boy, and he grew up as Alois Schicklgruber. (When Alois was forty, Hiedler, at the age of eighty-four, testified before a notary that he was the father of Alois, and he spelled his name Hitler.) Alois's mother died when he was ten, and he then lived with his uncle, Hiedler's brother. He was probably not treated as an equal; it

---

*The old families of the Waldviertel region of Austria, near the Czech border, included the Schicklgrubers, the Pölzls, the Hiedlers, the Hüttlers, and the Hytlers. In *Hitler's Lost Family*, Timothy W. Ryback quotes an Austrian writer who called the Waldviertel "the Appalachia of Austria."

seems safe to assume that his childhood was not happy. When he was eighteen, he left the village to join the border police in the Austrian customs service near Salzburg. He wore a uniform with gold buttons stamped with the imperial two-headed eagle; he carried a pistol at his belt; he guarded the border; and he hunted smugglers.

Alois married three times. His first wife was the daughter of a local customs official—a more prestigious position than that of a mere border policeman. Eleven days before the marriage, Alois was promoted. His new wife, Anna, was forty-one—fourteen years older than he was. She had a small dowry, her social status was a step up for him, and she was ailing. The marriage was unhappy, but as Catholics, they couldn't divorce; they separated after some years. They lived apart until her death from tuberculosis in 1883. She was sixty; Alois was forty-six.

His second wife had already borne him a son, Alois Jr., and she was pregnant at their wedding, a month after his first wife died, Angela was born three months later. Within a year, his second wife was also dead. Six months later, Alois married for the third time. Again, his new wife was pregnant at the ceremony. Klara Pölzl was twenty-five; Alois was forty-eight. Klara was his cousin's daughter, and they had to apply for an episcopal dispensation for the marriage to be permitted.

Alois and Klara knew each other well. Alois and his first wife had taken Klara in as a foster child; when that marriage ended, Klara went to Vienna to work as a servant. She returned to nurse Alois's second wife and to care for her two children, Alois Jr. and Angela. After the second wife died, she stayed on to keep house for Alois.

Four months after their wedding, Klara's first child, Gustav, was born; their second child, Ida, was born just over a year later, and was followed in turn by a third child, Otto, who died as an infant. Gustav and Ida each died two years after their birth. Adolf was the fourth child, born on April 20, 1889, and he was the first to survive. The next, Edmund, born in 1894, also died young. The last child, Paula, was born in 1896. Paula and Adolf were the surviving children. Now there were four children, altogether, in the household: Adolf, his younger sister Paula, and his older half brother and half sister, Alois Jr. and Angela.

Adolf was a sickly infant, born after the death of three siblings. Inevitably, his mother must have coddled him, protected him, adored him, spoiled him, overfed him. There is only one extant photograph of him as a small child, and he is fat.

It's hard to imagine that Klara married Alois with stars in her eyes. She had already lived with him *and* his first two wives; she was pregnant by him when they married. When he was sober, her husband was the very soul of German respectability. He was a petty bureaucrat; he wore his customs official uniform long after his early retirement from the service. He moved his family from village to village while he tried to make his way as a farmer, and wherever they went, he insisted on being called by his title, Herr Oberoffizial Hitler. At home, the children called him Herr Vater (literally, Mister Father). Some say that he looked down on his neighbors because they were peasants and that they laughed at him because he was silly.

According to several historians, Alois was a pompous ass and a lout. A friend reported that he hardly spoke to Klara. The love she had to give, she gave to Adolf—in excess. To the older two children, Adolf's half brother and half sister, she was something of a wicked stepmother. Alois Jr. was blamed for everything that went wrong, especially if it was really Adolf's fault.

When he was drunk, Alois was brutal. He beat his children regularly. Adolf's older half brother, Alois Jr., was beaten into unconsciousness; Adolf was once beaten so severely that Alois thought he was dead. Adolf and Alois Jr. frequently carried their father home from his drinking bouts at the local tavern. When they reached home, Alois would beat them and his wife; according to Alois Jr., he even beat the dog.

Alois probably died of a stroke, some say while reading a newspaper at home, others say while on his way to a tavern. By then, Adolf was fourteen years old, and the damage had been done.

Alois Jr. left home when he was fourteen. He served two jail terms for theft, and then left Germany for Dublin where he worked as a waiter. Reportedly, he was handsome and he dressed nicely—he wore white waistcoats and had a pocket watch on a gold chain. When he was twenty-eight he met Brigid Elizabeth Dowling at a horse show; she was seventeen. They eloped. Their son, William Patrick, was born in Liverpool in 1911. William Patrick is the source of many of the stories about Adolf and Alois Jr.'s childhood.

Like most who have themselves been abused as children, Alois Jr. beat his own child, and William Patrick's tales included stories of his father's drunken rages. Alois Jr. eventually deserted his Irish family and went back to Germany, where he married again, bigamously.

When William was eighteen, he visited his father, by then running a Berlin restaurant with his second wife. That summer, in 1929, William saw his Uncle Adolf at the Nuremberg Rally. After he returned to England, he told local reporters that he was Adolf Hitler's nephew. Newspapers picked up the story; eventually, it reached Germany, and Hitler was furious.

Publicly, Hitler refused to acknowledge the existence of his half brother or his nephew. "No one must drag my private affairs into the newspapers," he had roared at William. "I have never said one word they can use. And now there is a 'nephew' to tell them all the miserable little details they want to know." One report is that Alois Jr. was eventually sent to a concentration camp because he talked too much.

Brigid and William returned to Germany several times—blackmailing Hitler, in effect, for jobs and money. Eventually, they ended up in the United States. Brigid went to Hollywood, where gossip columnist Louella Parsons reported that she was working as technical advisor on *The Mad Dog of Europe*. Later, she worked as a volunteer with the British War Relief Society in New York City.

William was taken on as a lecturer by the William Morris Agency, giving talks across the United States and Canada, telling stories of his family's incest, bigamy, and plans for world domination. He registered for military service in the United States and was classified 1-A, but was ultimately rejected because his Uncle Adolf had been a corporal in the German Army during World War I. He wrote to President Roosevelt, asking him to intervene; Roosevelt passed the letter to J. Edgar Hoover; the FBI investigated William and found nothing subversive in his record, despite his relatives, and in March 1944, William was inducted into the United States Navy, where he served for two years as a seaman first class. After the war, William changed his last name to Hiller, married, changed his name again, settled on Long Island, and had four sons, all of whom shun any kind of publicity. Brigid died in 1969. William died in 1987. His tombstone bears no last name.

Hitler's half sister Angela had a happier life than her brother, Alois Jr. After her first husband died, she worked in Vienna as a housekeeper, and possibly for a time as a cook in a Jewish charity kitchen. One source has her as the manager of the Mensa Academica Judaica. In 1928, she moved to Munich and became Hitler's housekeeper. She took over the management of Berchtesgaden. Hitler resented her second marriage (to a professor of architecture in 1936) and her departure, with her new husband, for Dresden; he refused to give her a wedding present.

Angela had been, with a single notable exception, the only person in Hitler's family with whom he kept a connection. The exception was Geli Raubal, Angela's daughter by her first marriage. Hitler became a vegetarian after Geli's death by suicide.

Geli was, Hitler often said, the love of his life. She had come, with her mother, to live with him in Munich. She was young—there was about the same age difference between Adolf and Geli as there had been between Alois Senior and Klara. At Hitler's request, Geli called him Uncle Alfi; he referred to her as "my niece Geli." Hitler's parents had also called each other "Uncle" and "Niece."

Hitler controlled Geli's life; he went everywhere with her, choosing her clothes, the people she could see, the places she could go, the things she could do. Helm Stierlin, who wrote *Adolf Hitler: A Family Perspective,* called their relationship an "intensely possessive, sexualized, ambivalent and quasi-incestuous relationship that evoked, repeated and concealed what once—on the *feeling* level—had gone on between him and his mother." (The italics are mine.)

Like Rene Mueller, Geli was also quoted about Hitler's sex habits—his preference for the bottom over the top. When they made love, she said, she had to "squat over him in such a way that he could see everything." A friend of hers claimed that Geli was desperately unhappy because she could not bring herself to do "what he wants me to." (A friend of Hitler's testified that the physician who examined her body found her to have been a virgin.) Her suicide was sudden and unexpected.

Hitler was devastated by Geli's death. He locked the door to her room and turned it into a shrine. The only other person allowed to enter was a servant who placed fresh flowers in the room every day. For many years, he spent Christmas Eve alone there. He commissioned portraits to be made from photographs of Geli, and he kept a portrait or a bust of her—and of his mother—in every one of his bedrooms.

Hitler's mother had died much earlier, when Hitler was nineteen. The cause of death was breast cancer, which recurred after one breast was diagnosed as cancerous and removed. One source reports that as part of her treatment, Hitler encouraged her doctor to use idoform-soaked gauzes directly on the cancerous wound. The treatment was not unusual then, but it was painful and it was ineffective. It was also—if given in large enough doses, as it was, poisonous; the chemical was absorbed directly into the bloodstream.

Hitler worried about poison constantly: in his food—two SS men tested his food before he ate it; inside his body—decaying, corrupting; in society, in the fatherland. This was not the realistic nervousness of a ruler with enemies. It was the fear of a disturbed man who must worry about those body functions which are most intimate, most primal, most revealing. All the lime blossom tea in the world could not wash his body or his soul clean.

His beginnings are sufficiently strange—illegitimacy, sordid drunkenness, tyranny, brutality, and humiliation—for a man who became history's worst tyrant, the personification of evil. In him were the contradictions of an apparently meek man, somewhat silly looking with his little moustache, a man who was polite to women, fond of dogs, careful about dinner, horrified by meat—a man who killed millions, waged global war, hypnotized a nation, and built slaughterhouses for human beings that will never be forgotten. He was the son of a brutalized, overindulgent mother and a bestial, distant father, and to identify with either one of them was disastrous. He emerged neither male nor female nor androgenous, but as asexual as he was amoral.

And he ate what he did, and refused what he didn't, because of the imperial psyche, as tyrannical in the führer as in the humblest peasant, cashier, or clerk.

In one of the books written by an ex-servant, a sort of backstairs at Berchtesgaden, there is a description of Hitler's fondness for nuts. Every day after lunch, this woman brought her leader an enormous bowl of assorted nuts and "the Fuehrer simply stuffs himself with these." An autopsy was performed on Hitler's charred body by Russian doctors in that memorable May of 1945. "The left testicle could not be found either in the scrotum or on the spermatic cord inside the inguinal canal, nor in the pelvis." Hitler, in short, in the words which English soldiers sang to the melody of "The Colonel Bogey March," had "only got one ball."*

No wonder he stuffed himself with nuts.

*"Hitler / has only got one ball.
Goering's / are very, very small.
Himmler's / are very sim'lar,
and poor old Goebbels
has no balls
at all."

Chapter 18

- -

THE BIG APPLE

And when the woman saw that the tree was good for food, and that it was pleasant to the eyes, and a tree to be desired to make one wise, she took of the fruit thereof, and did eat, and gave also unto her husband with her; and he did eat. And the eyes of them both were opened, and they knew that they were naked; and they sewed fig leaves together, and made themselves aprons.

—Genesis

You first parents of the human race . . . who ruined yourself for an apple, what might you not have done for a truffled turkey?

—Brillat-Savarin

Almost anything that can appear on a menu has a tale or two in its family tree, but apples go back the farthest and have the classiest pedigree. They started out, after all, in the garden with Adam and Eve and the snake.

The apple isn't mentioned as such in Genesis. It's the fruit of the tree of knowledge that is forbidden. There have been votes here and there for apricots—which don't seem large enough or hard enough or beautiful enough to be sufficiently tempting—but apples are generally agreed upon as the forbidden fruit.

The knowledge hidden inside their red, crunchy skin is usually taken to be fleshy, that is, carnal knowledge ("...and they knew that they were naked...."). More broadly, it is the distinction between good and evil that Adam and Eve discovered when they bit into the apple, crossing the line between innocence and sophistication, purity and sexuality. It is the knowledge of infallibility and of eternal life. It is knowledge hidden in a fruit which grows on a tree which blooms in the garden of the gods who never die.

It is also knowledge acquired in the most basic way: by eating. The first human knowing is through the mouth, as infants gum and lick and suck and squeeze their way through their first hungry, sleepy world. Knowledge is oral first, and the knowing of the apple is oral knowledge.

Women became, with Eve's bite into the apple, the first sinners. Adam was one step removed. In the Bible, Adam gives his alibi: "And the man said the woman who thou gavest to be with me, she gave me of the tree, and I did eat." What a weasel! It was her fault, he said to God, she gave it to me, she did it first, I never would have done it myself, but she did, so I did. He even blames God: "the woman who thou gavest to be with me"—why didn't God choose a different rib? There were plenty to choose from.

And so it comes down to us: Because Adam said he was tempted by Eve rather than by the fruit itself, women became the handmaidens of evil. We're told: It is women who tempt men. That's much more important than the fact that it is men who are tempted. It is women who must wear the veil. It's not men who shouldn't look. Or linger over what they see. It's not men who should learn how to deal with temptation. It is the nature of women to tempt; it's the nature of men to be weak and to take no responsibility. Adam was the victim, because he was seduced by Eve. Man is powerless against women, so it must be made that women have no power. Only then can men be safe. And so we learned, and so it has been.

Poor Adam! Born first—the mother, as it were, of his own wife—he was still too naive, though he was the elder, too innocent, too weak to resist the outstretched hand of the temptress. It was Eve who took the giant step, who tasted what had never been known, who leapt out of innocence in order to learn. Because she was the first adventurer—and what a brave woman she was to taste the unknown, to dare to solve its mystery, to defy God!—and Adam was simply standing around and led astray, women through the centuries have been branded with guilt while men have labored weakly to resist. Or to have revenge. The *A* is worn by women. *A* is *The Scarlet Letter; A* is for adulteress. But *A* is for adventurer and *A* is for apple.

Obviously it is women who hold the *real* power. Women seduce; men are seduced. Women have the active role, even if they do just have to lie there. Prostitutes are sent to jail; their customers get dressed very fast and walk away, scared stiffer than they were before. We still believe when a woman is raped that in some way we don't know about yet, it is *she* who is guilty. (She shouldn't have been wearing that outfit; what was she doing in *that* place? How come she led him on that way? Why did she drink so much? It all means it's her fault.) Women go along with that thinking because it's more comfortable. We think that if it was *her* fault, then we ourselves are safe, like Adam. (*We* would never wear that; *we* couldn't possibly go there, *we'd* never drink that much. *We're* safe. Or so we think.) Thus it was in the garden and so it has been ever since. "Since the first moralists were men," Bertrand Russell has written, "women appeared as the temptress; if they had been women, man would have had this role."

There have been other gardens and other trees, and we have always been born innocent, men and women alike, before we come to inherit that original sin. (Why does innocence always have to be tested? Why can't it just *be?*)

The Greeks had the Garden of the Hesperides, and in it grew the apple tree of eternal life, which had been given to Hera by Mother Earth as a wedding present when Hera married Zeus. It was in the care of the Hesperides, who were the three daughters of Atlas. Their garden was on an island at the end of the world, guarded by a serpent.

Sidur, the Sumerian goddess of wisdom, ruled over another garden. Our word *paradise* comes from the Persian word for garden—a garden like the one in which man and woman were born and all the fruits grew and all, save one, were given to them.

And there have been other apples—orchards full—aside from that first one, though their symbol is always the same: eternal life, knowledge, eroticism, sexuality, and fertility.

There were even other apples in the Bible, aside from the one that Eve bit into. Apparently one bite is too much and a hundred is not enough. "Comfort me with apples," says the Song of Solomon, "for I am sick of love," and it returns again and again to the image of apples—and other fruits and berries and nuts—in the beautiful rhythms of its erotic poetry. "As the apple tree among the trees of the wood," says the Shulamite, "so is my beloved among the sons. I sat down under his shadow with great delight, And his fruit was sweet to my taste." "Under the apple tree I awakened thee," says King Solomon, and, "Let thy breasts be as clusters of the vine, And the smell of thy breath like apples."

Apples can be seen in the wall drawings of cavemen, plainly used as fertility symbols. For the Greeks, apples were the symbol of Aphrodite, goddess of love. A golden apple inscribed "To the Fairest" was thrown into the gathering of guests at a wedding party by Eris, the goddess of discord, who somehow, like the bad fairy at Sleeping Beauty's party, hadn't been invited to the bash. No one could agree on who was the fairest, so Zeus gave the apple to Paris, son of Priam and Hecuba, king and queen of Troy, and left it up to him to decide who was the fairest of them all.

Three ladies were especially avid to win the golden apple, and they tempted Paris with all their considerable charms and powers. Hera offered him wealth and authority if he would choose her. Athena suggested glory and fame in war. But Aphrodite said she would give him the most beautiful woman in the world for his wife if he would give the apple to her, and Aphrodite won the apple because she had the best bait.

Unfortunately for the city of Troy, Paris chose Helen, who as luck would have it was already married. Her seduction led to the long Trojan War, and by the time it ended, all of Troy was in ashes.

The Romans also believed the apple to be the fruit of love, and they exchanged apples as part of their marriage rites. Horace wrote that one should flick apple seeds upward, using the thumb against the index finger to propel them, and if they stuck to the ceiling, it would mean that one's love was willing. "To hit with an apple" meant to make love.

Apples were equally potent in the Middle East. *The Kama Sutra* gives a recipe for an ointment made with the fruit of "Adam's Apple Tree." The tree is *tabernaemontana Coronia,* not a true apple, but one which bears especially sweet-smelling flowers that turn into beautiful fruit, shaped like apples, out of which a bite has been taken. They say the fruit was excellent before Eve bit into it; ever since, it has been poisonous.

There is a lovely ninth-century Arabic poem, which clearly shows the power of the apple in the imagery of love:

> The apple
> which I received from the hand
> Of the most charming
> gazellelike maiden,
> Which she had plucked herself
> from a branch
> That was as supple as her own body.
> And sweet it was
> to place my hand upon it
> As though it was the breast
> of the one who gave it.
> Pure was the fragrance of the apple,
> Like the breath of the giver
> One could see
> the color of her cheek on it,
> And I thought I was tasting her lips
> When I began to eat the apple.

The power of the apple has ruled through the centuries. Thirteenth century nuns were warned in a handbook written for their guidance. "This apple," says the *Ancrene Riwle,* "is a token of everything that arouses lust and sensual delights."

In the old Welsh tongue, *aval* means apple, and Avalon is the Isle of Apples. According to Geoffrey of Monmouth, when King Arthur was fatally wounded, he was carried from Camelot to Avalon, where he lived forever, protected by the magical power of the apple trees.

Rabelais called the breasts *pommes d'amour,* apples of love. In slang in

England, breasts are soft as apple dumplings; an apple monger is a pimp; and apples, in the United Kingdom as in France, are what Americans call the nuts. "You're playin' in my orchard, now don't you see," sings "The Hesitation Blues," "if you don't like my apples, stop climbin' my tree."

New York City is the biggest apple of them all—the very nuts, you might say. That doesn't mean it's a modern Sodom, swarming with sin, but it *is* a sexy city, and it has always been full of people on the make. On the other side of the country, Los Angeles has fewer nicknames and a different kind of sex image. With all that bright sunshine all around, sex on the West Coast ought to seem healthier. Instead, it sounds seamier—hidden in dark places on dreary streets in a city with no downtown, or on casting-room couches, or in smoky rooms filled with dirty glasses—kinkier and more self-indulgent. It just isn't like New York's big avenues, a place to strut your stuff. The Big Apple is in better shape than it used to be, but on a good day, it has always been sunny and crisp. Like an apple. And sexy. Like an apple.

There are various theories about the origin of the image of Manhattan as the Big Apple. One is that it stems, via New Orleans, from a Spanish phrase, *manzana principal. Manzana* means apple, but it can also mean a tract of land or a city block. *Manzana principal,* then, means the big block, downtown, the main stem, the place where it's at. Jazzmen translated it as the big apple, or the big time, and put it where it belonged. Equally musical is the theory that the name for the city derived from a dance, or the jazzman's saying that there are as many cities for one-night stands as there are apples on a tree, but New York is the biggest of them all.

Another theory from New Orleans has it that black stable hands there (who may have themselves heard the phrase through music) called New York City's racetracks "the Big Apple," and the Big Apple racetracks were the main goal of every trainer and jockey in the horse world. A New York newspaper writer named John Fitzgerald had a horse-racing column called *Around the Big Apple,* and some word sleuths say his usage predated the jazz term by a decade. In that case, the stable hands brought the phrase to music, instead of the other way around.

Fitzgerald first used the phrase "the big apple"—before he adopted it as the name of his column—in the *New York Morning Telegraph* in 1921. In 1924, when it had become the title of his column, he explained the phrase for the first time; he explained it again in 1926. Both times, he reported hearing a conversation between two stable hands at the New Orleans fairgrounds. One asked the other where he was going next. "We're heading for the Big Apple," the second answered. "Then you'd better fatten up your horses," the first one said, "or all you'll get from the apple will be the core."

Horses love apples—was it that? Or the jazz phrase? No way to know. But other uses followed. The big apple dance craze started at a club in South Carolina called the Big Apple; the club opened in 1936, a year after Harlem's Big Apple club opened, and the national dance fad followed in 1937.

William Safire, writing in *The New York Times,* says it started earlier. He notes that Edward Martin, founder of the *Harvard Lampoon,* first editor of the humor magazine *Life,* and author of a 1909 book, *The Wayfarer in New York,* wrote about the attitude of Midwesterners toward New York City: "Kansas is apt to see in New York a greedy city.... It inclines to think that the big apple gets a disproportionate share of the national sap."

Another possibility is that the apple is an analogy with the shape of the world, with New York City right at the center; the main stem. The image of the apple, with its flesh and skin, is a human one. In Greek, the stem of the apple is called *omphalos,* navel—as in our navel oranges. That would make New York City the belly button of the world.

New York is certainly an apple in the biblical sense—a mecca of forbidden fruits, lust, and temptation. The apple brought sin to man; New York is full of sinfully luscious pleasures swinging ripe and juicy from the tree, waiting to be plucked and eaten.

Once picked and bitten into, there are some apples that stick in the throat, as Adam and Eve learned. Snow White, for one, succumbed to the lure of a bright red beauty. She managed to sleep through the action that followed, falling to the floor with what must have been a graceful sigh, rather than a guttural gasp. The Seven Dwarfs paid the price for her sin (as women have paid for Eve's). When the Prince happened along, bless him, he took care of everything, falling in love with Snow White, making the apple pop out of her throat in what was undoubtedly the first recorded Heimlich maneuver, rewarding the Dwarfs, and punishing the nasty queen. So shall it be on Judgment Day.

The apple that stuck in the throat of man, worse luck, is still there. Unable to resist his wily wife, Adam took his bite, but it lodged in his throat and he never even got to digest it. Men have that lump still, and they call it Adam's apple after him, an expression which goes back to the original Hebrew. It is supposed to be visible proof of a deep voice, which is audible proof of potency. Thus, we like to think of it as a sign of masculinity and virility rather than a reminder of gullibility or fallibility or weakness and hypocrisy. After all, it is Adam's apple. He ate the apple—"she gave me of the tree, and I did eat"—and he is the father of us all.

A FEW RELEVANT RECIPES

Eggs with Eggs

In Germany, Russian eggs are hard-boiled, served with mayonnaise and with caviar—eggs with eggs—and eggs are, after all, as feminine as you can get.
—Chapter 2, "The Sex Life of Food"

The first eggs in this recipe are from chickens; the second from fish. They go together very nicely. Adjust the quantities according to the number of people you wish to serve. Use one egg for each person, plus one or two extra for the bowl.

FOR THE BASE LAYER:
Hard-boiled eggs, shelled and chopped
Chopped onion
Hellman's mayonnaise
Salt and freshly ground black pepper

FOR THE TOP LAYER:
Sour cream (NOT no fat. Low fat (30 or 40% less fat) is fine.)
Garnish: A sprig or two of dill or flat-leaf parsley.

FOR THE MIDDLE LAYER:
Black lumpfish caviar

1. Make egg salad just as you would usually, mixing the chopped eggs and onions with the mayonnaise, adding salt and pepper to taste. You can make the egg salad ahead; keep it covered and chilled until you're ready to serve.
2. Just before serving, make the three layers: Begin by spreading the egg salad in a serving bowl (a glass bowl is especially nice, if you have one, so the layers show). Thinly spread the caviar over the eggs. (If you use a glass bowl, make sure the caviar reaches the edges so it's visible.) Cover with a layer of sour cream and garnish with dill or parsley.

Serve with quartered slices of whole-grain bread or pumpernickel, or with crackers.

Faux Chocolate *Pots de Crème*

Ranked against statements of love, chocolate is a keynote speech.
—Chapter 6, "Dinner in Bed"

These *pots de crème* are down to basics: chocolate, milk, sugar, and vanilla. The end result is dense and rich; a little whipped cream on the side is lovely. And perhaps a few berries, rasp or straw? You could use Cognac or rum instead of vanilla, yes. The original recipe was from *The New York Times*, and included a raw egg. I'm willing to risk all sorts of things, but not a raw egg. Not even one that has been tempered with hot milk.

¾ cup milk

1 cup (6 ounces) semisweet chocolate bits

1 tablespoon sugar

1 teaspoon vanilla or Cognac or rum

Tiny pinch of salt

Garnish: whipped cream

1. Heat milk to the scalding point.
2. While the milk is heating, place all the other ingredients except the whipped cream in a food-processor bowl or a blender.
3. Add the hot milk. Holding paper towels or a kitchen towel around the processor bowl so it won't leak, process until the chocolate is completely melted, between 10 and 20 seconds, longer if needed.
4. Two choices: Pour the chocolate into tiny cups—demitasse cups work nicely if you have them; *pots de crème* cups, with their little covers, are perfect by definition. Or pour the chocolate into a pretty serving bowl and spoon out portions from there. Refrigerate for at least 4 hours. Serve with whipped cream.

Serves 4 to 6

NOTE: It's very lavish to serve this with Russian Cream (recipe on page 245) for a black-and-white choice.

Eau-de-Vie

*There's a long gap, after all, between the moment of love and the
moment of birth.*
—Chapter 8, "A Bun in the Oven"

Eau-de-vie means, literally, water of life. In France, eau-de-vie is usually
made from fruit—raspberries, plums, cherries, pears.... This recipe is a remarkably simple version; its main requirement is patience. Once you start
making it, though, if you're anything like me, you'll want several varieties.
My favorite so far is quince, but unfortunately, it's hard to find quince —
even harder than it is to cut one up once you've found it.

FIRST:

Fruit—organic is best

*Alcohol: brandy or Cognac, rum, or
vodka*

SIX WEEKS LATER:

1 cup sugar

1 cup fresh cold water

1. Use one kind of fruit—raspberries, cherries, apples, pears.... Cut large
   fruit into halves or quarters. Place fruit in a bottle, and cover generously
   with Cognac, rum, or vodka—whichever you think matches best. Close
   the bottle, and place it in a closet for 6 weeks.
2. At the end of the 6 weeks, make a simple syrup: Heat the sugar and water together over medium-low heat without stirring, until the sugar is
   completely dissolved and the syrup is clear. Boil for 1 minute. Cool.
3. Using a larger container, add the sugar syrup to the fruit alcohol a bit at a
   time, tasting, until it reaches a taste you like. Be careful—it shouldn't be
   too sweet—there should be just enough to take the alcohol edge off. Remove the fruit; bottle the alcohol. It lasts for a very long time, if you let it.

NOTE: Leftover simple syrup can be used to sweeten cut-up fruit, or to
make lemonade or limeade, or for any number of other purposes. Keep it
in a clean jar in the refrigerator; it, too, lasts and lasts.

Basil Cheese with Walnuts

Comfort food stays fairly firmly on the feminine side of food—eggs, soups, puddings, chicken, potatoes, ice cream, sweets. . . .
                    —Chapter 11, "Comfort Me With Apples"

Cream cheese and butter: Unctuous and smooth, they slide right down—and in their richness provide loving comfort to the body and the soul. As if that weren't enough, there are also walnuts and olive oil, and a bit of rice vinegar for sweetness. It's lovely.

*1 tablespoon unsalted butter plus
    4 ounces (one stick), at room
    temperature
½ cup crushed walnuts—save one
    walnut half for a garnish
8 ounces cream cheese (NOT no fat;
    low fat is fine) at room temperature*

*¼ cup fresh basil leaves, lightly packed
1 clove garlic, minced
2 tablespoons extra virgin olive oil
1 teaspoon rice vinegar
Salt and freshly ground black pepper*

1. Using the tablespoon of butter, toast the walnuts gently over medium-low heat for about 5 minutes. In a pinch and a hurry, this can be made without toasting the walnuts—it's still delicious.
2. Add all of the remaining ingredients (except the saved walnut half) to a food processor and pulse just a few times until well mixed but *not* pureed. (To make by hand, chop the basil finely and mix all the ingredients in a bowl)
3. Mound in a small serving bowl or on a dish; top with the walnut half, and chill, covered with plastic wrap until ready to serve. This works nicely as a dip for sturdy vegetables when at room temperature and spreads smoothly when chilled.

Serve with quartered slices of whole-grain bread or wheat crackers.

Yields 1½ cups

Russian Cream

Whatever one wishes for—violence, perhaps, which is bloody red—or deserves, white food keeps the slate clean.
        —Chapter 10, "I Say It's Spinach"

I've treasured this recipe for years, and have only seen a few like it—but none better, and none as simple. It's related to *panna cotta*, but it has the delectable tang of sour cream, and to crème brûlée, only not as eggy, and again, with the tang of sour cream. Obviously, it's not low fat. Few among us are. But if you have it on a day when you've had little fat to speak of, you can throw caution to the winds. It's that kind of recipe.

1 tablespoon gelatin
½ cup cold water
½ cup sugar
1 cup heavy cream

2 cups sour cream (low fat is fine; do
NOT use no fat)
1 teaspoon pure vanilla extract

1. Sprinkle the gelatin over the water and let sit for 5 minutes, until the gelatin softens.
2. Add the sugar to the cream and heat gently (in the top of a double boiler or over low heat, stirring often and watching carefully) until the mixture is warm.
3. Still over low heat, add the gelatin mixture to the cream and stir until it and the sugar are completely dissolved.
4. Chill the mixture until it begins to thicken, and at that point, add the sour cream and the vanilla, folding them in well.
5. Pour into a serving bowl or individual dessert cups, or, if you don't mind unmolding at the last minute, into a mold that you've rinsed with water. Chill until well-set.

Serves 6

NOTE: This is especially good served with a sauce made of raspberries or strawberries blended in the food processor, sieved to eliminate the seeds, and sweetened to taste, or of blueberries cooked with a tiny bit of water and sugar until they're soft, and then chilled.

Artichoke Hummus

Some people are reluctant to eat beans at all because of their inevitable by-product, which strikes about four hours after they've been eaten. Some beans are worse than others. . . .

—Chapter 12, "Mine Own Petard"

Strictly speaking—even loosely speaking, for that matter—this isn't hummus at all. Hummus has chickpeas in it; this does not—though you could certainly use them if you like. Both recipes are based on beans, with added garlic and lemon juice, but here there is also the flavor of artichokes. It's a fast, easy, and good recipe. And if you keep cans of beans and artichokes in your pantry, you can always make this at a moment's notice.

1 15-oz. can artichoke hearts, drained
1 15-oz. can cannellini beans, drained
* and rinsed*
1 clove garlic, minced
Juice of a quarter lemon; more if
* needed*

Salt and freshly ground black pepper
¼ cup extra virgin olive oil
Optional garnish: paprika, extra virgin
* olive oil, and flat-leafed Italian*
* parsley*

1. Place all of the ingredients except the garnishes in a food processor and pulse until well-mixed but *not* completely smooth; some chunkiness is best. Taste for seasoning. There should be a slight tang of lemon—add a bit more juice if needed.
2. Place into a bowl; if you like, spoon a little olive oil on the top and sprinkle with paprika. Add some parsley leaves and serve.

Yields 2 to 3 cups

Index

genitals, (*continued*)
  and oral sex, 61–62
  and scent, 66, 67
Germany, 27, 29, 76, 116–117, 187, 210
gifts, 184, 187, 198, 202
Golden Ass of Apuleius, The, 45
Gopnik, Adam, 139, 151
Gore, Albert, 169
Gore, Tipper, 169
Gould, Lois, 97
Gourmet (magazine), 94, 143, 150
Grafton, Sue, 46
Grant, Cary, 154
Great Depression, 143, 160
Greece, 25, 66, 73, 186, 207–208, 235
Greene, Graham, 68
Gregory, Dick, 13
Grimm's fairy tales, 84–88. *See also* fairy
  tales
Guerlain, Jean-Paul, 67–68
Guggenheim, Peggy, 97
guilt, 100, 102, 103
Gurney, A. R., 103–104
Gutman, Robert W., 221
Guy's Hospital, 55

Habits of Good Society, The, 182
Hades, 208
Hansel and Gretel, 50, 86–88. *See also* fairy
  tales
Harris, Frank, 126, 136
Harvard Lampoon (magazine), 239
Hayward, Brooke, 94
Hayward, Leland, 94–95, 162
Haywire (Hayward), 94
headhunters, 57–58
heart disease, 64
Hecuba (queen), 236
Hell Fire Club, 152
Heller, Joseph, 201
Henry VIII (Shakespeare), 184

Hepburn, Audrey, 154
Hepburn, Katherine, 132
Hera, 208, 235
Herrick, Robert, 74
Hershey's, 30
Hestia, 208
Hiedler, Johann Georg, 226
Hill, Reginald, 43
Hinsdale County Museum, 207
Hitler, Adolf, 163, 222–235
Hitler, Alois, 226–228, 230
Hitler, Alois, Jr., 228–229
Hitler, Angela, 229–230
Hitler, Paula, 227
Hitler, William Patrick, 228–229
holidays, 13, 108–109, 138, 165, 181, 217
Holliday, Judy, 119
Hollywood Hayes code, 130
Holocaust, 216, 225. *See also* Hitler, Adolf
Holy Communion, 204, 216
Holyfield, Evander, 200
Hoover, Herbert, 160, 177
Hoover, J. Edgar, 229
hormones, 66, 68
Houseman, A. E., 81
Hungary, 211–212
hunger, 21, 40, 57–58, 80
  and cannibalism, 197, 210, 218, 219
  and comfort foods, 108
  and fairy tales, 86
  and food eccentricities, 96, 98, 101–102,
    105
  and love, 154
  and politics, 166, 167, 169
  strikes, 98, 218
  and table manners, 176
"Hunger Artist" (Kafka), 98, 218
hunter/gatherer societies, 27–28

In the Night Kitchen (Sendak), 84
incest, 196. *See also* child abuse

Index